Reverberations

Reverberations

The philosophy, aesthetics and politics of noise

EDITED BY
MICHAEL GODDARD,
BENJAMIN HALLIGAN AND
PAUL HEGARTY

continuum

Continuum International Publishing Group

The Tower Building	80 Maiden Lane
11 York Road	Suite 704
London	New York
SE1 7NX	NY 10038

www.continuumbooks.com

© Michael Goddard, Benjamin Halligan, Paul Hegarty and contributors 2012

Library of Congress Cataloging-in-Publication Data
A catalog record for this book is available from the Library of Congress.

ISBN: HB: 978-1-4411-9605-7
PB: 978-1-4411-6065-2

Typeset by Fakenham Prepress Solutions, Fakenham, Norfolk, NR21 8NN
Printed and bound in the United States of America

Contents

Illustrations

Acknowledgements

The Editors thank: David Barker and his team at Continuum/Bloomsbury; the Communication, Cultural and Media Studies Research Centre of the School of Media, Music and Performance at the University of Salford; Professors George McKay and Ben Light, and Dr Deborah Woodman; Bridget Hayden, Stephen Lawrie and Julie Kane; the staff and habitués of the Salford King's Arms, and especially Livy and Ken for their assistance with facilitating the noise gig associated with the University of Salford conference 'Bigger than Words, Wider than Pictures: Noise, Affect, Politics', from which this collection emerged. Work on the conference and this book was partly supported by a Research and Innovation Strategic Fund grant from the Faculty of Arts and Social Sciences at the University of Salford.

Cover image: from the installation *Vortex II* (2011) by Bridget Hayden.

Notes on contributors

José Cláudio Siqueira Castanheira is a soundtrack composer and sound designer for films and television. He is currently undertaking his doctoral studies in Communication at Universidade Federal Fluminense and obtained his Masters degree at Universidade Estadual do Rio de Janeiro. Recently he has performed in England and Scotland with the experimental musical group Simbiotecnoise, about whom he has also written. He is also developing research into the constitution of different models of listening and their relation to technologies and social practices, and is currently lecturing in film sound at Universidade Federal de Santa Catarina.

Felicity J. Colman is Reader in Screen Media at Manchester Metropolitan University, United Kingdom. She is the author of *Deleuze and Cinema: The Film Concepts* (Berg, 2011), editor of *Film, Theory and Philosophy: The Key Thinkers* (Acumen, 2009), co-editor of *Sensorium: Aesthetics, Art, Life* (Cambridge Scholars Press, 2007), and has a forthcoming book on Robert Smithson's work.

Daniel Cookney currently teaches within the University of Salford's School of Media, Music and Performance and School of Art and Design. His activities at the Popular Music Research Centre are based around the intersection of music and graphic design, and his current doctoral study examines records by electronic artists as visual artefacts. Prior to this, he worked under a pseudonym as a journalist contributing to a number of local, national and international publications.

Rob Gawthrop is an artist and musician who works with sound, film, improvisation and performance. His films, made between 1976 and 1990, have been screened widely and his recent sound work is concerned with the physicality of sound and its visual/aural perception (*Moving Air*), and films that deal with location as sound source, site and separation (*Remote*). He is a collaborator on regular programmes of improvised and experimental music in Falmouth as The School of Noises. As a researcher he has been exploring contemporary aesthetic theory and the interstices between noise, music and the audiovisual. Publications include 'Film Noise Aesthetics' in *Experimental Film and Video Anthology* (ed. Jackie Hatfield, John Libbey & Co, 2006) and 'One' in *Diffusion* (ed. Giles Lane and Catherine Williams, Proboscis, 2000). Since 2010 Rob has been the Award Leader for the BA and MA Fine Art Contemporary Practices at University College, Falmouth.

GegenSichKollektiv was founded by no one, nowhere, and hosts dissidents of reality as it appears to us. GegenSichKollektiv works towards subjective depersonalization by using nihilism as a form of cognitive discipline to reconsider our relationship to the structures of reality beyond the multiplicity of readings of post-structuralism. So far noise and improvisation has only tried to express the self. What we need now is the dissolution of the self as we know it in order to produce a form of revolutionary collectivity.

Michael Goddard is Lecturer in Media Studies at the University of Salford. He has published research in media and aesthetic theory, Eastern European film and visual culture, and anomalous forms of popular music. His book *Impossible Cartographies: The Cinema of Raúl Ruiz* is currently in press and he is co-editor with Jussi Parikka of the recently published special issue of *Fibreculture* journal, *Unnatural Ecologies*. He has also published articles on Throbbing Gristle and Laibach as well as co-editing, with Benjamin Halligan, *Mark E. Smith and The Fall: Art, Music and Politics* (Ashgate, 2010). Currently, Michael is working on a research project on radical media ecologies in radio, music and radical politics in the 1970s.

Benjamin Halligan is Director of the Graduate Programme for the School of Media, Music and Performance at the University of Salford. His publications include *Michael Reeves* (Manchester University Press, 2003), *Mark E. Smith and The Fall: Art, Music and Politics* (Ashgate, 2010; co-edited with Michael Goddard) and *The Music Documentary* (Routledge, 2013; co-edited with Rob Edgar and Kirsty Fairclough). He has published on disco music and science fiction, The Sarajevo Documentary School, Dušan Makavejev, Frank Zappa, Andrei Tarkovsky and the British Royal Family. *Resonances: Noise and Contemporary Music*, co-edited with Michael Goddard and Nicola Spelman, is forthcoming from Continuum/Bloomsbury.

Paul Hegarty teaches philosophy and visual culture in the Department of French, University College Cork. He is the author of the book *Noise/ Music: A History* (Continuum, 2007), and co-author, with Martin Halliwell, of *Beyond and Before: Progressive Rock since the 1960s* (Continuum, 2011), as well as numerous pieces on theory. He co-directs the record label dotdotdotmusic, and performs and records in various groups, most often as and with Safe.

Saeed Hydaralli holds a Ph.D. in Sociology from York University, Toronto, Canada. He is currently the 2011–12 Visiting Fellow with the Great Works Symposium at Drexel University. Saeed has been a Project Researcher with the Culture of Cities Centre for City Life and Well-Being: The Grey Zone of Health and Illness, University of Waterloo, Canada. He has also, over the previous five years, been Sessional Faculty at OCAD University and the University of Guelph (at Humber), both located in Toronto, in the areas of Urban Sociology, Material Culture, the Sociology of Consumption and Social Theory.

Dean Lockwood is Senior Lecturer in Media Theory at the University of Lincoln, United Kingdom, where he coordinates and teaches undergraduate and postgraduate modules in Media and Cultural Studies and Audio Production programmes. His publications include 'Presence-Play: The Hauntology of the Computer Game', with Tony Richards, in *Computer Games as a Sociocultural Phenomenon* (ed. Andreas Jahn-Sudman and Ralf Stockmann, Palgrave, 2008), 'All Stripped Down: The Spectacle of Torture Porn', in *Popular Communication: The International Journal of Media and Culture*, and, with Janice Kearns, 'As If We Didn't Know Who He Was: Mark E. Smith's Untimeliness'; in *Mark E. Smith and The Fall: Art, Music and Politics* (ed. Michael Goddard and Benjamin Halligan, Ashgate, 2010).

Cécile Malaspina is a Ph.D. student at Université Paris Diderot, Paris 7, supervised by Prof. Alain Leplege and Dr. Iain Hamilton Grant, University of the West of England. She holds an MA in Philosophy and Contemporary Critical Theory from Middlesex University. Currently she is contributing to the translation of the *Cahiers pour l'Analyse*, an AHRC-funded project realized by the Centre for Research in Modern European Philosophy and her article on 'The Axiomatic Ambition of Gilbert Simondon', is forthcoming.

Brian Massumi is a political theorist, writer and philosopher, and is currently a Professor in the Department of Communication Sciences at the University of Montréal in Quebec, Canada. Brian is well known for his translations of several major texts in French post-structuralist theory, including Gilles Deleuze and Félix Guattari's *A Thousand Plateaus*, Jean-François Lyotard's *The Postmodern Condition*, and Jacques Attali's *Noise*. Brian has authored several books including *Semblance and Event: Activist Philosophy and the Occurrent Arts* (MIT Press, 2011), *Parables for the Virtual: Movement, Affect,*

Sensation (Duke University Press, 2002), *A User's Guide to Capitalism and Schizophrenia: Deviations from Deleuze and Guattari* (MIT Press, 1992) and, with Kenneth Dean, *First and Last Emperors: The Absolute State and the Body of the Despot* (Autonomedia, 1993).

Bruce Russell is a New Zealand experimental musician and writer, and a founding member and guitarist of the noise rock trio The Dead C and the free noise combo A Handful of Dust. He has released solo albums featuring guitar and tape manipulation. He established the Xpressway record label, which was active from 1985 until the early 1990s, releasing mostly cassettes and a few records. He then founded the *Corpus Hermeticum* record label. A collection of his writings was recently published as *Bruce Russell: Left-Handed Blows: Writing on Sound 1993–2009* (Clouds, 2010).

Marie Thompson is a Musicology Ph.D. candidate at Newcastle University. Her thesis examines affectivity, sensation and the gendering of noise. She previously studied at the University of Liverpool, where she completed her Masters in Musicology in 2009. When she is not writing about noise, she will often be found making noise, and currently plays solo as Tragic Cabaret, in the duo, Ghostly Porters and in the band Beauty Pageant.

Robert Walker is a practising sound designer, re-recording mixer and musician with credits across independent feature films, television, short films, animation and installations. He holds a BA in Film and Media Studies from Stirling University and a PG Cert in Film Production (Sound) from UCLA. He currently teaches Film Sound at Screen Academy Scotland in Edinburgh and is a member of the Association of Motion Picture Sound. Recent publications include a chapter in *Mark E. Smith and The Fall: Art, Music and Politics* (ed. Michael Goddard and Benjamin Halligan, Ashgate, 2010) and an essay on the use of sound in *The Wire*. His research interests are primarily in the uses of sound and music in film and television.

Khadijah White is a Doctoral student in the Annenberg School for Communication at the University of Pennsylvania, and holds a MA in Communication. Previously, she worked as a journalist at 'NOW' on PBS and served as a White House Intern on the Obama administration's Broadcast Media team. As a student with a focus on culture and mass/interpersonal communication, her body of research has concentrated on examining the ways in which race, gender and sexual identity impact upon political rhetoric, symbolism, intergroup/intragroup identity construction, media panics and rumours.

Laura Wilson is a Ph.D. candidate at the University of Manchester. She has presented her research on Michael Haneke, *Irreversible* and other examples of extreme cinema at several international conferences. Her thesis is titled 'Body Horror and Physical Spectatorship' and it concentrates on the different ways in which cinema produces a particular physicality through graphic representations of violence directed towards the human body.

Scott Wilson is a Professor in the School of Humanities, Kingston University, London. His two most recent books are *The Order of Joy: Beyond the Cultural Politics of Enjoyment* (SUNY Press, 2008) and *Great Satan's Rage: American Negativity and Rap/Metal in the Age of Supercapitalism* (Manchester University Press, 2008). Scott is co-editor, with Michael Dillon, of the *Journal for Cultural Research* (Taylor & Francis).

Introduction

Michael Goddard, Benjamin Halligan and Paul Hegarty

Such a satisfying idea – noise annoys – at once simple-to-grasp kernel and yet capable of inflation into the most grandiose theories of subversion. But... who is there to be annoyed and in what ways?

REYNOLDS, 1990, 57

From the loud lawn-mower that shatters the suburban peace to the intrusive noise of unthinking neighbours to the unceasing cacophony of the post-industrial metropolis, noise is conventionally apprehended, in social terms, as an irritant. John Stewart *et al.*'s recent study of noise (2011) immediately frames the phenomenon in terms of 'problems, policies and solutions' in respect of planning, pollution and health, and argues that noise has been overlooked by Green and environmental campaigners and by politicians. Yet at the same time noise has functioned, since the industrial era at least, as a powerful pole of attraction, and not only in the articulation of theories and practices of noise music from the Futurists' early twentieth-century 'Art of Noises' to exponents of 'Japanoise' such as Merzbow. Noise 'annoys' then, to continue Reynolds' paraphrase of the Buzzcocks song, but in this annoyance (of others) it also provides new forms of pleasure, not least of which are the pleasures of transgression and subversion to which Reynolds alludes. Beyond this initial duality however, noise opens up on to a variety of levels beyond the simple consideration of whether noise practices are, or even can be, subversive.

The social level with which we began is arguably already a departure from a merely sonic apprehension of noise, since what counts socially as noise in an urban environment is not only relative to the position of the perceiver but also dependent on a number of extra-sonic factors such as social norms, temporality and duration. Thus the loud party may be tolerated before midnight on a Saturday but the same 'noise' is less likely to be treated with such indulgence in the early hours of a Sunday morning. Similarly, a car alarm is a useful device for its owner, and a screaming menace for those subjected to its insistent wailing when it malfunctions. And even, or especially, children can function as pathological agents of urban noise, however much their 'noise' is adored or at least tolerated by their doting parents – and hence the Victorian advice (of the time when families began to live cheek-by-jowl) that 'children should be seen but not heard'. In all these instances noise operates on the thresholds of normative social interaction as a potentially disruptive agency, but this tells us very little about what noise in its sonic forms really constitutes.

Another approach to the sonic aspects of noise is to consider it as disorganized or, more appropriately, 'unorganized' sound. In this respect noise functions as the 'other' to both language and music, considered as so many systems for organizing noise into meaningful or even beautiful modes of expression. Noise, on the other hand, is considered ugly and destructive of meaning or, in other words, functions as the disturbance or interference of a meaningful sonic system. In this way noise, which remains a pejorative term, would typically be understood to be a kind of metastasis or anarchic proliferation of audio occurrences, unwanted and unpleasant, and making for a discord that becomes disorientating. The ways in which we shape our soundscape to what we favour, or into something upon which we rely, and that therefore become an essential aspect of our habitus, are disrupted by noise that intrudes into our subjective or personal or virtual/digital soundscape, and that cannot be organized in this way.

And yet this negative potential already indicates the nature of the positive dimension of noise, in that innovations in musical form ranging from new forms of classical music, via jazz, rock, punk and hip-hop to industrial and electronic musics, from ambient to dance, have often initially been perceived as ugly and rebarbative noise, meaning simply that they departed from the norms of a previous system of sonic organization. Noise music itself could be said to represent or capitalize on this tendency, even to the extent of forming a genre (as these categories and subcategories indicate), and as such requires a particular set of coordinates for its reception and discussion. The subject of noise musics is therefore better suited to specific studies. In addition to noise music, something similar could be said of linguistic phenomena such as new forms of slang or dialect, equally perceived by outsiders as a horrible noise, relative to 'proper' languages and their rules of organization and articulation. This may even apply to groups of deaf people communicating in sign language in pubs, who on occasion are subject to discrimination for so doing.

Equally, it may be the 'insider' who hears noise, say, in the form of a foreign language being used.

It is questionable, however, whether this account of noise as a lack of sonic organization, or the irruption of another mode of organization, has not already passed into another level of noise that is the technical and communicational account of noise as the Other of information. From classical theories of information, such as that of Claude Shannon, noise is perceived as the shadow of or resistance to a signal being passed between two points in a system, from a sender to a receiver. In a technical system of communication, therefore, the aim is to maximize the signal-to-noise ratio, to attain the most perfect possible transmission of the message. Nevertheless, no technical system is ever perfect, and there are no messages free of their accompanying characteristic forms of noise or interference. This also highlights the crucial role of technology in accounts of noise. It is not that it is impossible to conceive of noise outside of technical systems, but rather every technical system of communication is accompanied by its own characteristic forms of noise, from which no complete separation, or perfectly transmissible message, is possible.

What is covered over in this account, however, is the generativity of noise alluded to above in relation to musical and linguistic innovation. Far from being a mere residue of a communicational system, noise is primary, or even primal, and we are always already 'in' noise or, as Michel Serres puts it, 'we are surrounded by noise. And this noise it inextinguishable [...] We are in the noises of the world, we cannot close our door to their reception' (Serres, 2007, 126). For Serres, at least, noise comes before any meaningful system as its transcendental field, which is why noise can never be fully eliminated. In this perspective all living systems in their negentropy are temporary escapes from entropic noise, but escapes that are destined to failure by the laws of thermodynamics. In more aesthetic terms we might think of noise as ground, and meaning as figure, rising from the ground, but caught within its field in order to function. More basically, what any system necessarily excludes as noise are all the levels of organization above and below it that include its own conditions of possibility, hence the informational account of noise as a lack of organization being a state of fundamental distortion. Noise is indeed static or interference but not that of an unorganized chaos so much as patterns of organization alien to the norms of a specific system – that which Serres refers to as 'the parasite'.

This abstract yet materialist account of noise brings us back to the social and political dimensions of noise, as so many interferences among differing systems of organization, however they might be defined – whether in relation to urban and civic environments, differing and even antagonistic subjectivities, or modes of sonic expression. The Public Enemy track 'Bring the Noise' (from the 1988 album *It Takes A Nation of Millions To Hold Us Back*) self-identifies a decisive 'blackness' to the group's noise ('Turn it up!/[spoken]: "Hey, yo' Chuck, they're saying we're too black, man."/Bring the noise!') which in turn hampers or discourages disseminations of these 'truly' black sounds and militant subjectivities ('Radio stations I question their blackness/ They call themselves black but we'll see if they play this'). Such a social and political mapping of noise is no more and no less than what Jacques Attali accomplished in his now famous book *Noise* which, according to Russo and Warner, aimed to 'expand the range [of noise] to cover virtually any cultural channel' (Russo and Warner, 2004, 48). Of particular interest to Attali was the ways in which modes of the sonic organization of noise in the form of music were not only explanatory of historically specific modes of power but even premonitory, as if noise was first organized sonically, before becoming organized socially and politically.

The experience of our research into noise adds credence and nuance to this idea of noise as the forerunner: sound-waves before matter. Disarmingly, in the first instance, noise seems to deftly deflect critical attention or analysis. Rather than presenting itself as an area ready for exploration and mapping – at least from a philosophical or sociological rather than scientific position – noise signals continually towards its seeming polar opposite: silence. It is telling that the piece of 'music' to which the authors in this volume return time and again is John Cage's celebrated *4'33"* of 1952: the 'silent' performance arising from an empty musical score. Noise may represent an acoustic disorganization, as argued above, but what noise is not, then, is silence. And so silence becomes the natural measure of noise.

Silence would seem to represent a series of disturbing absences just as noise represents a series of disturbing presences, with the habitus soundscape, our 'middle way', seemingly only the temporary and fluctuating passage between the two. Upon encountering noise in cultural texts and events, the question that suggested itself time and again was simply: What, then, is silence? What needs to be detracted from the habitus to achieve silence? What is perfectly audible, and yet is taken as the sound of silence? And what, then, is an unacceptable level of silence? And yet silence itself has become equally contested, and the index of a contemporary symbolic order: as a valuable commodity in the post-industrial city, as the condition assumed as prerequisite for 'thinking', as an architectural imperative, and as demanded and imposed in its courts of law.

But if noise and the systems to which it gives rise are immediately political, they are also aesthetic, and this aesthetic is in no way limited to musical or sonic arts. Already in information theory the concept of noise is by no means a necessarily sonic one and can be equally applicable to a blotch on a page of newsprint or to the visual static on a television screen, as phenomena that, like sonic noise, obstruct and interfere with an intended message. Elsewhere, in conspiracy theories seeking to address 'numbers stations', it is the short-wave static noise itself that delivers coded information with the spoken word merely illustrating the clarity of frequency. Noise aesthetics, then, can be textual and visual or, rather, audiovisual and tending ultimately in digital conditions towards synaesthetic, 'glitch' phenomena.

Nevertheless, the question that noise aesthetics raises, and that was already touched upon in Reynolds' account of noise cited at the beginning of this Introduction, is that if noise, as the supposed 'other' of any meaningful system of communication, is desired – and in the digital context even designed – does it still even function in a subversive sense *as* noise, or has it already been fully domesticated as a new system of meaning? In Reynolds' terms (1990, 58),

[T]o confer the status of value on excess and extremism is to bring these things back within the pale of decency. So the rhetoricians of noise actually destroy the power they strive to celebrate; they are the very start of the process by which subversion is turned into contribution, which is absorbed as a renewal for the system.

This is less, however, the contradiction that Reynolds sees it as, locating it in so many 'anti-pop gestures' and 'reality effects', than a productive paradox generative of numerous fields of sonic, aesthetic and even political experimentation. Rather than a subversive fallacy, what Reynolds identifies points to the ways in which engagement with noise necessarily opens up specific technical or meaningful systems to outside interferences, to systems and durations other than our own. This process, rather than disqualifying noise as a subversive paradigm, opens its specific modes of subversion from a restricted system-defined economy to a general economy, whether conceived in terms of Bataille's 'accursed share', or Serres' account of noise as parasite.

Such multiple levels and domains of noise prompted and informed the event 'Bigger than Words, Wider than Pictures: Noise, Affect, Politics' held at the University of Salford in Summer 2010, and from which several of the chapters in this collection derive. While some academic papers explored multiple forms of noise music (ranging from avant-classical musics and jazz improvisation to psychedelic rock, punk and industrial musics, to the noise musics of Furudate and Karkowski or Filthy Turd), others engaged with some of the more philosophical dimensions of noise alluded to here, for example, in the work of theorists like Attali, Steve Goodman and Gilbert Simondon. Still other presentations were concerned with the social and political aspects of noise as a constitutive element of everyday urban life, while there were also engagements with a range of aesthetic practices beyond the strictly sonic ranging, from the fiction of H. P. Lovecraft, via the cinematic deployment of noise to digital glitch aesthetics. These presentations were accompanied by an evening of noise performances, including the Brazilian noise group Simbiotecnoise, iPollytouch (who attacked various objects with electrified shears), Safe and The Telescopes (Infinite Suns). These performances were enough in themselves to indicate the multiplicity of conceptions of noise and produced both pleasant and unpleasant sensations and responses in their auditors, which in turn fed back into the event. The questions raised by these diverse levels, practices and experiences of noise have been expanded upon in this collection, according to the three sub-domains of the philosophy and aesthetics of noise, audiovisual noise practices and the ethical and political dimensions of noise. Underlying all these areas, both in their distinctions and their many interrelations, are questions of the affect of noise, both its capacities to affect us, and our capacities to respond to noise, be that on an ontological, aesthetic, social or political level.

The philosophy and aesthetics of noise

In Part One, contributors examine the what, the how, the where and the when of noise. The question 'What is noise?' is of course central to the whole project of using noise as an analytical, artistic or subversive tool, but in these chapters, the writers also begin to open up questions of noise as a function, a locatable process, event or sequence. Paul Hegarty opens by thinking about the question of noise's relation to time, on individual and historical timescales. This is reflected in the duration of 'musical' noise pieces and performances that create barriers to our common-sense understandings of quotidian time. Bergson, Nietzsche, Deleuze and Guattari all help formulate the question, and in turn the noise of 'harsh noise wall' in particular responds to these philosophies to offer its own theorization of time. In Chapter 2, Scott Wilson looks at noise as an internal processing of an unreceivable exterior, opening with the thought of 'amusia' – the incapacity to hear/understand music. A Lacanian reimagining of this phenomenon unleashes the hidden desire of and for music transformed into the unlistenable, become threatening. From an Oliver Sacks case study, through rock 'n' roll, Edvard Munch and arriving at Jacques Brel's hatred of the accordion, a pattern of an audio unconscious emerges, in which the ineffability of music turns to abjection, to a continual process of 'othering'.

In Chapter 3, Brian Massumi opens up the field of communications theory, via the exemplar of Rafael Lozano-Hemmer's light signal-based artwork, in which communication is revealed to always need a third, a 'more' than the two ostensibly speaking (as William Burroughs and Brion Gysin suspected). Language comes to be about thirdness, about the sea in which communication drifts. The piece also signals that the drift, the sea, are themselves communication – above and below the material of shared speech. Language's sociality is revealed to operate through constant iterations of signal and noise, each inflecting the other. In Chapter 4, Cécile Malaspina takes us further into notions of communication and cybernetics, with a strong push from Gilbert Simondon, and also the drive of Ray Brassier's idea that noise is productive, and does not need to be an object/area of confusion once we look to certain radical sound practices, which in turn feed socio-political action. Malaspina takes this and the idea of noise in systems theory to ask whether (and how) noise can work as a cross-disciplinary tool, or even a 'cross-discipline' in its own right (what Dick Higgins might have included in his idea of 'intermedia'). As well as looking at sound and noise informing each other, sound and non-sound also play off one another, and noise offers itself as an open-ended paradigm, the *prospect* of a crossing.

In Chapter 5, Dean Lockwood hears just such a crossing in the writings of H. P. Lovecraft, which are riven with odd sounds, impenetrable and threatening alien tongues, and the menacing combination of advanced technology and alien essence. In contrast to Wilson's chapter, where noise is mobilized internally in a kind of ecstatic repulsion, for Lockwood, Lovecraft feels the noise creeping ever inward. Noise as ingress is encouraged and feared simultaneously. The coincidence of the then new presence of radio in homes and the noise of 'the other' is brought into the present by José Cláudio Siqueira Castanheira, in his piece on how analogue and digital models of sound production play with our sense of noise (Chapter 6). The more we become digital, or are exhorted to be, the more we can understand the history of audio technology and of our ideas of noise and music as intertwined. There is mutual mediation, but above all, our attention is drawn to recall that what is sound/noise/music is always technologically and culturally mediated – and, in fact, our bodies are only one more type of sound-processing technology. These bodies are in turn shaped by cultural and technological expectations and discourses.

All of the above attempt to address not just an aspect of noise, but address it in all its aspects while acknowledging that a different set of parameters could have been selected. For that reason, the chapters in Part One are modellings of noise that are far from irreconcilable, for all their different approaches, examples and methods.

Audiovisual noise practices

Part Two presents a number of theoretical approaches to the presence of noise in the visual arts. Rob Gawthrop, Benjamin Halligan, Robert Walker, Felicity J. Colman and Laura Wilson all discuss film, from the mainstream (Halligan), to art house (Walker and Wilson), to the avant-garde or under-ground (Colman, Gawthrop). Colman, Daniel Cookney and Gawthrop consider site-specific artistic practices – investigating them, interacting with them and, in Cookney's case, presenting the processes of capturing these findings. Gawthrop and Halligan also consider theatre and performance.

A frustration shared by the majority of these writers is apparent: the question of sound in film per se, let alone noise, is often overlooked or marginalized, and so lags far behind the visual in terms of aesthetic import in the academic disciplines associated with film. In part this is due to the relatively recent innovations in sound design and sound reproduction – innovations brought about, as discussed here, by unlikely figures in the mainstream and that, as Halligan argues, immediately require spectrums of noise rather than, or even over, norms of diegetic sound and incidental music. As Colman and Cookney illustrate, investigating acoustics represents the opportunity to overturn the given coordinates and sets of meanings and readings, and so enact a radical 'breaking open' of the found environment or artistic text. This potential may also be seen in evidence in the chapters that substantially discuss film too: audio-mapping, audio analysis, its aesthetics, affects, ambiguities and negations.

In Chapter 7, Halligan contextualizes sound innovations as an effective second 'expansion' of cinema (where the first, which failed, was associated with the counterculture), and dates this from the late 1970s. But noise, for Halligan, is seen to function in an ambiguous and even dissembling way – as denoting or circumnavigating impossible dramaturgical demands, and often working to censor what is seen. Following this line of thought, Halligan finds common ground between theological conceptions of the problem or impos-sibility of divine art, and post-structuralist thought on the 'impossible image'.

The dramatic impact of the image is enhanced or even transformed by the use of noise in the analyses mounted by Walker and Wilson, and both present considerations of what to this end might be termed the 'sound affect' rather than 'sound effect'. In this instance, noise enables the break from the secondary roles more typically allotted to sound in terms of film – as emphatic, incidental, as a 'reality effect' – and may best be understood as establishing a second dimension to cinema-going: that of biological as well as neurological response. In Chapter 8, Wilson argues that the experience of *Irreversible* (Gaspar Noé, 2002) is founded upon the ways in which sub-audible sonics alter the physical state of the viewer from one of relaxation to anxiety. She identifies this experience as 'physical spectatorship'. Wilson then approaches the centrality of the rape scene in the film to regenerate the more familiar debates in film studies concerning voyeurism and violation, the gaze and assault, and the therapeutic uses of seeing or revisiting trauma.

In Chapter 9, Walker surveys cinematic renditions of the condition of tinnitus, but does not find the rendering of the loss of hearing simply a matter of sonic equivalents. Rather, the resultant hearing-loss noise comes to constitute a subjective aesthetic mode that reorders the world presented, and is best considered in relation to silent cinema. In this, Walker is indebted to the pioneering work of Michel Chion, as are Wilson and Halligan. The image of violence against hearing – the blood that trickles from the ear in both Elem Klimov's *Come and See* (1985) and James Mangold's *Copland* (1997) – recalls and reprises the celebrated image of violence against seeing: the human eyeball, sliced by a razor, of *Un Chien Andalou* (Luis Buñuel, Salvador Dalí, 1929).

In the chapters by Colman, Cookney and Gawthrop, the focus is more on noise and event or place. In Chapter 10, Cookney presents a series of investigations into that which may be termed the noise of silence. The provocative rationale and methodology which follow, and the discussion of the investigation of noise that is nominally outlawed in the institutions of silence, illustrate the ways in which noise itself functions as the entry point into otherwise unheard (rather than invisible) aspects of the governance of public spheres. As with Cookney, Gawthrop (Chapter 11) also considers the ethics and mores of noise, of what is and what is not deemed acceptable, and how this collective position may be seen as representing a collective policing of aesthetics in the public sphere. Noise therefore retains a potential or even a will to usurp, and Gawthrop's concern is the use of noise in avant-garde and underground art and film as a conceptual wedge that calls into question, in philosophical terms, assumptions about the fixedness of the image, the author as creator, art and happenstance, and the tenuous but dominant analogue relationship between sound and image that has been the principal point of departure for the examples considered in Part Two. Likewise, for Colman (Chapter 12), noise possesses the possibilities of liberation, both against 'fixed' readings of works of art, but also against the assumed perspectives or positions of readings of works of art. As noted elsewhere in Part Two, the 'point of view' and 'point of audition' may be some way apart. For Colman, noise is intrinsic to the shift in art practice – historical, conceptual, financial and institutional – from the canvas and the site-specific installation. Noise restores an individual experience and regenerates subjectivity when it comes to considerations of art. Colman's model is Lee Ranaldo's noise responses to Robert Smithson's artworks, and her thesis is that noise can function as an inter- or transdisciplinary dialogue or tool. Such a notion of reverberation, which is shared with Cookney and Gawthrop, represents the integration of a situationist or psychogeographic element into the theorization of noise.

Noise, ethics and politics

Part Three switches attention to the political, ethical and social dimensions of noise without, for all that, abandoning its aesthetic and philosophical resonances, which is hardly surprising considering that several of the authors are also noise practitioners themselves. In Part Three, though, there is a shift, less away from aesthetics than towards practices that interrogate, in a number of contexts, noise practices and 'performances', in relation to subjectivities, experiences and contemporary social life. Whether this is in the context of noise musics or everyday urban coexistence, these chapters trace the rudiments for a politics of noise, and show how a rigorous engagement with the latter has the potential to transform conceptions of the former.

Chapter 13, written by the anonymous GegenSichKollektiv, considers performances of noise and silence within and against the context of the contemporary capitalist commodification of all experiences, including transgressive aesthetic ones. In a highly speculative yet materialist analysis that brings together Marx's accounts of machines and labour with the latest developments in speculative realism, and especially the work of Ray Brassier who has also engaged directly with noise, this chapter articulates an experience of noise as one of 'anti-self', against the commodification of noise as yet another medium or material for consumption. Following on from this, in Chapter 14, Marie Thompson begins with two noises, that of the car alarm and the opening of a Melt Banana performance. Thompson uses both of these experiences as a springboard to the affective plane of noise as it has been theorized by post-Deleuzian theorists like Massumi and Steven Shaviro. This is done in order to pose the question clearly of the differences between everyday noise, largely perceived in terms of 'negative affect' and 'threat', and noise music which is also part of a framed experience with positive connotations, at least within a certain community, arguing that noise musics convert the negativity of noise into something desirable and generative, operating within a 'theatre of affect'.

The register shifts in the next two chapters towards the social and the everyday, via two different accounts of the problematics of urban noise. In Chapter 15, Saeed Hydaralli begins his investigation by situating social noise as an urban phenomenon, but one that is highly problematic for planners and policy makers. Complaints about noisy neighbours, for example, often go against any objective metrics, suggesting the need for a qualitative account of social noise. For Hydaralli, noise is a relational term, referring to the relations between the sounds of foregrounded and background activities, with sound becoming perceived as noise when it crosses these borders, producing interferences between different spaces. In Chapter 16, Khadijah White begins from similar premises of the relativity and unmeasurability of urban noise but explores less its everyday experience than the metaphorical language that is used to refer to noise. As in Hydaralli's chapter, noise's capacity to trouble boundaries is emphasized here, in this case pointing to ethnic boundaries at work in differing responses to the 'noise' of the 'Harlem drummers', which have as much to do with temporal as sonic expectations of appropriate urban behaviour. In these negative responses to urban noise, White detects a number of metaphors of noise, ranging from 'noise as a prison' to 'noise as a contaminant' to 'noise as an invader' used to condemn and marginalize sonic practices and practitioners deemed to be violating social mores, while at the same time pointing to the activist potential of noise for claiming social territories for marginalized groups.

The final chapter in the collection returns to questions of sonic and noise practices, in a polemical reactivation of the work of Walter Benjamin, Guy Debord and other iconic figures of twentieth-century radical thought and practice. In Chapter 17, Bruce Russell, a member of the legendary New Zealand noise group The Dead C., embraces rather than rejects the apparent anachronism at work here, arguing that it is only by activating the apparently outmoded that a cultural practice can be fully critical, radical and even revolutionary (and one could also extend this approach to the use of 'modern' radical theory, made in the chapter itself). That this new habitus is based precisely on an active relation with the past and the outmoded renders this provocative argument both paradoxical and compelling.

PART ONE

The philosophy and aesthetics of noise

1

A chronic condition:
noise and time
Paul Hegarty

Human time, clock time, work time, progressing time: all order our action and perception. With time, the amorphous duration of endless becoming is moulded, and locked away, even if never to be fully dissipated. The other time, the other times outside of 'our', human, time (for there are many), make up a perpetual residue, ready to swell over the bows of clock time. Noise has often been dealt with in terms of its effect on the body, or on parts of it. This means that noise is generally treated as a spatial problem or proposition. As noise is not autonomous but occurs through being perceived, defined, legislated for and against, as noise, this prominence of the physical encounter with noise has led to deep phenomenological insights about its working, but the embodied is not just 'there' in space, it is also 'there' in time.

Noise offers the hope of times improper, the prospect of unending, of non-linearity and the dream of non-death. Noise opens up the sense of what Henri Bergson identifies as 'duration', often in very literal form, and it is through very long, very short, and very static noise pieces that I will address the idea of noise as not just another kind of time, but noise as a questioning of time. Noise does not just disrupt clock time, it brings clock time out in its full reality. Neither does it immerse us in Bergson's optimistic dream of a true human sense of durational being. Instead it is a time that is subtly different from 'our' time. Once we let noise take us through Deleuze and Guattari, and then return to Nietzsche, noise will have told us something about time, and time about noise. In an untimely fashion.

It is with the sound of a hammer falling repeatedly that Bergson begins to round up his thought on time and duration, in *Time and Free Will*: 'when we hear a series of blows of a hammer, the sounds form an indivisible melody in sofar as they are pure sensation, and they also give rise to a dynamic progress' (Bergson, 1960, 125). Two types of time are brought into being through the perception of the blows: first, the purer, truer sensation of something happening which impacts upon our senses; second, the idea of time as a sequence of events, a sequence of moments. In the first type of time, being responds through an acceptance that something is happening of which I am aware; in the second, understanding structures the something into a set of things where discrete events have their own moment and combine into a greater event. Bergson's sloppy use of the word *melody* should not distract us; what he means is that the hammer blows are one entity. This one entity is perceived within 'duration' (the essence of being) in multiple ways, which is how time passes unequally depending on our reaction to what is going on during that time. The division of time into seconds and minutes is a homogenization of the truer time, an imagined objectivity attributed to time. While this is a betrayal of the multiplicity of duration, it is not meaningfully bad; it is more of an inevitability. It is what frames the truer duration, so that duration can truly be. This suggests that Bergson is proposing a deconstructive idea of time, and certainly that is the point of interest for writers like Deleuze who brought out this subtle, perhaps even unconscious self-reflexivity in Bergson.

The idea of 'dynamic progress' is essential, and it is why sound is the privileged encounter of sense and event. Sound offers the prospect of sequence – and even an isolated sound suggests a narrative to which it belongs or disrupts. Bergson's use of the hammer is meant to indicate 'a sound people hear' rather than a historicized activity. The same goes for the sound of tolling bells. Here, Bergson talks about how the person hearing a bell ringing attributes a meaningful sequence to the rings, through counting them, in order to know what time it is, and more profoundly, to understand not only the meaning of the chimes, but that a sequence of humanly produced sounds has a meaning due to its being a sequence (1960, 86–7). The clock tower with its bells measures out time (or represents that measuring), gives it form, tells people that time has form, has predictable form that is always the same. It lets people know that time is as measured by humans, and constantly reminds us of how to process time as something *external* as opposed to being about an internal encounter with external events. Elizabeth Grosz goes further, arguing, after Bergson, that time is embodied, negotiated in processes and interactional, and the other type of time is the one we have constructed as 'empty time', 'time in itself' (Grosz, 2004, 244).

For all the interesting possibilities of evolutionary development of how we, as units of humanity, process time, Bergson ignores the social construction of time: hammers and bell towers are far from neutral as they tie into labour and religion. If sound is the privileged connection of being with the world, then how those beings interact, how their culture informs their hearing, will matter. Both of Bergson's examples belong to the world of order, discipline, productivity and moral goodness. These are good, proper sounds, in their place. At least as described by Bergson. But let us take the bell tower. This turns out to be a more complicated situation than one involving only listening and counting. Church time was connected to rural cycles of activity in times when there were very few large-scale urban environments (i.e. pre-eighteenth century). As well as shepherding Christians to their regular celebrations, the bells marked longer periods of time, in the form of religious and local festivals. Bells would be used for all manner of tasks, a pre-industrial-era mass medium. For that reason and with them under the control of the Church, the French revolutionary governments of the 1790s led a campaign to not only ban bell tolling but also to melt many of them down. They would instead be purely secular (and this would lead to the clock towers' function as marking progress of the day as rationally divided time). In the interim, the bells become noise, the site of resistance, as they go from regular and clearly understood signals to being occasional disruption (see Corbin, 1994). So bells are neither neutral nor fixed in meaning, even if we are talking about a particular bell in a specific village. So, from sound as the driver of experience and perception, we can move to recognizing that whether or not that sound is regarded as noise is important.

Jacques Attali starts from there, in terms of music and public performance. For him, the history of noise is a history of what is not allowed, what is deemed illegal and subject to exclusion. If noise is not a 'thing in itself', then it must alter or come into and out of being as historical time progresses, so noise is synonymous with avant-gardeness, and what is noise now will not necessarily remain so (Attali, 1985, 5–6, 11). If we take Attali's almost entirely cultural reading of how sound is noise or not and apply it to the types of perceptual encounter that interest Bergson, then the implication from Attali is clear: as the listener listens, things lose their noisiness, and acquire meaning or at least sense as to their purpose. This may occur in the course of hearing a particular piece of noise music, or in the course of hearing more and more and beginning to listen instead of hearing, or as certain types of noise become standardized into genres. This endless and inevitable recuperation of noise is why the sometimes misunderstood idea of noise as failure is quite common in noise writing.

To return to Bergson, we can maintain his idea of duration, but historically situated. We then need to think of the two types of time: duration and quanti-fiable, simple yet false time. Noise music or anything that aspires to the condition of noise can have nothing to do with the latter; and yet something that is very long can stimulate the other type of duration. Furthermore, noise music occurs in quantifiable time: on recordings, in performances. Deleuze helps Bergson out here. True duration is multiple, and part of this multiplicity is its encounter with 'standard' time, which is socially connected to order:

> [Duration is] an internal multiplicity, one of succession, of fusion, organi-zation, heterogeneity, discrimination as to quality or of a *difference of nature*, a multiplicity that is *virtual* and *continuous*, incapable of being reduced to number.
>
> (Deleuze, 1966, 31; my translation)

This sounds like the kind of thing noise aspires to, but it is primarily about music. Both Bergson and Deleuze see music as suspending quantitative time in favour of being as duration. For Bergson, music removes us from our constructed illusion of quantitative time. Rhythm and measure interrupt it and bring us into duration, a sensation of time, being and sound as an intensity (Bergson, 1960, 12). On the face of it, this is just stupid, since rhythm and measure seem to exist to reinforce quantitative time, and we will be told by him that our attributing sequentiality to sound is the way in which our true experience is deviated into a limited conception of time and therefore of reality. The point is that the explicit structuredness of music somehow initiates sensation out of time for the listener, as opposed to the more mechanical structuredness of clock time. This too is unsatisfactory, but if we explore intensity as an idea it becomes rather more interesting, as intensity is both inside and outside of duration. On the one hand, intensity is the sense that something is entering the mind to a degree that measure is lost. On the other, intensity implies lack of intensity elsewhere and is always already quantitative. Either way, intensity is not a property of sounds, or a piece of music, but how that input is experienced. The constant movement of music fuels the multiplicity of thought and sensation, and endless becoming of duration, rather than just wallowing in the specific duration of music. This is where Deleuze subtly parts from Bergson, as the latter talks explicitly of the 'cradling' effect of music (Bergson; 1960, 16; trans. modified from 'bercé' to 'lulled and soothed'). Deleuze and Guattari's take on intensity, as developed in *A Thousand Plateaus* (1988), is different: intensity is the quantitative transformed into a plateau or rhizome where connections are reconfigured so as to prevent the arrival of meaning and narrative. Bergson's multiplicity of intensity is one of transformation, Deleuze's is of simultaneity. Where

Bergson imagines music as the way of mobilizing sound so that listening beings move into duration, Deleuze looks to avant-garde music based on disruptions and atonality, as well as to literature of cut-ups or streams of consciousness. Deleuze seems to suggest a way for noise to affect time in a way that Bergson hints at but does not reach, but, even with Deleuze and Guattari, we may still be talking of an 'intensity' that plateaus into a safe cradling despite its formal intent and strategies, as the plateau represents a location that allows dwelling, a certain sort of settling that veers away from the more deconstructive implication of 'the impossible' found in Nietzsche, Bataille or Derrida.

The idea of intensity is implied in all noise: noise is the too much, the unwanted, the excess – in terms of volume, performance practice, simple duration, difficulty. But perhaps too much of this intensity has already been identified as problematic by Bergson: it suggests that something is more intense than something else, (i.e. it is quantitative and therefore removes the intensity as something felt, perceived, sensed or suffered). If intensity is an aim in noise, can it be maintained? Let us look at this literally: intensity in noise consists of volume, duration, unpredictability, loss of reference points. Noise often claims to *be* intensity, an excess that is always more, and therefore capable of inducing an ecstatic reception of the sounds encountered that goes beyond listening. To get even more literal, noise music aspires to be a seemingly permanent condition, and needs time to be noise and music, rather than just a pile of noises; thus this results in long performances or recordings, unrelenting sequences of moves that go against music (arguably in the name of a higher, but I would say lower, musicality). Neither sound nor auditor is to be allowed to settle. This is the reason for Japanese noise artist Merzbow's prolific output – the endless proliferation of *merz* sound takes away the possibility of mastery. On individual albums there may be track divisions, but there is very little in the way of let-up or release. Where there is calm, it is only to act as an undertow of anticipation of noise to come – like being bound and awaiting blows that bring pleasurable pain but not release. Some of his albums sprawl over several CDs, and there have been playbacks of the entire 50-CD *Merzbox* (1999). The endless proliferation of his releases (usually double figures every year) creates both a sense of pre-emptive fatigue and the possibility of continual surprise, as well as the impossibility of keeping up with everything and controlling the Merzbow *oeuvre*. But – is more always more? I would argue that actually noise music's attempts to always be more are precisely an attempt to always be less – less than meaning, less than an object of contemplation. In so doing, the excess, the 'more', becomes low rather than something spiritual and consciousness-raising like Pauline Oliveros' idea of deep listening ('the result of the practice [of deep listening] cultivates appreciation of sounds on a heightened level, expanding the potential for connection and interaction' [Oliveros, mission statement, deeplistening.org]). But we do settle, at least after some initial shocks, and the sheer range of sounds on offer at any one time leads to the sort of duration an untempered Bergson suggests for us – one where organized sounds stand in place of the distractions of everyday life and open up a sense of our own being as duration. The task for noise is to not let this happen (even if noise music occurs in the awareness, it is always going to have to fight for this).

Two examples: Hijokaidan's *Romance* (1990) and Vomir's *Proanomie* (2009), both single-track full-length CDs (77 and 76 minutes respectively), and very different in terms of how they structure and destructure time around them. *Romance* is a constantly changing mess of howling feedback, residue overpowering the possibility of a musical centre to fix upon. Moments cannot fall into a narrative (except of fragmentation), and permanent suspense replaces the ebb and flow of noise and not-noise or different types of noise. In this work, we catch a glimpse of the broken time of noise, which occurs at both individual (this piece) and historical scales (the history of noise) – making them interact. Following Bergson, we can see history as something external that imposes the quantification of events, but we still do not get the sense of the permanent revolution through what is judged to be noise by Attali. Where we do find this is in Walter Benjamin's 'Theses on the Philosophy of History'. Here, he writes that 'where we perceive a chain of events, he [angelus novus] sees one single catastrophe which keeps piling wreckage upon wreckage' (Benjamin, 1992, 249). The angel is an idealized observer, not a moralizer, whose act of observing structures time differently from humans, and may be seen in earthly historical terms as history being made up of disruptions, with historical continuity only the residue. In a way that recalls Bergson, Benjamin goes on to argue that 'the concept of historical progress of mankind cannot be sundered from the concept of its progression through a homogeneous, empty time' (1992, 252). For noise, we can see this working at the level of a history of noise, or of the movement of a piece, or the reaction and reception to either one piece or to a genre.

Romance holds us in an unsettled version of duration, where we are exposed to what Benjamin calls 'jetztzeit' – now-time – a time removed from linear chronological progression, and is precisely not homogeneous. In addition, though removed from the most ordered time, its removal is still in relation to standard time – it is specifically 'duration that is removed from time', not autonomously other. If we go to the other extreme, though, we again encounter a removal from time – as with the case of Vomir's *Proanomie*. This album, like the vast majority of Vomir's pieces, is entirely white noise.

Or something not-quite-white. It comes across as a mass of shifting layers, seeping into one another and in and out of perception. It is as full as possible, but also dramatically empty. Its radical stasis, while being ostensibly noise, is a purposeful rejection of the time that music and organized sound (or sounds recognized as organized – hammers, clocks, bells) structure for us. Non-moving music is often a goal of 'spiritual' music, to create trance-like states, or to reveal an essence of the emptiness of time, as in American minimalisms ranging from Morton Feldman to La Monte Young. Noise music can certainly create this state, but once it happens, are we really in the presence of noise any more? A relentless wall of noise with no prospect of its ever ending (both in terms of overall duration and at any one point not being able to hear where it is going) could create a sense of continually altering absence of satisfaction, like the different pains when shifting around in stress positions. But if we settle on this, I think what we have here is too pure a Bergsonism, too much an attempt to restore an authentic if difficult duration. Once again, Deleuze, this time in the company of Félix Guattari, has a more interesting take on how time can both move and stop (without changing position or halting).

> This proliferation of material has nothing to do with an evolution [...]. It is on the contrary an *involution*, in which form is constantly being dissolved, freeing times and speeds. It is a fixed plane, a fixed sound plane, or visual plane, or writing plane, etc. here, fixed does not mean immobile: it is the absolute state of movement as well as of rest, from which all relative speeds or slownesses spring, and nothing but them. (Deleuze and Guattari, 1988, 267)

This fluctuation between movement and non-movement maps on to and across the lump of once-layered sounds in Vomir's work. That fluctuation then refers back to the empty time of clocks, hinting at pure duration. It is anything but pure duration, however. It is internally compromised, its fullness making it empty of the qualities of music that permitted Bergson to imagine humans rejoining the world of duration. Here, duration is also made empty, made nothing, replaced by a failing authenticity of nothingness.

Vomir frames his recordings (through nihilistic titles and occasional accompanying texts, along with bleak, simple artwork) as a removal from the world, a nihilistic withdrawal assumed as a 'positive' value. But the empty time of the quotidian is not replaced by something better, just the realization of a clearer nihilistic reality – or as his 2010 cassette album puts it, *No Eternal life, Just Endless Annoyance* [*Pas de vie eternelle, juste un emmerdement permannent (sic.)*]. *Proanomie* is not doing noise through its long duration, but in how duration is never allowed to supersede empty time, and this through the collapse of the vertical (the recorded layers) so that the horizontal is always thwarted, returned to the banality of the CD player's clock.

Where we may have to look for noise in terms of time is at the other extreme of the scale, in repetition, or fleetingness. If noise can only ever be fleetingly perceived as noise, however long a specific piece is, and less so the more it is accepted (e.g. in the form of noise genres), then perhaps we should be looking at pieces of noise that are just that – fragments, short works. The ultra-short track offers no literal time in which to settle – it is only attack, its entirety transformed into disruption. Ths isolation of a tiny group of sounds removes the prospect of narrative from inside the track; the only possible sense is one of its coming into existence, only to vanish before being processed. However, stick a whole sequence of these together and you have a pattern (especially on compilations of short tracks). There is still interruption, and huge variety (such as on Naked City's hardcore jazz splurge of micro-cosmic noise pieces *Torture Garden* [1989]) – and often the most impressive short tracks are ones that seem to do away with all the 'unnecessary bits' – think 'perfect pop', hardcore, early Hüsker Dü or Wire. But that would hardly make something noise; instead it would be an attempt to capture some sort of essence of music, or rock, or pop. This might be unavoidable: if noise and music are intimately connected from the outset, then any attempt to get at the core of the functioning of one will tell us something about the other – as if one was the other.

The short track is even more effectively noise when isolated. Organum, like several 'noise music' bands – the Haters, Merzbow – have issued many records in seven-inch format. This format allows a concentration to the point where one track acts as its own world. Many tricks are played with the material of the releases, but what is striking about Organum is the shortness of the records. The material form is a central part of how this works – because we are not talking about a whole series of short tracks, but one short track per side. The Organum collaboration with The New Blockaders, 'Der Graben' (2002), is 1.37 on each side, and the track is basically the same. What we have is an excess of the material side, a luxuriating in the limits of the form, only to fall so far within those limits as to be comical and/or offensive. The second side of the 'Crusade' single (1997) is fewer than 50 seconds long, and this is almost impossible to see due to the transparency of the vinyl. The second side of the 'Horii' 12-inch (1986), 'Keloid', is even more 'extreme' – one side of this 33rpm record is 1.10 long. These tracks have specific noise functions in how they relate to the first sides, using the same material, collapsing it, sucking out developments hinted at on side one, and which we would expect to continue as the piece progresses or has a second part or a different version. With 'Keloid' we also get a huge run-off that takes nearly half as long as the track, and this is a visible 'fuck you' to the listener and to the sounds accumulated on side one. The noise in all these short tracks is not in the content, but in the material form, which adds to the temporal play proposed by Napalm Death or Extreme Noise Terror. The shortness is materially visible, and comments on the material, at the same time as the material element offers insight into the sound part.

But actually we do not need to insist on shortness to the detriment of the extremely long – it is the arbitrariness of time taken that reconnects these tracks to the 70-minute punishment CDs, which leaves us in a duration that is about becoming. After all, a CD can contain one track only and be any length at all: is the 51 minutes of Vomir's *Renonce* (2010) any less hermetic than the 76 minutes of *Proanomie*? Once we accept that duration is not about how much clock time is used, then no. Once we accept that Bergsonian duration is exposed as an insufficient recasting of time, then the 'involution' which Deleuze and Guattari spoke of can occur in however short or long a moment as it structures. The structuring of that time is not just in the sound, but also the material form. If each piece is a blast of thick, swarming yet seemingly static matter, then there is no reason for a piece to end (or begin) other than arbitrarily. The arbitrariness works, first, as an immersive technique (even more in the live context), a disorientation from clock time. Second, it is a fragment of 'now-time' that seems to be exposed temporarily. Third, it is a return to 'empty time': this one is 6.30, this other one 61.42, yet another 23.05, often seeming to be timed simply according to the standards of the recording format. That Vomir is resolutely not about a communing duration is easily seen in the absence of a piece that would last forever, or at least some ridiculous length of time, gauged in days or weeks (although *Claustration* [2007] occupies five CDs).

Vomir's complexification of time needs Nietzsche in addition to Bergson and Deleuze. Nietzsche's eternal return suggests a parallel with Vomir in that to return is to be both caught in a moment, like an insect in amber, and also to be between moments, always only about to be glued into place. Becoming is not about arriving, or even travelling as if to arrive, but something to do with being as irregular pulsation. Grosz signals this when she teams up Darwin and Nietzsche with Bergson, to create a complex idea of time as generative movement that is only ever its own embodied generation:

The eternal return cannot be understood, as [Arthur] Danto reads it, as a doctrine of the repetition of all things, acts and identities. It is not being, matter, things that return: rather, it is returning that is the being (i.e., the becoming) of things and of matter in its particular configurations, including those constituting life.

(Grosz, 2004, 143)

Noise, like time, is no more separate from bodies, from judgements, from listeners, than time is from those that perceive time. But empty noise is not the same as empty time: empty noise undoes time, by expanding it vertically (now) and flattening it horizontally (in linear time). But noise as noise music does not wish to be empty like this, to imagine it can step outside time, music, and even noise, to simply occur as some sort of 'bare noise'. Noise music flits continually around and entwines with what it is not, creating either a jarring sense of time that does not settle, or, in Vomir's case, the very presence of this impenetrable mass empties empty time.

'"Timelessness" to be rejected', writes Nietzsche in *The Will to Power* (Nietzsche, 1968, §1064), amidst his thinking on the eternal return. Eternal recurrence is a removal from time as standard, linear, forward-progressing units of time, in favour of a temporality that is both stuck and permanently moving. Each moment repeats forever, and all time occurs at every moment. So, in Vomir, we see this in the form of the compression of layers of noises into a rolling lump whose movement is illusory. With Hijokaidan, we have the permanent prevention of one moment defining the next moment as the next step in a sequence. With Organum's tracks on seven-inch the moment is all there is. Its prevention of the buildup of repetition is precisely how it leaves minimalism behind in favour of a crushing of time.

It is not that noise is the eternal return, and music the limited sense of time. It is this at first, but noise and music interact in the multiplicity of duration as suggested by Deleuze's Bergson, and for Nietzsche, the eternal return is not permanent war but the struggle between war and peace: 'you resist any ultimate peace; you will the eternal recurrence of war and peace, man of renunciation, all this you wish to renounce? Who will give you the strength for that?' (Nietzsche, 1974, §285). It is a struggle about whether contradiction, opposition, difference can occur. Even then, the idea of the eternal return is not an answer to how noise makes time or vice versa, but a way of situating it as a question, or more accurately as something that will not be solved. Even as the prospect of noise time recedes, Nietzsche holds out the thought that even if we cannot get to the essence of how time structures being, something similar to noise will bring us closer, bring an actively nihilistic non-understanding:

To *endure* the idea of recurrence one needs: freedom from morality; new means against the fact of *pain* (pain conceived as a tool, as the father of pleasure; there is no cumulative consciousness of displeasure); the enjoyment of all kinds of uncertainty, experimentalism.

(Nietzsche, 1968, §1060)

Perhaps Nietzsche wasn't talking about noise. But, if he wasn't in *The Will to Power*, he was in *The Gay Science*, where he writes that 'the whole musical box repeats eternally its tune which may never be called a melody' (Nietzsche, 1974, §168). And this means every tune which does not attain melody, every fractured moment, condensed in on itself, over and over, without ever coming to the pleasure world of order.

The hammers of the bell and the worker do not necessarily cede to the philosopher, but they will perform a new philosophy nonetheless, because Nietzsche also has a hammer for us. He describes his book *Twilight of the Idols* as a 'great declaration of war' (Nietzsche, 1998, 3), but the hammer is not one for smashing. Instead it is a diagnostic hammer, one for tapping the idols to demonstrate their inner emptiness, 'to hear in response that famous hollow sound which speaks of swollen innards' (ibid.). This auscultation is also present when noise stretches or compresses itself, making it a questioning of time, as opposed to music which is the structuring of time into clock time. Vomir's mass of noise endlessly recycles and never attains a moment in which it can dwell. The listener is brought to the idol of music which was supposed to help reveal time through chronological development, periodicity, narrativized sound sequences, and invited to touch 'with a hammer as with a tuning fork' (ibid.). This empty time is brought out as always already having been the condition of music through the empty and emptying saturations of noise. Not that this will change anything, or provide a cure. Noise has not brought us to time, to a time or out of time. This is in fact time as a rejection of 'being in time', noise becoming time that smothers the listener while fending him or her away.

2

Amusia, noise and the drive:

towards a theory of the audio unconscious

Scott Wilson

Amusia and *amusia*

It all sounded like screaming.
– D.L., on going to the opera
SACKS, 2007, 105

Well, you get in that kitchen make some noise with
the pots 'n' pans.
BIG JOE TURNER, 'SHAKE, RATTLE AND ROLL'

Judging by the cases of neurological amusia collected in Oliver Sacks' book *Musicophilia* (2007), the condition never concerns simply a case of deafness or indifference to music. Amusia does not describe a world of silence so much as the presence of noise where there ought to be music. Music, or an aspect of it, is perceived as noise. Sometimes the condition affects melody, sometimes harmony producing a dysharmonia. Elsewhere it affects rhythm but not metre, or the reverse. Even in the more extreme instances, it remains the case that music is not absent but experienced as a dissonant negativity that is sometimes overwhelming. In a classic example from the neurological literature, Henri Hécaen and Martin L. Albert described one man, apparently a former singer, who 'complained of hearing a "screeching car" whenever he heard music' (cited in Sacks, 2007, 101). For Vladimir Nabokov music was agony and he complained of feeling 'flayed' when he heard orchestral music. The condition of amusia therefore describes the occasion of music as the experience of a tormenting noise that causes subjective fragmentation, even heralding death.

Sacks' examples are all presumed to have biological causes, but they are expressed in highly subjective forms sensitive to music as a mode of subjectification, even of power and violence. In Western culture at least it seems that noise is a source of more annoyance and distress than vision. The phrase 'noise pollution' does not have an optical equivalent in spite of Western society being bombarded by visual stimuli. This pollution does not just concern aircraft or traffic noise, car alarms, ring tones, advertising jingles, repetitive pop music, the percussive hum of personal stereos, iPods and so on. There is perhaps nothing more annoying than the sound of other people as in the case, for example, of the Parisian psychoanalyst Jacques-Alain Miller's Islamic neighbours whose music perfectly evokes for him the *jouissance* of the Other that lies at the 'extimate' core of a racism that no rational understanding or liberalism can erase (see Miller, 1988). Music may be perceived as an unbearable noise when it is experienced as the expression of the Other's *jouissance*. Perhaps this also applies where the Other is the locus of the law in an institutional as well as symbolic sense, not just when its alterity is figured in signifiers of ethnicity. Since 'music can organize our bodies and keep our minds in order' (Hegarty, 2007, 11), this musical expression of order may well, like Sartre's gaze, be experienced as nauseating, unbearable. Could something like this be behind Nabokov's problem with orchestral music? No doubt a certain form of amusia arises as an effect of sensibilities that are as much political as musical. For Brian Eno, 'classical music [...] represents old-fashioned hierarchical structures, ranking, all the levels of control. [...] I have to say that I wouldn't give a rat's ass if I never heard another piece of such music' (Eno and Kevin, 1995, 12).

Sacks's main example of amusia in his book is a 76-year-old woman to whom he was introduced in 2006. 'D.L.' is the daughter of a very musical family who did everything they could to teach and acculturate her into a world of melody and song, but to no avail. Sacks does not consider whether or not the woman's amusia could in some way be related to the music of family romance and a father who made her listen to and play music 'again and again'. Nor does he comment on a school and social circle that not only failed to recognize or take seriously her condition but also forced her to sing publicly and attend regular concerts in musicals such that when her amusia was recognized she lamented that an earlier diagnosis 'might have saved her from a lifetime of being bored or excruciated by concerts' (Sacks, 2007, 106). When asked what music sounds like to her, Sacks writes that Mrs. L. always answers: 'if you were in my kitchen and threw all the pots and pans on the floor, that's what I hear' (106). Later, Sacks adds, she noted that she was 'very sensitive to high notes' and that the opera 'sounded like screaming' (105). Opera, of course, is quite an acquired taste and I suspect Mrs. L.'s sentiments in this regard may well be shared by others who have failed to acquire it, but it does not necessarily imply a lack of taste or appreciation of music.

Indeed, her view is shared by some people with a highly developed sense of musical taste. In a heated debate in the letters page of *The Times* concerning the introduction of jazz and world music on Radio 3, the BBC's classical music channel, a correspondent wrote: 'I have always enjoyed the jazz and world music content. The problem for me [...] is opera and operatic singing [...] I get great pleasure from most forms of music, but not from maniacal screaming. Give us music, Radio 3, and we will return' (*The Times*, 7 May 2008, 20).

D.L.'s description of thrown pots and pans is as interesting an example as operatic screaming. Sacks does not give enough information to ask questions concerning any personal or idiosyncratic reasons for such a description, but it inevitably throws up cultural connotations. A kitchen's pots and pans are not normally thrown on the floor without also signifying some kind of crisis, producing a cacophony shattering domestic order. For many women like D.L. born in 1930, the order of domesticity to which they were confined, willingly or not, was shattered, at least symbolically, by the 'sexual revolution' of the 1960s. This revolution was heralded in the 1950s when young women of D.L.'s age were invited by Bill Haley and his Comets to 'get out of that kitchen and rattle those pots and pans' in a version of the rock 'n' roll classic 'Shake, Rattle and Roll' that failed to diminish the suggestive tenor of Big Joe Turner's original. For many of D.L.'s father's generation attuned to the Classics, such a vulgar form was of course not perceived as music at all but a racket, a hideous noise that, in the generational antagonism it represented, similarly shattered domestic order.

For D.L.'s generation, 'Shake, Rattle and Roll' provided the noise music that precipitated the relation of non-relation of sexual, social and generational antagonism. Rattling pots and pans in the context of sexual suggestion and the disruption of social order has long cultural roots, of course. Charivari, for example, as a form of popular power, was sometimes the source or catalyst for revolt; and in France it remains a term for the noise of public ridicule. Charivari is therefore an important example of how noise is not exterior to music but the same thing. It may be 'rough' but the banging of pots and pans in charivari is music, an amusical music that exposes its violence and power. In the unfortunate instance of Mrs. D.L., all music seems to have become a charivari, forever summoning up, through the sound of the shattering of domestic order, discordance with her own social reality. D.L.'s amusia turns classical music into noise, screaming and the banging of pots and pans, the very sound, for her father's generation, of the rock 'n' roll of Jerry Lee Lewis, Little Richard, Big Joe Turner and so on. In classic Freudian terms (and a certain Freudianism was at its height in America in the 1950s), D.L.'s amusia is the symptom of a repressed desire, the message of her father's generation being returned in reverse form.

Music, as amorous promise, celestial harmony, other enjoyment or inordinate joy is also a singular locus of discontent. In order to explore what is both singular and common with regard to the affective power of music, it seems to me to be helpful to appropriate the neurological notion of amusia for psychoanalytic cultural theory. In this notion of *amusia* the *a* denotes the subjective intensity of the unconscious in disharmony with the world. The *a* marks the point of noise, tunelessness, the pain of the pots and pans, that music is to me or my music, my sound is to others. I am that dissonance, that shattering explosion of pots and pans. It would be easy to dismiss the suffering that is frequently involved in the amusical perception of noise as a symptom, perhaps a symptom of hysteria. For Lacan, the symptom is not a call for interpretation but a pure *jouissance* addressed to no one. A symptom is a particular way in which the subject enjoys and suffers from the unconscious. If neurological amusia is a symptom, then it is one that experiences music as a pure *jouissance*. While *jouissance* emerges in the default of speech, occupying the place vacated by the absence of meaning, with *amusia* suffering is related not just to absence but to a form. Amusia establishes the subject in a negative relation to a form that it recognizes through suffering, through an experience of painful noise. In amusia *jouissance* is correlated to a form – music – that communicates without saying anything. It is thus more like Lacan's notion of the sinthome in which the *jouissance* specific to a subject may be embodied in an art that Lacan elaborated in relation to James Joyce (Lacan, 2005, 38). Like the sinthome, the amusical relation to music denotes a singularity, a singular *jouissance* or rather joy exterior to, or foreclosed from, the symbolic order and the metaphors and metonymies of a purely linguistic unconscious. Perhaps this is why, even though they may be foreclosed from the name-of-the-father, psychotics can sustain an approximate relation to symbolic systems through music, and indeed through mathematics and numerology (see Wilson, 2011).

A considerable tenor in his day, James Joyce produced a remarkably musical form of writing that, in *Finnegans Wake*, exceeds all possibility of understanding and interpretation – to the intense irritation and frustration of many readers, if not literary scholars happy to be kept infinitely busy. The text is afflicted with an *amusical* musicality that points towards a different relation to the auditory sphere than language, or indeed vision. For the almost blind Joyce, the field of vision (and all the discursive metaphors it gives rise to: clarity, clearness, lucidity, transparency) was not his favoured domain. *Amusia* occupies a different register to language, vision and self-reflection if not to echo. Without reflection, amusia nevertheless relates the question of the subject, devoid of all subjective qualities, devoid of being, substance, form, content, essence, to the affectivity of music, to what affects itself and affects with music. The '*a*' of *amusia* both denotes and places in question, in horror and joy, the critical and clinical locus of a certain form of life. This very question is the one that reverberates in the auditorium of unconscious desire, a question posed in the eruption of an operatic scream. 'I scream'. Or rather there is screaming. Someone or something screams.

The Scream

I was walking along a path with two friends – the sun was setting – suddenly the sky turned blood red – I paused, feeling exhausted, and leaned on the fence – there was blood and tongues of fire above the blue-black fjord and the city – my friends walked on, and I stood there trembling with anxiety – and I sensed an infinite scream passing through nature.
EDVARD MUNCH, *Journal*, Nice, 22 January 1892

Whether it is the volcanic scream that burst from Krakatoa to leave a blood-red sky from 1883–4, the scream of nature red in tooth and claw or the scream of the dying God, the strange figure in Munch's famous painting presses its hands against its ears in horror and agony. *The Scream* is of course not just a single image created in 1893, but a series of images produced between 1893 and 1910. Or rather, it is a series of repetitions of the same image of profound dissonance with one's sonic environment. It is one of the most resonant images of the twentieth century and beyond, reverberating in all aspects of culture from the most exalted to the most disposable. Among many other things, it is a powerful statement that the heavens no longer resound with the music of the spheres but with a primal scream that echoes from the dawn of time. While in this muddy vesture of decay we cannot hear the harmony of immortal souls, nor do we believe in them any more, we do sense an in-human voice: a scream passing through nature. And the more we cup our ears against its background radiation, the more loudly it resonates throughout inner and outer space like cosmic tinnitus.

Munch was almost the exact contemporary of Sigmund Freud and like *The Scream* psychoanalysis hears only the voice of suffering where there might be music. In psychoanalysis, music is always subsumed into the category of 'voice'; it is 'a voice and nothing more' (Dolar, 2006). But in this, psychoanalysis is no different from the history of Western philosophy. If epistemology privileges sight and light (insight, concept, theoria, enlightenment and so on), ontology privileges voice; it is 'phonocentric', as we know from Jacques Derrida. 'There has only ever been one ontological proposition,' wrote Gilles Deleuze famously: 'Being is univocal' (Deleuze, 1997, 35). From Parmenides to Heidegger, Duns Scotus to Deleuze himself, 'it is the same voice that is taken up, in an echo which itself forms the whole deployment of the univocal' (ibid.). Psychoanalysis is the symptom of this general amusia even as it diagnoses its suffering, since it remains constrained within the same condition. This is why psychoanalysis needs to open itself to an 'amusianalysis' in which music is regarded as heterogeneous to language and speech. Music is not a subcategory of language. It is not a pre- or proto-language; it is not the pure materiality of language, lalanguage or the excess of language.

Very little of the sound in the world is speech, even when some or all of it is called music. To the music of the spheres could be added the music of the oceans and the creatures within them, on land and sky that crawl, skip, hop and fly across the earth, borne by the music of the wind, of the tectonic plates, and further, from the assemblages of musical milieux, those co-evolutionary domains of multi-cellular beings to the unimaginable subatomic domain of super strings, the secret vibrations supposedly constitutive of all matter including dark and anti-matter ... all the various strata of *natura musicans* that never stops resonating in the impossibility of silence. Of course, through being named as such, music becomes the subject of speech, but that is the essential limitation of language – to reduce music to speech is to fail to hear it.

That music and speech are heterogeneous is evident in the profound desire that music speak, that it say what words cannot say. Conventionally, music is attributed with a special power of speech, such that it can address the question of existence in a way that escapes language. That this is a delusion does not dispel the desire for musical speech. This is one of the reasons why it is essential that psychoanalysis speaks of voice rather than music and its relation to desire. It is possible that music has significance for speaking beings only insofar as it is misperceived as voice, only insofar as it is attributed with meaning. But music says nothing and has no meaning, any more than mathematics. The correspondences that are found in mathematics and music seem to suggest that they must mean something, but they do not. 'To extract a natural law is to extract a meaningless formula', says Lacan. Formulae consist of 'pure signifiers,' and 'the idea that such a signifier might signify something [...] means that God is present in natural phenomena and speaks to us in his language' (Lacan, 1993, 184). Since music has no propositional content, no reference to anything other than itself, no predication, it makes no sense to say it is either meaningful or meaningless, since 'music does not even have the *possibility* of being meaningful' in a linguistic sense (see Patel, 2008, 304). Language and music are heterogeneous forms and forces, different particulate systems that trace out two different domains of the unconscious, or two different unconscious tracks that may overlap and block the path of one another, occupy its space, but not at the same time.

Dissonance and repetition

For convenience, in order to stress both the similarity and the difference between the audio unconscious and the unconscious supposed to be structured like a language, I propose to trace Lacan's famous schema of desire that is, appropriately, broken up like a sonata into three or four movements. Desire is an effect of speech, but here I want to attempt to demonstrate topographically, following Lacan, how desire also operates as an effect of an audio unconscious where speech is absent or misperceived and music is the privileged form harnessing the drive. The following schema, the structure of relations which I retain only to change the terms, are of course reproduced in the essay 'The Subversion of the Subject and the Dialectic of Desire' (Lacan, 2006, 671–702). The myth that provides the point of reference throughout Lacan's essay is Hegel's account of self-consciousness that produces the dialectic between master and slave in *The Phenomenology of Spirit*. Lacan's subject of the unconscious is of course defined against both Hegel's philosophical subject of self-consciousness and the subject that is ejected from the discourse of science. While the latter assembles its regimes of knowledge, its laws and formulae, this is at the cost of closing the borders to the regime of revealed truth that might enable them to mean something to somebody. It is this gap between truth and knowledge that psychoanalysis hopes to bridge. While Hegel's dialectic offers a structure, it is not, for Lacan, self-consciousness that defines the subject. The knowledge that defines the subject for Lacan is the knowledge that is borne by the letter whose agency directs the subject without its knowing. It is still a subject of knowledge; it just doesn't know that it knows. It is the job of psychoanalysis, therefore, to try, by means of its own dialectic of desire, to reveal the truth of unconscious knowledge (or at least *wo es war*) in the speech of the analysand as an effect of the process of analysis.

Heterogeneous to speech, music also ties together knowledge, in the form of *savoir faire*, and a truth about which one can say little other than that one experiences it. For there to be people ignorant of the knowledge it takes to make music, who can nevertheless become passionately affected by it (in love or hatred), no doubt implies the presence of unconscious musical knowledge, but further it also suggests the opening to a truth in the affective, revelatory experience that exceeds all knowledge including musical knowledge. Coming from elsewhere, what it reveals (perhaps all that it reveals) or exposes is the finitude that is shared by everyone it affects and passes through. The graphs in Figures 2.1 to 2.4 attempt to show where desire is situated in relation to something or someone that is defined in relation to sound. The first graph is the 'elementary cell', sometimes known as the 'quilting point' or 'button-tie' that shows the stitching of a mythical drive into the signifying chain.

The vector S→S' describes the locus of virtual sounds that is brought into actuality through an initial encounter with sound (a 'big bang', say). The trauma of this first aural explosion is missed, however, and is only perceptible in the echo that follows, the repetition that occurs when the

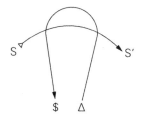

Δ→$ = the drive
S→S' = the locus of sound

Figure 2.1 Graph 1: The elementary cell

vertical vector re-enters the locus of sound. This establishes a point of aural perception in relation to a locus of dissonance and repetition. Repetition establishes the rule that gives consistency to the locus of sound in two ways: first, through the rhythm and spacing that establishes sound in a temporal line of different tones and beats, and second, through the more profound echo of the event of dissonance that sustains, in repetition, experience and memory. In the second graph (Figure 2.2), therefore, there is no Big Other other than the locus of repetition in which repetition is the echo of originary dissonance. This locus and its principle of differentiation and organization that repetition brings to sound (promising harmony, melody and so on as well as the repetition of dissonance) provide the possibility of music.

Jacques Brel's hatred of the accordion

In Jacques Brel's famous song 'Vesoul', the sound of the accordion provides the point of amusia that articulates the singer's ambivalent relation with bourgeois Paris. In the song, the marital complaint that male desire is being pulled hither and thither by the desire of his spouse, that is itself driven by the 'mad dash tourism of the bourgeoisie', accelerates, upon the dissonant scream of the accordion, as it becomes purely the effect of a machinic oscillation, such that even the key sites of bohemian Paris become just another tourist attraction. It is a perfect musical performance of Walter Benjamin's famous essay, 'Some Motifs on Baudelaire' where the former suggests that the latter makes the basis of lyric poetry 'the shock experience', characteristic of modernity, that 'has become the norm' (Benjamin, 1999, 158). This is music beyond the pleasure principle. At first, the relatively sedate opening of the song merely supports the highly rhythmic here-and-there of Brel's lyrics, his poetic persona being pulled along by an alter ego that is itself indistinguishable from the 'fort-da' of the signifier, the names of the towns. But upon the dissonant screech of the accordion, the music starts going like a train, becoming indistinguishable from the noise music of urban travel. The oscillating movement accelerates, noise becoming continuous with music, in such a way that the subject of twentieth-century travel becomes wired into the shocks and rhythms of systemic motion: 'D`ailleurs j`ai horreur/ De tous les flons flons/De la valse musette/et de l`accordéon.' Even as the noise of travel becomes music, music itself becomes noise, particularly the unbearable wailing of the accordion, yet Brel (or his persona) demands more of it: 'Chauffe! Chauffe, Marcel!' Turn it up: faster, louder, harder, in a self-flagellating racket that propels the musical locomotive, untrammelled, along the tracks of the death drive and the inevitable crash – itself systemic – that is nothing but the anorganic pulse of (re)generation, dissonance and repetition.

At this point Brel seems to merge into his bourgeois persona – as the bohemian Paris of Baudelaire and *Les fleurs du mal* that, as a Belgian bourgeois, Brel desired and came to embody himself, becomes disclosed as yet another heritage site, just a sordid little train stop at Gare St Lazare. The noise of the accordion, clichéd signifier of Parisian romance, is abject, unbearable, the superegoic means by which the bohemian punishes himself. In TV spectaculars, Brel presented the spectacle (of himself) as the bohemian poet who, even as he sneers at the bourgeoisie, becomes captured and propelled by an 'auratic' logic of sound: the desire for noise, for increased shock and sensation that ultimately leaves one fatigued, emptied-out, yet again arriving at Vesoul, the most boring place in the world. '*Mais, je te préviens/le voyage est fini!*' But, no, *encore!*

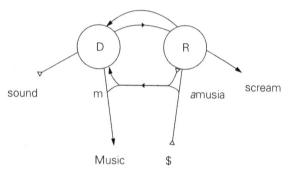

Figure 2.2 Graph 2: Dissonance (D) and Repetition (R)

Music, as a particular organization of sound, offers a certain symbolic form, in its difference from the non-music that is disorganized sounds, in which may be sensed a momentary unity, harmony or order. As such, music occupies the position of Ego-Ideal that hooks the imaginary on to the symbolic. The lower part of the graph that in Lacan's original maps the mirror stage, here describes the process of individuation [*m*] that is produced in the relation between music and dissonance in an experience of *a*musia. The example of Jacques Brel's 'Vesoul' above may be mapped on to the figure in the following way: $ marks the point of the Belgian *petit bourgeois* Jacques that is repressed by Brel the celebrated Parisian musician and the object of parody in the form of the alter ego, the bourgeois husband afflicted by his wife's touristic wanderlust. The extimate point of *a*musia denotes the ambivalence towards the accordion with which Brel/his persona punishes himself in his demands

('Chauffe! Chauffe, Marcel!'). From the point of *amusia* the vector goes in two directions: towards the 'originary' (missed) event of dissonance that grounds the subject as an effect of its repetition, and the symbolic form 'Music' in the position of Ego-Ideal.

Brel, as celebrated ego, is an effect of the vector $\rightarrow$Music where the latter denotes the music/poetry of bohemian Paris (Baudelaire's *Fleurs du mal*), the Ego-Ideal that provides the form and context for Brel's work and identity. The 'screaming' of the accordion that marks the break in the song is of course the symptom of petit Jacques's discomfort with this symbolic mandate evident in the self-consciousness of the parody and, perhaps, by the fact that in the song he never makes it back to Antwerp but is propelled along a trajectory of noise music, the anorganic pulse of dissonance and repetition, over which he has no control.

The three delusions

In his perception and image of the locus of sound as an infinite scream, Edvard Munch testifies that the space in which the extimacy of sound passes is voice as much as nature. Because the locus of sound passes through the voice of speaking beings it is misperceived as speech, an effect of general *amusia*. The scream that 'passes through nature' is therefore misperceived as an appeal. But the question arises as to whom the appeal is addressed.

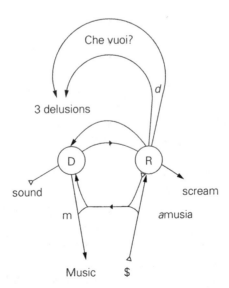

Figure 2.3 Graph 3: The three delusions – love, hatred and ignorance

In speech, the appeal is a demand to the mother or father that becomes alienated as infinite desire when its specific needs are met and all that remains is the demand for love. Desire, that is always desire of the Other, remains eternally posed concerning the question of existence. Che vuoi? What do you want of me? Who am I? What am I for?

The failure of the Other to answer these questions in any adequate way means that the burden can fall on music. In its ineffability music paradoxically suggests a locus of more profound meaning. Desire [d] emerges, in relation to music, through the delusion that it speaks, that it can convey things – feeling, emotion, truth – more than words can say. As such it seems to promise that it can directly address the question of existence through affect and tell me, or make me feel, who I am. This essential delusion, at the end of desire, takes the various forms of love, hatred and ignorance (in the position of $\$\lozenge a$, the structure of fantasy). The delusion of love believes that music speaks directly to me, or indeed that it is only through music that I can express myself. My guitar, piano, lyre, speaks of the longing of my soul that mere words cannot express. Alternatively, music speaks not to me but to my rival, and I hate it. The delusions of love and hate are, of course, essentially the same where the rival is nothing other than an alter ego. In the delusion of ignorance, music speaks neither to me nor to my rival but purely to itself in its own language of which I am ignorant. My ignorance, however, implies that it has some special access to knowledge and consequently to knowledge about me about which I wish to know nothing.

Audio unconscious

At the upper level of the graph (Figure 2.4), the vector that runs parallel to the locus of sound marks the place of the audio unconscious. The term 'joy' should replace Lacan's term 'jouissance', however, just as 'death' replaces 'castration'. Death does not here refer to the empirical end to someone's life, but to the continuous death of someone or something that music denotes as the defining sound of a life. This does not just refer to the funeral song or desert island discs that one carries around in pleasurable anticipation of death and the celebration and commemoration of one's life; it refers to the music that for better or worse in joy or in agony marks the indeterminable, endless possibility of the death of someone or something. It refers to the music that reduces us to waste, to noise that is framed by the silence of death, which returns from the past in the form of repetition in the clamour for being. It is the music of an indeterminable joy before death.

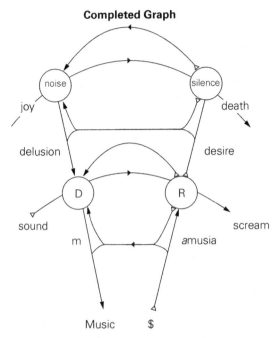

Figure 2.4 Graph 4: The audio unconscious

For Lacan, 'the drive is what becomes of demand when the subject vanishes from it' (2006, 692); that is to say, the subject of language, speech. The drive is pure, speechless demand; as such it is usually characterized as silent. While 'Eros is sonorous', suggests Deleuze, 'the death instinct is silent' (Deleuze, 1990, 241). For Georges Bataille, Eros is inextricably bound to death, hence 'eroticism is silence' (Bataille, 1986, 264), except in the case of 'those people whose very presence in the world is a pure denial of silence, a chattering, a neglect of potential solitude' (ibid.). The place of the death drive ($\$\lozenge D$) is therefore denoted by silence. However, silence is impossible, no doubt in the same way that the experience of death is impossible (since death takes away the consciousness necessary to experience). John Cage discovered when he was placed in an anechoic chamber that silence is precluded by the noise of the body that inhabits it. Consequently, when Cage staged a piece of music that consisted of a motionless pianist at a silent piano, music became whatever noise could be perceived in the 4 minutes and 33 seconds that were allotted to the performance. In the redefinition of music to whatever sound may be audible within a particular temporal frame, the noises of the bodies of the audience are conjoined with their ambient environment in the demand for music.

A number of processes have been designed into the installation to come between the sender and the receiver of the message. The bipolar transmission usually considered to lie at the heart of human communication is complicated to such a degree that one is forced to say either that what is being made visible here is not human communication (or not only that), or that human communication is not definable by the dual subjective structure – between sender and receiver – that is almost universally assumed to characterize it.

The first complication is that the message appears in an entirely different mode than the code that enables it. It is present in a purely visible way. It is seen before it can be read, and it cannot be read as it is seen. This is because the flashing in the sky is a translation of the digital input into an analogue signal that preserves only selected characteristics of the digitally encoded linguistic meaning. Each letter in the message corresponds to a change in the intensity of the beam. Letter by letter, different light intensities daisy-chain without interruption, in a continuity of variation. There is a moment of near darkness between words, but this interval is in no way comparable to the off-state of the digital code. It is more a punctuation between the conti-nuities of variation on either side than merely one half of the on-off binary. The off-state of the interval makes a threesome: the two series of intensities, with the interval between.

This 'thirdness' (to speak like founding semiotician C. S. Peirce) is the basic articulation of the signal. But three's a crowd. Each of the variations punctuated by the off-state is multiple, consisting of a population of inten-sities. This complexity translates as a pulsation. The result is very different from the strobe effect ordinarily used to transmit code visually. Most if not all of the messages will consist of more than two words. Coming irregu-larly in the midst of a series of changes in intensity, the moment of near darkness will meld into the continuing pulsing, its threeness into the multi-plicity it parses. Rather than an off-state that is the opposite of an on-state, it will come across as the low note on the same scale (brightness). In other words, the compositional principle of the signal, as experienced, is more a continuous modulation of a dimension of perception, than an encoding of separate pieces of data or a sequencing of units of meaning. Modulation is the very definition of the analogue signal – a continuous variation in amplitude and time (that is, a smoothly varying value).

Something like language

So what value is being analogically varied here? The changes in intensity are based on the frequency with which the corresponding letter occurs in the language of the message. The higher the frequency, the brighter the pulse. Letter frequency is a socio-historical variable. It materializes in statistical form the particularities of a culturally specific linguistic evolution. In Amodal Suspension, this cultural-frequency variable pulses into view as a visual rhythm. The encoding of letter frequency into the beam attaches it geneti- cally to culture-specific rhythms of speech. But the encoding is not visually decodable by the viewer, any more than the meaning of the message can be seen in the pulse and flutter. What comes across is, simply, the rhythm. A language-like rhythm – without the actual language.

Rhythm is the most perceptually salient dimension of language. Phonemes disappear into their meaning. You don't hear them to the exact degree to which you understand them. But their rhythm asserts itself, an experienced something-extra that conveys an emphasis, accent, tone or mood. The rhythm carries the force of the phrase, above and beyond its structure and meaning. *Amodal Suspension* uses encoding to make visible this extra-linguistic effec- tiveness: the force of language. This is the variable that is being analogically presented. The display conveys the feel of a statement's impact without its meaning. We get the same feel from the firefly's inhuman light show of exoskeletal love. It is impossible to watch them and not get the uncanny feeling that they are 'talking' to each other.

The installation makes human language visible at a rhythmic limit where it shades into a dimension of experience that is necessary to its workings but is not of its mode, since it is also the province of the bug. The work creates a visual analogue of human language, something 'like' it, that reattaches it not only to a particular cultural evolution but also to the biosemiotic background from which it emerged. The meaning and structure of language are 'suspended' in the beam, against the forceful background of their own emergence. What is positively experienced here is a transitional zone where language in its human mode rhythmically returns to the animal fold from which it came, at the same time as its sound mode translates into a visual mode akin to gesture (which beckons to speech, heralding its possibility, in the human as in the animal). What lies transitionally between modes is 'amodal'. Hence the title of the piece.

The force of a statement never fails to make itself felt. But it also always fades, making way for the next utterance. The beams slowly rise into the sky and decrease in intensity while preserving the original rhythm. In the meantime, other messages are received and displayed. With 20 towers, up to 10 messages can beckon at once, each with a signature pulse. The air crowds with the sight of language rising. The properly linguistic dimension is not lost. It is still there, latent as a definite possibility in the code that is never shown, though it enables the display.

To see the latent content, the addressee must 'grab' the message from the beaming crowd as he would pluck a point of light from a summer cloud of fireflies. This is done by clicking on the beam on the real-time website simulation of the event, or on-site by cell phone by entering the number of the tower currently carrying the message. To access the coded content, the participant must perform a digital analogue of gesture, beckoning delivery of the meaning content. And it has to be done fast. As soon as the message is grabbed, the beam abruptly disappears. If someone beats them to it, they receive a message informing them of the name and location of the poacher. The message may still be accessed from the public log archived on the server.

Language to the third power

The base definition of linguistic communication is often considered to be the transmission of a syntactically coded content from a sender to a receiver. The problem with that bipolar transmission model is that it is incapable of distinguishing between insect communication and human language – and not because the model has complexly returned to their transitional zone, but merely because it has oversimplified. There may or may not be a syntax to firefly flashes, but there certainly is to the dance of the bees. The reason commonly given to explain why the bee does not have language even though it is capable of communicating syntactically coded message content is that the message cannot be retransmitted to a third party.

The communicational system found in nature best able to do that is human language. Human communication is defined by this linguistic 'thirdness', by its capacity not for linear transmission but for indirection. This complicates things: with the third party in waiting down the line comes the possibility of that party jumping the line and intercepting the message. Indirect relay and message poaching, or hacking, is the true ground of human communication. With indirect relay comes the inevitability of noise and the accompanying distortion of message content. A fuller model than sender and receiver, with a coded message passing between them, would be a combination of the games of 'telephone' and musical chairs.

'Third' parties never come in ones. Where there's one third, there's bound to be another down the noisy line. Three's a crowd again. But this time the triadic multiplicity separates human language back out, returning it to its proper mode. Lozano-Hemmer's installation also makes visible the re-arising or re-emergence of specifically human communication, in its first flush, or flash, seen for what it is: a nonlinear crowd phenomenon. The rising community of poachable beams is Lozano-Hemmer's visual analogue of what he calls the chaotic 'social soup' of many-party thirdness: a literal flash mob.

Earlier it was said that a number of mechanisms interjected themselves between the sender and receiver in a way that complicated the linear model of message transmission. Also mentioned was the possibility of message poaching, which interjects between the sender and receiver the potential presence of a third party on the line. There was the further necessity of catching the message with a flick of the thumb or finger. This alloys the verbal dimension of language with the bodily dimension of gesture, bringing into the experience of the installation an experiencing of the limit between the linguistic and the extra-linguistic, human thought and the body, the human and the non-human. It brought what we normally tend to think of as mutually exclusive domains into a proximity, a convergence that is not stated or displayed but rather performed. To participate in the installation, one has to perform this limit of language. Speech and bodily action brush up against one another and relay into one another, in a way that redirects attention at least momentarily away from the message content, to the speech act as performance and as event. Embodied social performance becomes more noticeably, in fact unmissably, a part of the speech act in a way that brings to the fore the accompaniment of the linguistic by the extra-linguistic – in convergence, but not necessarily entirely at peace with one another. The need to interrrupt the understanding of the message content with the effort of the catch produces interference patterns between content and performance context.

There is a third mechanism of meaning interference built into the installation: translation. Messages could be entered in English or Japanese. If, for example, a message entered in Japanese is poached by a third party using English, the message is automatically translated using an off-the-shelf automatic translating software system widely used on the Web (Systran's Sherlock). As anyone who has used the translating feature on the Web knows, automatic translation is not a very advanced art. Errors inevitably slip in, often to comic effect. Using automatic translation in this context brings interference into the very heart of the message, again frustrating the possibility of transparent communication. The linear transmission of message content is scrambled, in a technologically assisted version of the telephone game.

All of these mechanisms for interrupting transmission and creating interference make *noise* as much a part of the installation's content as the meaning of the messages conveyed.

Sea of noise, crest of words

There are different ways of thinking about noise. The most widespread is native to information theory and corresponds to our everyday understanding of the term. Noise according to this definition is the opposite of signal. It comes at the signal from outside its structure and disrupts it. On this view, the structure of the signal is clear and self-sufficient. Its meaning is as unambiguous as it can be made by the code used to construct it, unless it is perturbed from without. The extra-linguistic element of noise is cast as the simple opposite of linguistically formed message transmission. It is its negative: the unstructured and unstructuring.

But in *Amodal Suspension*, when we approach the extra-linguistic, we aren't moving into the simple opposite, outside or negative of the linguistic. We are moving into a zone of indistinction where language shades back into what it emerged from – gesture, body, animality, the multiplicity of the population whose collective life gives rise to the need for communication, whose endless reserve of third parties ensures its continuation and plasticity, and whose history is sedimented in the structure of its language and the frequency of its elements. This zone of indistinction is not the negation of language but rather the field of its emergence – not its unstructured opposite, but the event of its coming into being. The installation returns language to its generative or constitutive field, its field of emergence.

There is another way of understanding noise that dovetails with Lozano-Hemmer's use of it in *Amodal Suspension*. It comes from certain philosophies concerned with ontogenesis and emergence, and has also been explored in some avant-garde art of the twentieth century, such as the work of John Cage. In this alternate view, noise is as constitutive of the signal as its code. The following discussion of this conception of noise is based on Aden Evens' analysis in *Sound Ideas*. The book is primarily about music, but its discussion of sound and noise is written to apply as well to language – as it must. For the line between music and language is another of the zones of indistinction belonging to language's field of emergence. Language meets multiplicity in thirdness, it meets body and animality in gesture – and it meets music in sound, and in the fact that it shares sound's own emergent relation to noise.

'It is noise,' Evens writes, 'that binds the signal, that serves as a medium, a baseline, a plane of relief against which signal stands out' (Evens, 2005, 15). He describes noise as a background to signal, but not so much in the visual sense, where the background is in contrast with the form that stands out against it. His use of the word 'relief' suggests a *geological* image. Noise is like the underlayer from which signal, with its message content, rises in relief, under pressure from tectonic forces. Signal stands in relation to noise as a mountain rises from the continually shifting ground. A mountain is mute testimony to the past action of forces of emergence of the earth, and to the certainty that future tectonic shifts will continue to reshape the landscape. Like a peak, signal stands out against the generative, and regenerative, forces of its own tectonic formation.

The idea that *Amodal Suspension* makes perceptible the force of language may be articulated with this concept of noise. Central to that concept is the fact that a sound never entirely disappears. It dissipates. It relaxes, spreads out, becoming less and less contracted, but it remains, hanging in the air, a breath away from silence, fused with the relaxation of every other sound that ever rang out. This noise of near-silence is an imperceptible background buzz, a vibratory limit *of* sound at which a sound rejoins all sound. Evens calls it a 'cosmic echo': a universal history of sound.

When a new sound rings out, it ripples the surface of this cosmic echo. From the rippling, it peaks. Its own vibration resonates with the silence-nearing background buzz, or forms interference patterns with it. The resonance and interference of the background noise is a condition of the new sound's emergence, but also becomes an ingredient in it, contributing to its timbre or giving it an undertone. The emerging signal peaks from the background of noise. Given the energetic, vibratory nature of its ground, it is perhaps less like a mountain peak than a wave, cresting on the sea. A wave may be thought of as contracting the calm of the sea into a new swell. The cresting of the wave gives new focus to the imperceptible stirrings of the deep, whose potential energy is brought once again to forceful expression. The emergent wave gives focus and expression to the forces of the sea; and the sea gives direction to the wave: towards the shore. Similarly, a sound signal may be thought of as contracting noise, the near-silent universal history of sound, into the clarity of a newly emerged meaning. It gives focus and expression to the reservoir of all sound, whose spreading depth reciprocates by giving the signal direction: toward sense.

A signal, to become meaningful, to become a linguistic sign, must be contracted a second time. It must ripple another reservoir, and bring it to a crest of focus and expression. This second reservoir is that of our perceptions and memories, our habits of attention and learned responses, our innate animal tropisms and acquired tendencies, our skills, hopes and desires, as socially instilled, and as embodying a variation on the long and continuing history of nature and culture, and nature in culture. Each emergent meaning contracts this universal history into the clarity of its individual meaning, bringing its potential energy once again to forceful expression, and, in return, receiving direction from it. Quoting Evens (2005, 15–18):

Every string plucked, every throat cleared, vibrates a [background] vibration, modifies an existing difference [and is modified by it]. Sound is a modulation of difference, a difference of difference. [...] Noise is the uncontracted, the depth from which these contractions of perception are drawn, and, though sense-less and insensible [in itself], it makes sense or gives sense to sound, by providing sound with its direction and focusing it to a point of clarity. Noise is the reservoir of sense, the depth in which sounds connect to each other, the difference whose modulation is signal. [...] Sounds only have sense when what is heard includes not only what is heard clearly, but includes also the implicated in what is heard [the obscurity of the background from which the clear and distinct stands out]. To hear meaningful sound – be it the articulate meaning of speech or the ineffable meaning of music – is to hear sound in motion, heading somewhere. [...] Noise draws along with it a residue of obscurity, lines of relaxation which anchor sound to the noise it modulates. Sound implicates these obscure tethers, which connect sound to noise [...] implicating worlds of forces not yet unleashed, but whose reservoir powers the music [or linguistic expression], driving it along. [...] Implication pushes [language] forward [...] and this motion is not created by the [words] but produces them as [the expression] of its force. [...] Implication is what connects isolated elements to each other, in a creative synergy.

Words upon words

V. N. Vološinov echoes this in his formula that 'expression organises experience' (Vološinov, 1986, 85). The organizing centre of any communication, he says, is not within the individual but in a collective outside (93). This is not the kind of outside that stands against, as opposite to or the negative of the inner life attributed to the individual through which it expressively crests. It is the outside constituted by the whole of communication, its sea. In Vološinov, this whole of communication is defined not as bounded but as a boundary region (96): a region of contact, a crossing point (76) between the linguistic structure of the message carried by the signal and the extra-linguistic noise of gesture, body, animality, our perceptions and memories, our habits of attention and learned responses, our tropisms and acquired tendencies, our skills, hopes and desires. The 'whole' of communication is the ensemble of modulations of individual expression, in a churning zone of indistinction.

Like Evens, Vološinov describes this zone of indistinction as a connective current of self-regenerating expression. 'Language,' writes Vološinov, 'cannot be said to be handed down – it endures, but it endures as a continuous process of becoming. Individuals do not receive a ready-made language at all, rather, they enter upon the stream of communication' (1986, 81). Our individual communications crest like waves from the sea-streams of speech. He goes on to say that there is a reservoir of past communications into which each message dissipates. A message never disappears, especially in this digital age where everything can be recorded and automatically archived. A speech act doesn't disappear; it relaxes into the archive. Every message ever produced subsides in the potential for reported speech – the potential to be taken up again and re-actualized in a third party report of what was said.

Reportable speech is the sea of communication. An archived message is a 'crystallization' of a wave-crest of communication that once broke on its shore (Vološinov, 1986, 118). But an archived message is not exactly inert. Its crystalline structure retains a potential energy: it can be re-expressed and brought into focus again. The archived reservoir of reportable speech is a stilling of communication. But it still retains an organizing force, one that inflects each new expression, giving it an undertone and contributing to its orientation. No utterance, as Derrida argued, is ever entirely original. A speech act is always a 'citation' that regathers the force of the already-said, but with a difference, repeating it with a variation – modulating it (in analogue fashion).

Reported speech, Vološinov reminds us, bears testimony to an 'active relation of one message to another'. That active relation is the condition of emergence or potential ground of communication: 'words reacting upon words', to new but analogous effect, in a continuity of variation (Vološinov, 1986, 116). In the archive, that active relation becalms itself. Words already-said relax back towards the collective sea of communication, settling down again into Lozano-Hemmer's social soup. The archive is a reservoir of what Maurice Blanchot called the anonymous 'murmur' that is both the moving ground of language and its outside limit (Blanchot, 1989, 26, 47, 50; 1993, 159, 242, 329). Archived words are in communicational reserve, poised for reactivation. Upon reactivation, they leave their backwater of repose to re-enter the active stream of language. They come back in citation, undertoning and inflecting the cresting of new events of language. Words regained, reacting again upon words. Language ebbing and flowing, relaxing into stagnant eddies and contracting again into the wave-crest.

The extra-effect or force of language staged in *Amodal Suspension* is the power of language to rhythmically regather its active relation to itself and its modulatory outside, in a pulsed continuation of the always-crossed line of communication. The project includes its own automatically compiled archive. The project archive is in many ways the heart of the installation. It will be very rare that the person to whom a message is addressed manages to catch it out of the air. The mass of messages will settle into the online archive. The addressee will have to extract it from the archive. Once again, the process is designed to have a strong element of tactility. The messages populate a 3D space that recedes in all directions. The further away they are, the more blurred the words. To bring the words into focus, the participant has to navigate through the space with the mouse. The navigation has the feel of swimming. Using the mouse is like paddling with your hands in a liquid medium. You agitate the cursor to create eddies in the liquid archive of communication. The eddies will catch a message on their swell and flush it towards the front of the screen. When one washes forward, it crests into focus and can be read. The tactility of this eddy-fishing for the message gives the digital archive a turbulently analogue experiential dimension.

The archive also works to return communication to the zone of indisinction between gesture and language in exemplary fashion. Just beginning to access what the archive holds already reactivates the words at the regenerative border zone between the extra-linguistic and the linguistic, before their linguistic meaning reappears. It brings the infra-inhabitation of language by gesture to the fore.

The archive also exemplifies the return of communication to its constitutive 'thirdness', the power of relay that, processually speaking, is more fundamental to its operation than the explicit structure of linguistic forms, or the digital code of the archiving of words. The archive plays a central role in *Amodal Suspension*'s insistent thirding of communication. Messages transmitted directly from a sender to a receiver will almost inevitably reach the wrong party. They will be poached from the sky by an unintended recipient. They will then detour to the archive, where they will rest, in an ever-expanding reservoir of reported speech. The computer becomes the third party through which messages relay indirectly to the addressee. This detour of digitally reported speech gives new technological expression to the indirection that constitutes the force of human language.

Language caught in the act

What *Amodal Suspension* suspends is precisely the said-and-doneness of the cultural act, its determinate communicational achievement as a particularizable, individually ownable transmission of a message. Refracted into indefinitely prolongable third-party transmission and the indeterminate afterlife of citation, the language act is unmoored from the shores of finalized human communication. *Amodal Suspension* sets the achievement of noise-reduced intersubjective communication as its external limit. It contrives for the language acts it enables to remain on the near side of ownable human individuation. It also has an immanent limit, one that stirs its potential from within: the force of language as it enters a zone of indistinction with the animal. This side of finalized human communication, gesture remains tied to the emergent force of language. The participant act remains a grab at *words*. It is suspended in this reach for language, performed independently of the content of the words, which may never be known to any given reacher, and is in every case detoured, thirded and sea'd.

Vološinov distinguishes the 'theme' of language from semantic content. The difference is that a theme is singularly marked by the noisy 'whole' to which it emergently belongs (Vološinov, 1986, 99). It marks a speech act's belonging to the ever-changing whole through the particular 'evaluative accent' or affective tone with which it crests (Vološinov, 1986, 103, 105). The evaluative accent is enactive. It is performed, not just signified. It is performed extra-syntactically (in tone or rhythm), and often extra-verbally (in gesture or facial expression) (96, 100). Vološinov's concept of theme asserts that the enactive movement from indistinct potential whole to particular evaluative accent is the meaning of the speech act in its fullest sense. Theme is what effectively makes the speech act an act. It is the force of language as it pertains to content.

What *Amodal Suspension* suspends is the 'as pertains to content' in the semantic sense. The understanding of the semantic content of the messages is refracted and interfered with. The cresting in evaluative accent is deferred, if not lost in the ebb and flow. It is left in suspense. The speech act is suspended in the very act of reaching towards language. Language is caught in the incipience of its own act. What is left is the 'theme' of *language itself*. What participants are primed for is language as such, aside from any particular enaction of its content. Its force is felt, extra-verbally, in gesture, just out of reach of achieved content. The formative implication of language with the extra-verbal is gestured to, in a grabbing at words hanging out of reach at the tip of the thumb and the sweep of a beam. The medium of *Amodal Suspension* is this reaching toward language, finality of meaning deferred – the event of language compellingly incomplete. This, its event-medium, is performatively one with its content.

Sociability

What might we call the domain stretching from the immanent limit of the gestural zone of indistinction of human language with the animal, to just shy of effectively performed intersubjective communication? *Social domain* will do. The event-medium of *Amodal Suspension* is *sociability*. An act of sociability is constitutively open. It doesn't have to be begun again, for the simple reason that it never ends. It undulates across a continuous rhythm of words reacting upon reservoired words, in rippling waves. A social act doesn't perish; it subsides into the background noise of the sea of sociality. Sociability ebbs and flows with the vagueness of a continuous background murmur.

The social death of the personal

'Personality, from the standpoint of its inner, subjective content,' Vološinov writes, 'is a theme of language [...] *a word is not an expression of an inner personality; rather, inner personality is an expressed or inwardly impelled word.* [...] The inner personality is generated along with language' (Vološinov, 1986, 153). Human personality is a turning-inward of the generative 'thematic' movement stretching between the fusional whole of enactive potential and the determination of the particular act. Inwardly impelled, the word continues to eddy, but in the restricted confines of an identified coordinate position on the cultural map. Individually owned speech is a localized 'impletion' (94) of a recognized position on the cultural map. At a certain point in the history of culture, mechanisms are invented to 'abstractly segregate' localized cultural acts that have been channeled and mapped in this way from their social impletion (70–1). The result is an apparent individualization of speech: the invention of the 'sovereign' bourgeois individual occupying a determinate position on the cultural map and speaking only for himself. Theme in Vološinov's sense, with its immanently formative connection to extraverbal levels, is abstractly segregated on the side of the individual, and is construed as 'private' and subjective. A partition is thus instituted between the 'private' sphere, dedicated to the subjective manifestation of the 'inner personality,' and a 'public' sphere of intersubjective communication where statements are considered to be judgeable according to criteria of objectivity. The social is reconstituted, opposite the individual, as an objectively testable externality. Only the semantic meaning of language, embedded themelessly in its formal structure, is left for the public sphere.

There is only one word for language segregated from theme and reduced to its semantic content and formal structure: 'dead' (Vološinov, 1986, 73, 81). Society, understood as a public sphere at a decorous remove from the 'inner personality', is the death of sociability as enacted in 'Amodal Suspension'.

The quasi-public

The partition between public and private expression organizes a regime of mediation. Manifestations of the 'inner personality' must be formated for public expression by mechanisms of 'socialization' that interpose themselves between the individual 'in itself' and the intersubjective sphere of external self-representation, holding them at a remove from each other. In the public sphere, other mediating mechanisms maintain a dignified intersubjective distance between individuals' expression. Among these are legal and informal measures against unauthorized or unacknowledged citation. Third-party communicational drift becomes criminalized as plagiarism or theft of 'intellectual property', in an attempt to pin expression to clearly individualized acts, recognized as carrying incumbent responsibilities and entitled to the due rewards of ownership. By contrast to this regulation, the comparatively unregulated private sphere appears as an arena of 'direct' personal expression, experienced as more 'true' and 'authentic'. True life is only authentically found, it is felt, on the side of the personal. By Vološinovian standards, this 'life' is but a half-reflection of death by social partition.

'Life'. Vološinov insists, 'begins only at the point where utterance crosses utterance' (1986, 145). The life of the social is where words react co-generatively upon words. The mutual reaction of words upon each other survives in trace form even in the public sphere, in the way in which every expression 'constitutes a germ of a response' (102). If the present act of expression constitutes the germ of a response that may come next, then it stands to reason that it was itself a response which a preceding expression likewise contained in the germ. But might not that preceding expression very well have germinated into more than one response? There is, after all, a whole population of individuals cohabiting the public sphere. Could not that ancestor expression have contained two germs? Or three? Or four? Or n ...? Each expression is an infectious forking of the paths of sociality into a potential infinity of lines of transmission. In all that complexity, how could the lines not get tangled? How could each act of expression not resonate with any number of others? Is it not undeniable that every romantic pop song lyric is filled with the echoes of any number of other love songs, as if it were citing them *en masse* in its specific difference, as an individual variation on their never-ending, ever-branching collective theme? Is it possible to hear an individual political position-taking without a ring of the déjà-heard? The regulation of the public sphere is designed to background this endemic third-party noise on the line as much as possible, holding it to a residual minimum in order to safeguard the private/public split, its accompanying forms of individual recognition, responsibility and ownership, and their historic deadening of expression.

There is a kind of speech that from time immemorial has stealthily re-insinuated the tangled web of third-party lines into whatever sphere or technology of communication was available: gossip. Every piece of gossip purports to be a direct report of something specific said by a particular other. Its citational practice, however, is sloppy, to say the least. You never quite know if the 'he said x' is in fact a 'she said he said x'. Or even a 'he said she said he said x'. You never know how far down the line the utterance has actually come. The 'owner' of the speech reported is essentially vague. Because of this, what is ostensibly a 'private' exchange between two parties is on a party-line. Not only is there is a cited third speaker necessarily involved, because the statement presents itself as a report of another's utterance, there is the distinct possibility of a fourth person in line, behind what the reported-upon third person is reported to have said. Gossip is actually in the *fourth-person singular*.

And there is more. The receiver of the titbit of reported speech is not involved in the exchange with a clearly individual status. He or she is equally present as the representative of what 'people will think'. Where there is gossip, there is a teeming crowd of 'he saids' and 'he said she saids' and 'what people thinks' and 'theys'. In gossip, two's a crowd. The crowding is such that the distinction between social type ('they': people of an interested ilk, however ill-defined) and self-representing individual 'I' is expressively blurred. The vagueness of the subject of speech is compounded by the fact that the evaluative accent with which the speech is reported does not distinguish between the present speaker's individual accent and the implied evaluation of the third- and fourth-party speakers whose potential voices echo on the line, or between the present listener and the virtually overhearing 'they' that overpopulates the exchange. The 'theme' of the language act is collectively owned in its speaking and no sooner emitted than already recognized by a virtually listening multitude, pregnant (in the sense that a significant pause is said to be 'pregnant') with an oversupply of implied response.

Gossip is much maligned. It is commonly denounced both as threat to privacy and as a degradation of public discourse. But who are 'they' who can convincingly say they viscerally prefer a well-sourced news report to the latest gossip? Despite the tendency to stereotyping inherent in gossip's collapse of type and individual into each other and in the normative accent that often accompanies the gossipy evaluations of the virtual they, gossip is simply more socially alive. It brings us back to the sociable place where 'utterance crosses utterance' and words react with gleefully irresponsible abandon on other words. What is so threatening about gossip to defenders of privacy and regulatory watchdogs of public speech is that it is neither: neither private exactly, nor public. Its crossing of the lines between individual and type, its blurring of the lines between 'I' as this speaker and the third-person other, its collectivizing of the individual ear and socializing of evaluative accent, all of these things enable it to slip into the space between the two.

Gossip inhabits the zone of indistinction between the private and the public. It has special status. It is *quasi-public*. Which is much the same as saying 'quasi-private'.

Gossip is a machine for bringing expression a step back from the external limit of regulated intersubjective interaction towards that indistinctly potentiated fusional relation marking the immanence of the social domain (and of the sociability to culturability). Gossip backsteps the historic achievement of culture that is the speaking bourgeois subject into the ever-rolling, sometimes rollicking, movement of unregulated sociability. It brings the off-set between the cultural act and the social act back into their region of overlap.

A quasi-directness of expression

Vološinov saw something similar happening in the nineteenth-century bourgeois novel. A new mode of reported speech came into prominence. The conventional markers that formally separate the reported speech of a character from the author's reporting speech in traditional indirect discourse (he said *that* ...; she said, '...') are eliminated. The character's speech is directly inserted into the author's expression. This creates a 'paratactic' connection between the two utterances: a direct contiguity without any marked subordination, as if 'both the author and the character were speaking at the same time' (Vološinov, 1986, 144). 'The boundaries of reported speech become extremely weak', as if the two activities of speech generation were 'breaking into each other' (134–5). Each retains its own evaluative accents to some extent. These 'collide and interfere' (154). 'Two intonations, two points of view, two speech acts converge and clash' (135). The result is a single 'varidirectional' (80) stream of language which envelops within itself a social 'interorientation' (119–20, 125). This 'merging of differently oriented speech acts is *quasi-direct discourse*': 'speech *interference*' (137). Expressive social noise.

The literary use of quasi-direct discourse is one thing. What worries Vološinov is 'the social tendency it expresses' (158). He saw quasi-direct discourse gaining ground outside literature. It was clear to him that 'quasi-direct discourse lines on the main road of development of modern European languages, that it signalizes some crucial turning point in the social vicissitudes of utterance' (158). Without giving specific examples, he laments that in this tide of quasi-direct discourse, 'typifying and individualizing coatings of the utterance' become 'intensely' differentiated, hypertrophied to the point that they undermine the 'responsible social position implemented in it' (158). In other words, the extreme of typicality and the extreme of individuality converge and clash. Not unlike in gossip. The two extremes combine, without mediation, in a single interorientation, a vari-directional stream of de-positioned – deterritorialized – language from which 'serious ideational consideration' has been quasied out (158). What is left is the 'expression of an adventitous, subjective state' of indeterminate personhood, as intensely typical as it is hypertrophically individual.

Vološinov is attached enough to traditional notions of authenticity and truth in speech to see this development as a 'depression in the thematic value of the word' (159). He calls the tendency of quasi-direct discourse taken to this extreme the 'contrived word' (159). It might have been more in keeping with his own philosophy to see it, on the contrary, as a coming to performative expression of the theme of the sociability of language itself, in an exemplification of language's essentially contrived social nature: a surfacing of sociability for itself, in all its noisy inauthentic glory.

Sociability giganticus

Today we live out the far side of the social tendency which made Vološinov cringe. From this vantage point it appears much less frightening: as banal as Facebook. How more 'contrived' could the word get than when it is digitized and refracted through a technological apparatus of immense complexity and tentacular reach? The same clash and convergence between extreme typicality and the hypertrophied assertion of individuality is to be found on the 'personal' pages of social media. But the posts are not 'personal' in anything approaching the nineteenth-century sense, when there was a clearly contrasting 'public' for individual speech to be set against. Social media are the reign of the quasi-public. Facebook friends exist to interlink. The 'personal' connection is made to drift across the propagating links, rippling into expanding social circles, to the point where mutual 'friends' will often not know who each other are. Facebook posts are designed to relay, propagating indefinitely across the rippling sea of digital sociality. The relay function is taken even further with Twitter. Citations proliferate in paratactic contiguity with each other, merging at the limit into a single varidirectional stream of social expression. Evaluative accents clash and converge in multitudinous interorientation. As of April 2011, it was estimated that one billion tweets were being emitted each week. *Sociability giganticus*. Peer-to-peer sharing, for its part, has weakened the ownership of expression, sparking often draconian rearguard actions in defence of 'intellectual property'. Hacking even more so. This, as 'personal' expression on social media sites falls under the proprietary control of corporations (content posted by individuals on Facebook belongs not to them but to Facebook, Inc). The rules of ownership formerly in place have been scrambled by the predominance of a new operator: 'access' (a shift pre-diagnosed in Rifkin, 2000). In this brave new social world, gossip has attained a new level of prominence, not only in the content of 'private' messages but in dedicated 'public' sites which are among the most visited of all the internet.

The point about gossip is not that the gossipy content has increased. It was always high volume. It is that, with social media, the internet itself has brought to global expression and previously unheard-of prominence (at a level not even 'they' would have suspected) the tendency of which gossip has been the most historically constant and reliable agent: the quasi-directifi-cation of social relation. The internet has taken quasi-direct relation to a global scale, and made it unmistakeably the dominant mode of expression. Under the impulsion of social media, the internet has ushered in the reign of the quasi-public. It has massively backstepped the cultural act into the domain of sociability – 'pure sociality' as the 'field of immanence' of expressive variation, 'the intrinsic nature of association' (Deleuze and Guattari, 1994, 87).

The internet-led backstepping of the cultural act into pure sociality has been decried as the death of culture. The internet has also been lamented for undermining the objectivity of public sphere expression. It has been demonized for undermining the responsible social position implemented in speech and the serious ideational content of expression (just a minute, haven't we heard that before? Isn't that Vološinov's intellectual property? Except ... who did *he* get it from?). The internet's malevolent effects on the 'inner personality', particularly in its tender childhood shoots, have been voluminously fretted over (not least of all on the internet).

This last worry comes to the heart of the central issue that Vološinov raised in relation to quasi-direct social relation: the replacement of the responsibly self-positioning and seriously ideating socio-cultural subject by a quasi-direct 'adventitious subjective' growth. *Adventitious*: '1: coming from another source and not inherent or innate 2: arising or occurring sporadically or in other than usual location' (*Merriam-Webster*).

Ultimately, the question which the internet poses for culture and society is what this adventitious subjectivity, now unleashed, may become. Whatever it becomes, its singular quasi-public/quasi-private status, marked by ultimately disowned, depositioned, irresponsibilized utterances, will ensure that its becoming will be a *collective individuation* (Simondon, 2005). Will it rejig the respective limits of the social and the cultural? Will it refigure their overlap and immanence? Will its monstrous complexity and tentacular stretch take socia-bility itself to the pseudopodic 'cosmic' limit of culture? How will it redraw the map of the human territory? Will it rejuggle the zones of indistinction between the human, the animal, the technological and the generative forces for variation that crest from them? There is no paucity of noisy futuristic prognostications on these subjects. This chapter will refrain from adding more.

Jacques Attali famously argued that the evolution of music heralds what Vološinov called 'crucial turning points' in the vicissitudes of the social and the cultural domains. 'Amodal Suspension' raised the issue of the quasi-directness of social relation in 2003, a year before the founding of Facebook. Music is not the only art that heralds vicissitudes. Other arts, including the electronic arts, do so as well. The intensely participatory nature of electronic-art practices such as Lozano-Hemmer's relational architecture give an option that was not open to Vološinov but is to contemporary critics and prognosticators: that of refraining from arguing the points interminably. The option is to experience them. To experiment with them. Rather than forming words with the finality of a personal statement, to make a participatory grab at them at the quasi-public limit of the social. For 'it is undeniably conceivable that a beginningless series of successive utterers should do their work *in a brief interval of time*, and that so should an endless series of interpreters', such that 'before the sign was uttered, it was virtually present' (Peirce, 1998, 403). The option is to save ourselves the prolix embarrassment of futurist argument, and instead live the open-ended futurity virtually present, now, in the event.

4

The noise paradigm

Cécile Malaspina

Introduction

The analogy between noise, as a musical strategy, and the phenomena of noise in other disciplines, appears to trigger the idea of a paradigm of innovation. Yet it is perhaps no small paradox, if noise is thus thought to unite heterogeneous disciplines in a paradigm, if we think of the paradigm as Plato did, as an analogical method. If we think of noise as a principle of differentiation (because it implies the radically new that is different from everything you are used to) and as index of heterogeneity (because no two forms of noise would satisfy this criteria of novelty if they were the same), then what kind of a ground is noise for an analogical relation? If the idea of a paradigm on the basis of noise is not a contradiction in terms, then what kind of a relation can it promise to illuminate between historians, performance artists, musicians, sound engineers, cultural theorists, etc.?

The reason why the idea of a paradigm of innovation on the basis of noise is intriguing is that we seek in noise the shifting of paradigms and hence the continual transformation of the relations between cultural and scientific disciplines and domains. Its own functioning as a paradigm must be affected by this principle of innovation: it cannot merely assimilate the various disciplines in a paradigmatic domain and it cannot stay self-same, if it is based on noise.

The dynamic of such transformations between disciplines and domains finally animates a fundamental problem for the theory of knowledge, regarding the unity of and at the same time the heterogeneity among the sciences, but also among cultural and scientific practices, insofar as there is a traditional distinction between both. Noise is thus also an epistemological problem, of interest not only to epistemologists, but also to scientists in the human and the natural sciences alike, for which the moving boundaries between their disciplines and subdisciplines are a vital question for research.

The most apparent problem is that, in order to enable such a transdisciplinary analogy, the concept of noise needs to pertain to as wide an array of theories and practices as possible. However, it also needs to be conceptually specific enough to provide theoretical and experimental grit, without which it would gloss over these domains and their differences without consequence – precisely obliterating the heterogeneity and differentiation it promised to celebrate as a principle of innovation.

This is, it seems, the problem with a potentially weak notion of noise and the ensuing disenchantment with predictable tropes that have been associated with noise in musical praxis, brilliantly exposed in Ray Brassier's 'Genre is obsolete' (Brassier, 2007). Brassier's text will allow us to see the paradoxes attendant on 'noise', insofar as it implies a dialectic of negation. It will also open up some of the conceptual potential inherent in the innovative use of noise, in the form of a strategic use of ambiguity and the ascesis of a formalizing abstraction that potentiates difference, rather than suspending it.

Gilbert Simondon's reinterpretation of Plato's 'paradigmatism' (Simondon, 2005),[1] on the other hand, will go some way towards helping us envisage what could constitute an analogical relation between heterogeneous disciplines and domains, beyond the traditional idea of an analogy based on the logic of structural identity or resemblance. If we integrate Simondon's analogical method with what Brassier calls a relation between 'incompossibles' (Brassier, 2007, 8) then we are this much closer to thinking an analogical relation between the disciplines that is not only able to sustain noise, but is also precisely about the integration of noise as an innovative process.

To flesh out the analogy between cultural and scientific praxis, we will consult the French philosopher of biology Michel Morange (Morange, 2006), who gives us an account of the ambiguity inherent in scientific concepts imported from other disciplines, in this case biological concepts arising from information theory, like 'program', 'code' or 'message' – and which will enable our transition to the concept of noise, as it arises in information theory. Morange's account of this ambiguity resonates with Brassier's idea of 'strategic ambiguity'. Not only is ambiguity deemed not to hinder scientific innovation, but, on the contrary, it is shown to enable the metaphorical circulation of concepts between diverse scientific and cultural domains.

The potential inherent in this transdisciplinary ambiguity can be made more explicit by looking at the work of Henri Atlan, bio-physicist and philosopher, who was among the pioneers in the study of complex systems – a domain in which the concept of noise *and* the interplay between heterogeneous disciplines are both essential. 'Today,' Atlan says, such ideas are 'presented as self-evident, that is to say that the creation of information,' in other words, innovation, 'can only occur on the basis of noise,' but 'one forgets what it is that makes them relevant, namely [...] how and under which conditions the opposition between organized and random can be replaced by a kind of co-operation, where the concept of the organized and that of randomness inevitably acquire new contents' (Atlan, 1979, 63–4).

Analytical delirium versus postmodern disenchantment

In his text 'Genre is obsolete' (Brassier, 2007), Ray Brassier singles out Tom Smith's *To Live and Shave in L.A.* and Rudolf Eb.er's project *Runzelstirn und Gurgelstock* in order to discern the innovative potential in the paradox-ridden field of engagement with noise. For the rich account of Smith's and Eb.er's sonic orgies I invite you to read this beautiful text. What we will focus on here is the conceptual space he finds in their work, a space that carves itself out of a series of confrontations (concept versus proper name; construction versus negation; strategic ambiguity versus self-reflexive distancing; the fusing of 'incompossibles' versus the totality of all possibility; and finally ascesis versus eclecticism), which problematize the demand for ever new forms of noise, whose ensuing aesthetic criteria surreptitiously twist noise into a form of innovation freighted with orthodoxies.

What happens when the strategic use of noise that has characterized much of the musical innovation during the twentieth century, coalesces in the 1980s into a musical genre, is the following. While this moment appears to concentrate the essence of innovation that has driven sonic practice thus far, the noise it makes becomes familiar, an 'accumulation of stock gestures' entailing the 'slackening of the criteria for discriminating between innovation and cliché' (Brassier, 2007, 2). When noise becomes a genre, the plethora of specific practices that have fed into the richness of its sound and animated its recalcitrant appeal appears reduced to a name that holds a very slight conceptual weight, even none at all, when all it says is what it is not: anti-convention, anti-classification. Noise becomes 'the expedient moniker for a motley array of sonic practices [...] with little in common besides their perceived recalcitrance with respect to the conventions governing classical and popular music' (Brassier, 2007, 1).

As a proper name, 'noise' comes down to the absurd designation of nothing much: the blandness of a generic negation. Its nominal absurdity is disinherited of the rich history of forays into the sonically absurd – a history which fails to culminate in this moment. In Brassier's words, the practices converging around this label then oscillate 'between that of a proper name and that of a concept', equivocating 'between nominal anomaly and conceptual interference' (Brassier, 2007, 1).

The nominal anomaly is, of course, that of a genre predicated on the negation of a genre. Conceptually, however, the not very innovative idea of innovation bows, in our view, to a modern idea of progress. The new must supplant and disqualify what preceded it, jump-starting with every step what Brassier calls a dialectic of negation. Its ever more stringent requirement to innovate with respect to all it has already negated, paradoxically, yields to a neurotic orthodoxy of criteria for invention: the 'abstract negation of genre issues in the sterile orthodoxies of "noise" as pseudonym for experimental vanguardism, and the result is either the stifling preciousness of officially sanctioned art-music or (worse) the dreary machinations of "sound-art" ' (Brassier, 2007, 1).

Brassier sees Smith and Eb.er as representing an approach able to subvert this dialectic compulsion with 'delirious lucidity' (Brassier, 2007, 3). Rather than drowning out detail in an empty sonic abstraction, their work is described as being constructed from an 'overwhelming plethora of sonic detail, surfeit of information, excess, rather than deficit of sense' (5). Eb.er interestingly solicits a biological metaphor: '15 years of R&G sounds get divided and divided, grow and grow. I grow my sounds "biologically", like dividing cells. Cut and let grow' (8). Rather than progressing by negating what came before it, Eb.er's biological metaphor may perhaps be pushed further to describe noise as a sonic *biocenosis*, a continual autophagous rite of devouring and proliferation.

The 'nominal anomaly' of noise and its 'conceptual equivocation' thus fail to sing the swan-song of noise. Its on-going vitality is, in Brassier's examples, nourished by a constructive formalization that staves off formulaic reduction, and that appears to lead to an evolving complexification rather than the haemorrhaging of sense. Brassier opposes this construction of 'generic anomaly' (Brassier, 2007, 12) to the orthodoxy of negation, to the idea that innovation either suspends what precedes in a cliché of transgression or, as Brassier says, in the 'mannerism' of self-reflexive conceptualism (ibid.). 'Nominal anomaly' and 'conceptual interference' are instead recycled as tactical ambiguity, which differs essentially, for Brassier, from the ambiguity of 'self-conscious strategies of reflexive distancing' (Brassier, 2007, 3) emblematic of an academically condoned avant-gardist aesthetic. The conditions and legitimacy of expression are not only not put into question by Smith and Eb.er, they are fed into a sonic and psychic shredder: ambiguity no longer expresses a coy self-consciousness; it is, one might say, no longer subject to a degenerated Kantian twitch.

Strategic ambiguity instead becomes, in Brassier's words, the key for 'fusing hitherto incommensurable sonic categories in a way that draws attention to the synthetic character of all experience: dub cut-up, free-glam, electro-acoustic punk for Shave; cartoon musique concrète and slapstick art brut for Runzelstirn' (Brassier, 2007, 12). Smith's 'The Wingmaker in 18th Century Williamsburg' (Menlo Park, 2001) is said to forge 'previously unimaginable links between currently inexistent genres' resulting in a music of 'unparalleled structural complexity, where each song indexes a sound-world – compositions are conjoined in a monstrous but exhilarating hybrid' (Brassier, 2007, 8). Eb.er's events on the other hand are described as 'psycho-physical tests and training'.

By emphasizing Eb.er's 'psycho-physical training', the idea of construction, of formalization and that of Smith's 'sound worlds', Brassier arrives at the idea of an ascesis through noise. In our view this is about an ascesis towards a sonic holism – but a holism without totality. Rather than experiencing the unity of the all as a totality of all things, this form of ascesis leads, in our view, to a sonic ecology that considers the whole as an open system 'where all possibilities are extant, even the disastrous ones' (Brassier, 2007, 6).

Brassier opposes the idea of a 'totality of all possibilities', synonymous with God, Smith's paradigm of a PRE-aesthetic:

Since the totality of possibility is a synonym for God, whom we must renounce, the only available (uncompromisingly secular) totality is that of incompossibles. If all possibilities are extant, this can only be a totality of incompossibles, which harbours as yet unactualized and incommensurable genres.

(Brassier, 2007, 8)

What Smith calls a PRE-aesthetic is thus very different from what we might think of as a 'post'-aesthetic, its 'analytical delirium' literally worlds away from the dispersion of a postmodern eclecticism that is neither here nor there and whose transformational potential falters on a poorly eliminative understanding of Hegel's dialectical concept of 'Aufhebung' as simple negation.

While the 'analytical delirium' of a Smith or an Eb.er may promise a way out of the dialectical conundrum for sonic noise adventurers, it may still be difficult to see, at first glance, how Smith's PRE-aesthetic paradigm may convince epistemologists and scientists (in the human and natural sciences) that it has something essential to say about the combined unity and heterogeneity of the sciences, and of the cultural and scientific domains more generally. Yet this is precisely what we will try to envisage, by taking a closer look at Gilbert Simondon's renewal of Plato's 'paradigmatism', which will allow us to sketch out the possibility of an analogical relation that escapes a logic of structural identity and thus also that of a dialectic of negation.

Analogy

Gilbert Simondon's theory of individuation is characterized by the emphasis on a relative holism, whose paradigmatic concept is that of a 'field', which spreads from the natural sciences (invention of the concept of an electro-magnetic field) to the human sciences (concept of a field in Gestalt theory) (Simondon, 2005, 538). The concept of a field enables the analysis of inter-mediate systems: neither absolute totalities (the Parmenidian All), nor the generalized atomism of a Democritus.

Simondon understands ontogenesis as a process of differentiation and structuration that occurs within the 'pre-individual' state of such a system:

> The individual would thus be understood a relative reality, a certain phase of being that supposes before it a pre-individual reality, and which, even after individuation, does not exist on its own since individuation does not exhaust the potentials of the pre-individual reality in one strike, and what individuation brings to the fore is, on the other hand, not only the individual, but the individual-milieu couple.
>
> (Simondon, 2005, 25)

The structuration of this 'pre-individual' state is characterized by what he calls a process of 'analysis' (in analogy to chemical processes). The undoing of structures, on the contrary, is what he calls a 'modulation' (Simondon, 2005, 566). The pre-condition for the occurrence of both processes is, according to Simondon, a high degree of tension between incompatible orders of reality within the system – equivalent to the potential in a thermo-dynamic system.

While his concepts of the 'pre-individual' and its inherent tension would provide the basis of a worthwhile discussion of Brassier's concepts of 'incompossible' realities and of the notion of a PRE-aesthetic 'analytical delirium', we must for now press on with the question of a transdisciplinary, paradigmatic relation on the basis of noise. If Brassier is right to think that noise enables relations between hitherto 'incompossible' realities, then an analogy based on noise excludes a principle based on structural identity or resemblance.

For Simondon, thought association based on resemblance is precisely the characteristic of pseudo-scientific thought. Devoid of science's inventive capacity, he presents this resemblance-based form of analogy as sprawling with images and keywords, which invariably dissipate without consequences other than ideological ones:

> Pseudo-scientific thought makes extensive use of resemblance, sometimes even of vocabulary resemblance, but it does not use analogy. Pseudo-scientific thought thus produces a veritable debauchery of images and key words: wave, radiation [...] these words only cover confused images, barely able to ensure affective resemblance between the propagation of a mechanical tremor in a fluid and that in an electromagnetic field without physical medium.
>
> (Simondon, 2005, 563)

In his text 'Allagmatique' (ibid., 559–66) Simondon presents Plato's paradigmatic method as driving inductive discovery by transposing a known and proven thought operation to a situation, where the operation or function is identical but the structure is unknown. Simondon gives a mathematical example of this analogical method, namely the use of the fourth proportional (for numbers a, b and c, a number x is such that $a/b = c/x$). Plato's analogical method is philosophically relevant for Simondon, because it exceeds the scope of this mathematical form of analogy: Plato's paradigmatic method is able to transfer not only operations of measure, but every kind of operation. Plato compares the fisherman catching fish to the sophist catching the attention of rich youth. The ontological terms (the fisherman, the fish, the sophist and the rich youth) are arbitrary, while the operation subsists as identical.

The particularity of this method is that it compares operations and not structures; in other words, that it identifies the operational schema animating different structures. The structural elements that are compared for their similarity in the 'pseudo-scientific' use of analogy are precisely the ones from which this logical use of analogy abstracts – not to negate them, but on the contrary to enable a process-oriented understanding of structural difference.

This analogical transfer of an operational schema is, for Simondon, a motor of inductive discovery and an attempt to 'rationalize becoming' (Simondon, 2005, 562). Contrary to the traditional view of Plato's metaphysical exemplarism (a realm of immutable ideas of which reality is merely a corruptible copy),[2] Simondon sees in Plato's 'idea' the equivalent of his concept of the law, precisely, Simondon adds, in the way 'physical laws recall *invariants*' such as the preservation of energy (Simondon, 2005, 536). Simondon gives the example of Fresnel's discovery of the law of the propagation of light to demonstrate this form of analogy:

> If one supposes a structural identity between a light and a sound wave, one is obliged to dispose of the elongation of the vibration of the sound and the light wave identically; Fresnel's genius consisted in abandoning resemblance for analogy: supposing a different structure of the light wave and of the sound wave, he represents the light wave as having a perpendicular elongation in the direction of propagation and leaves the sound wave its longitudinal elongation, parallel to the direction of its movement. This is when analogy appears. Between these different structural terms, the operations are the same: the combination of waves, be they light or sound waves, occurs in the same manner in the case of sound waves as in that of light waves. But some structural results are different.
>
> (Simondon, 2005, 563)

Plato's analogy is thus the transfer of an operational schema. It is itself a movement, a *propagation* of operational schemas between different ontological systems and, by analogy, propagation of a conceptual schema between different epistemic domains. The term he coins for this propagation underlines its role in relating different orders of reality: he calls it a 'transduction' (Simondon, 2005, 532), a polyvalent concept that designates the transduction of analogue signals, as much as the transduction of mechanical momentum, or the transduction of genetic or other information across the cell membrane.

In epistemological terms the analogical process is equivalent to a conceptual transduction that entails a conceptual resonance and consequently the emergence of an epistemic domain defined by this resonance. The transdisciplinary appeal of the concept of noise must, at least in part, be inspired by the tremendous ability of a cluster of concepts from information theory, one among which is noise, to traverse and transform a growing web of scientific disciplines in such a transductive manner. What is more, these concepts have been able to bring about the emergence of transdisciplinary fields, such as cybernetics and later the study of complex systems. It is arguably this transformative and generative power that gives the notion of noise, even in the absence of an agreed definition, a paradigmatic aura.

Metaphorical ambiguity

What remains is to combine Simondon's paradigmatic method with Brassier's idea of the strategic use of ambiguity. This may go some way towards enabling us to understand how noise can inform a trans-disciplinary paradigm, how its abstraction can express the potentiation of specificity and detail, rather than negation of specificity, how its formali-zation can become a delirious analytical ascesis that fuels the formalization of invariants, rather than producing epistemic eclecticism and ideological relativism.

The idea of a paradigm based on noise raises a great number of problems, one of which is the slippage of the concept of noise. With what technical specificity does the concept of noise traverse thermodynamics, information theory and biology (never mind socio-economic or cultural theories)? What is the degree of cultural connotation that the concept of noise brings to these disciplines, here obscuring the clarity of a message, there causing genetic mutations or signifying the random input from the environment? The problem is not only the lack of a transdisciplinary definition of noise, but its indelible fluctuation between theoretical context, as, for instance, its quantifying role in physics and information theory (quantity of information), its metaphorical role in the life sciences, and finally its role in probabilistic or deterministic theories (Atlan, 1979)[3] – never mind its role in aesthetic or altogether speculative theoretical contexts.

That this transdisciplinary grey area has a high degree of potential is what Michel Morange appears to argue. Noise belongs to a cluster of information theory concepts, such as information, message, code, memory and network regulation, which have entered endocrinology, neurobiology or immunology, but 'without a trace of information theory's mathematical formalisation' and indeed intermeshing these different theoretical contexts in a hybrid theory such as cybernetics (Morange, 2006, 620). He sees cybernetic theory as emerging, precisely, at the intersection of existing lines of inquiry, like the study of physiological self-regulation (homeostasis) and the urgency of new requirements, such as the logistics of exponential growth of information in science and technology, communication or the development of a new generation of weapons during the 1930 to 1940s.

Despite the fact that the application of cybernetics to the nascent area of molecular biology was not immediately evident, its transdisciplinary momentum throughout the natural, the social sciences, linguistics and economy created, in Morange's words, a cultural 'mould' for the reception of the concept of a genetic 'code' during the 1960s (Kay, 1995, cited in Morange, 2006, 620).

In frank contradistinction to the commonplace interpretation of Gaston Bachelard's concept of 'epistemological obstacle', frequently understood as little more than the residue of imaginary and ideological projections that need to be eliminated in order to enable the progress of scientific thought (Renault, 2006),[4] Morange finds that the ambiguity of such concepts does not necessarily constitute an obstacle in the dynamics of scientific development. While their ideological recuperation can become a political threat, for instance, in the idea that our biological destiny is inscribed in our genes like a program, 'the use of such metaphors or of such concepts does not impede scientific progress: on the contrary, it gives it a space for freedom within which scientific knowledge can at all times transform and redeploy itself' (Morange, 2006, 620).

With the exception of the concept of a genetic code, which designates a 'chemically arbitrary code' that fixes 'a quasi-universal correspondence between components of two macromolecules of different chemical nature', all other informational concepts are, in Morange's account, metaphorical when transferred across scientific disciplines (Morange, 2006, 620). But what about the concept of noise? It is itself an ambiguous concept whose role in information theory arises from a disputed analogy with thermodynamics.

Entropy of the message

Shannon's formalization of the quantity of information measures the statistical probability with which a symbol, from a given alphabet, appears in a message (without taking the signification of this message into account). The more unlikely the appearance of a particular sign is in a message, the higher its quantity of information. Shannon also calls this entropy of the message (Atlan, 1979, 45), his formalism following that of Boltzmann's formalization of thermodynamic entropy. There is thus nothing intuitive about a concept of quantity of information, indexed by its measure of entropy, and it can be confusing to think that increased noise or entropy in a channel of communication compromises the clarity of a message, while increasing, according to this definition, the quantity of information in the system.

Boltzmann's formalization of entropy measures the distribution of submicroscopic particles in a closed physical system (i.e. an isolated piece of physical matter). Maximum entropy corresponds to the distribution towards which all closed systems invariably tend. This is because the tension contained in a system in the form of differences in energetic potential equalizes through interaction, until the system as a whole finally reaches a state of energetic equilibrium such that no flow of matter or energy can occur from one part of the system to another. Entropy is the statistically homogeneous distribution of submicroscopic particles: every particle is now as likely as any other to be anywhere in the system. Thermodynamics thus talk to us about a reality where maximum entropy equates with maximum probability: nothing is more predictable than this outcome in a closed system. The emergence of form or of the stability of a system other than that of pure entropy thus occurs with minimal probability; in other words, nothing is less certain than organization.

What makes Shannon's concept of information eminently analogical is the fact that it is identical to Boltzmann's, *except for one thing*. Boltzmann's formula is multiplied by a physical constant (k), which expresses entropy as a quantity of non-usable heat, in the form of flows equal to electrical currents or flows of matter in the form of displacements of thermal charges 'under the effect of a force or under the effect of a difference in potential, that is to say, here, a difference of temperature' (Atlan, 1979, 35). (k) is thus the reference to physical reality.[5] Without (k) Shannon's formula becomes a measure of pure probability and is thus ontologically arbitrary (it does not matter to what type of reality it is applied). Its measure of probability lends itself to the statistical analysis of any kind of mass phenomena, hence its great analogical value, or we could say its paradigmatic value (understood in Simondon's sense as an analogy of operational relations across structurally heterogeneous realities [Simondon, 2005, 544]).

It thus endows the concept of noise and of information with the ability to relate across otherwise heterogeneous or 'incompossible' (Brassier, 2007) domains of knowledge, from the physical to the biological sciences, from the socio-economic to political sciences in a transductive analogical relation. This analogical relation is thus not ontologically reductive and the epistemic domain it expresses is thus not delimited by what Simondon might have called the 'pseudo-scientific' criteria of resemblance or structural identity, but by the conceptual resonance that engenders a new epistemic domain.

'Ambiguity-autonomy' and 'destructive ambiguity'

Henri Atlan's approach as a biophysicist was to extend Shannon's formalism to the analysis of self-organizing systems and to ask: 'how and under what conditions can information create itself on the basis of noise; put differently, how and under what conditions can randomness contribute to create organizational complexity rather than being only a factor of disorganization?' (Atlan, 1979, 46).[6] Atlan's own analogy between information theory and the analysis of complex self-organizing systems implies, as he points out, that information in an organized system is comparable to information transmitted in a channel of communication. Insofar as it is transmitted to an observer, Atlan distinguishes between information transmitted in the channel itself and information contained in the system as a whole (in analogy to the observer for whom the channel of information is one among others).

Within the channel of communication Shannon's 'theorem of the channel with noise' applies: the quantity of information of a message transmitted in a channel of communication disturbed by noise can only decrease by a quantity equal to the ambiguity introduced by this noise between entry and exit of this channel. Corrective codes introducing redundancy can diminish this ambiguity to the point that the information transmitted is equal to that emitted, but under no circumstance can it be superior (Shannon and Weaver, 1949).

While the transmission of information within the channel (from A to B) breaks down if the amount of noise is equivalent to the information transmitted (the information arriving at B is autonomous from A), a perfect transmission makes B equal to A and B is therefore redundant. In a self-organizing system a compromise is needed between redundancy and variety: to reduce noise and enable the transmission of information, without which the system would break down, and yet allow noise which introduces variety, which in turn augments the number of possible responses of a system to random fluctuations of the conditions imposed on it by its environment. W. R. Ashby formulated this as the law of 'requisite variety': 'In an environment that is a source of diverse and unpredictable aggressions, variety in structure and functions of the system is an indispensable factor of autonomy' (Atlan, 1979, 43).[7]

Noise thus has different effects according to the level of organization we consider. Atlan designates the effect of noise within the channel of communication as 'destructive ambiguity' (since it threatens the transmission of information upon which the system relies). Yet it leads to an increase in variety in the system as a whole, which results in what he calls 'autonomy-ambiguity' (Atlan 1979, 46). A central condition is that the system is complex enough, that it has an extremely high number of subsystems and of relations between these components, to enable the positive role of 'autonomy-ambiguity' to coexist with its destructive effect on the subsystems. Edgar Morin was, according to Atlan, the first to identify these 'hyper complex' natural systems (Morin, 1973), in that the number of their components is extremely high (10 billion neurons for a human brain, we are told) and the interrelation among elements and functions is such that each element is in principle directly or indirectly related to every other. The resulting reliability of natural self-organizing systems is the envy of man-made machines.[8]

What is more, it is not only the homeostatic reliability of natural systems in compensating for noise that is at stake here, but the integration of noise as a constitutive factor of self-organization.

Noise on the basis of information

If noise is thus a prerequisite for complexity and self-organization, this will impact upon our idea of a paradigm shift, and with it that of a crisis that must provoke such a shift, or reversal/rupture/revolution. This is indeed what our analogy with Atlan's concept of organization on the basis of noise appears to suggest. Atlan warns of the temptation to attribute the emergence of a crisis to the effects of noise, since the effects of noise are, as a matter of fact, permanent constituents in the process of self-organization. In his view the eventual crisis arises as a result of an inversed function of the principle of complexity on the basis of noise. The origin of a crisis is to be sought at a meta-organizational level, in the absence of a code that translates the information contained in individual channels of communication into the code that enables the communication between these channels. The crisis is the consequence of noise on the basis of information.

Recuperating the operability of the system as a whole requires a reload of redundancy (an increase in repetition). Redundancy had diminished under the effect of ambiguity, and in doing so had increased variety (information) at the level of the system as a whole: 'the same factors that are responsible for the progressive disorganisation of a system, which ultimately leads to its death, are the ones that previously "nourished" its development with progressive complexification' (Atlan, 1979, 49).

There is thus a subtle difference between the normality of noise, or to adapt Brassier's expression, the 'generic anomaly' of self-organization and the requirement, signalled by a crisis, of new codes to ensure the continued communication between subsystems. Such a crisis would concern a meta-systemic level and would call for a code that has, to return briefly to Simondon, like the Platonic paradigm, the 'capacity to traverse, animate and structure a varied domain, domains that are increasingly varied and heteroge-neous' (Simondon, 2005, 544; emphasis in original). Such a code, or concept, is defined by what Simondon calls the 'quality of information' as opposed to the idea of the 'quantity of information'. For Simondon this 'quality' charac-terizes the enduring efficacy of a concept or a formalization to resonate over long periods of time and across changing scientific and cultural eras, as is the case with Plato's paradigmatism or Aristotle's concept of hylomorphism (the relation between energy and form).

The crisis is thus a meta-systemic – or, if you like, meta-physical – problem, provoked by a surfeit of information. It is provoked by 'noise on the basis of information'. And while the critical state of meta-systemic organization provokes a reload in redundancy, the meta-systemic or meta-physical codes/ concepts it calls for to relate its subsystems would (if we integrate Brassier's and Morange's points) require a strategic margin of ambiguity, allowing for the paradigmatic fluctuation that animates the circulation of concepts among its subsystems.

Conclusion

If it were possible to sustain such an argument epistemologically, then one may reach the conclusion that the idea of paradigmatic fluctuation, enabling perpetual regional reinvention, de-emphasizes that of a paradigm shift (be it the reversal of a set of conventions, as with Kuhn, or the idea of an 'epistemo- logical rupture', as with Bachelard). The traditional idea of scientific progress, cajoled into action by the cyclical re-emergence of epistemological crisis, may reveal itself to be the legacy of a dialectic of negation; its violent jolts from one paradigmatic code to another a symptom of its epistemological rigidity.

The idea of an epistemological crisis could instead be relativized as the fluctuation between creation and de-creation, or 'analysis' and 'modulation' (Simondon) of structures of knowledge, rather than a dialectic of affirmation and negation. This may point us in the direction of a much-needed alternative to our current idea of scientific progress, whose negative dialectic disperses cultural and scientific domains and its disciplines and subdisciplines in a postmodern kaleidoscope, tending to isolate the efficacy of change in the splintering of specializations. The traditional paradigm of progress thus appears to lead to increasingly paranoid forms of competitive self-renewal that are related to the whole only through the levelling equivalence of commercial profitability.

If the quantity of information in an epistemological domain could thus be understood as its capacity to sustain noise (variety), then the role of the paradigmatic codes/concepts it calls for, or its 'quality' of information, would *not* be to minimize this meta-systemic degree of uncertainty, to reduce its 'quantity of information' to the clarity of a message, which would ultimately increase redundancy at a meta-systemic level. Its role would instead be to create conceptual resonance able to sustain the transdisciplinary noise.

This approach would appear to suggest that 'epistemological noise' is proportional to a constitutive transdisciplinary ambiguity, in other words to a margin of uncertainty within which epistemological self-organization fluctuates between the two extremes of chaos and convention; an organizational fluctuation between, on the one hand, absolute noise, in other words the maximum probability and sheer homogeneity of pure sonic/epistemological entropy, in which all potential for transformation is terminally exhausted, and on the other, the unsustainable rigidification of conventions, whose probability of decline is proportional to its phenomenal claim to perennial certainty and universality.

Epistemic self-organization may thus be understood as occurring with the minimal probability with which noise nestles between the extremes of absolute scepticism and reductive determinism. The unpredictability we cherished in innovative musical practice, inspired by noise, would thus appear to point to a factor of organization that contrasts, obviously, with a purely negative definition of noise as entropy, disorganization, destruction, dispersion. Atlan's differentiation between the destructive effect of noise in a channel of communication and its beneficial effect at the level of the system as a whole thus appears to suggest that a transdisciplinary approach is likely to benefit from a positive effect of noise, or variety, while it is within individual specializations that clarity and the elimination of noise would be prioritized.

Perhaps we can go so far as to ask whether the requirement of necessary structural or deductive redundancy characterizes analytical approaches. Tending towards specialization, towards the concern with truthfulness or fidelity of a message, the analytical approach would therefore also require the critical analysis of the conditions of transmission or communication within one system. The use of strategic ambiguity, of 'epistemic noise' at a meta-systemic level, on the other hand, may be the characteristic of speculative, synthetic approaches. Analytical and speculative approaches would thus be joined by the epistemological equivalent of a topological limit between differentiation and integration. Such a view may lead to an epistemological holism that exceeds the equation of truth and clarity of message – without forgetting that we are talking about a relative holism, about systems that do not encompass the totality of possibility.

5

Mongrel Vibrations:
H. P. Lovecraft's Weird Ecology of Noise
Dean Lockwood

There has been a great deal of philosophical interest in the fiction of H. P. Lovecraft recently, based on the assumption that his 'weird realism' can help illuminate weird reality (see e.g., Harman, 2008). Weird fiction deals with impossible, awful encounters with otherness. It may be understood as radical in that it provides a space for the exploration of disturbing, ineradicable alterities haunting and undermining quotidian experience. It suspends the actual, opening up lines into the virtual. Discussion of Lovecraft's fiction, though, has involved little recognition of the importance of sonicity in the weird. This is my focus. I wish to connect my reflections on this to the concept of vibration, leaning on Elizabeth Grosz's observation that '[v]ibration is the common thread or rhythm running through the universe from its chaotic organic interminability to its most intimate forces of inscription on living bodies of all kinds and back again' (Grosz, 2008, 54). Through a discussion of the nexus of noise and horror in Lovecraft's major works, this chapter will argue that he sketches a weird vibrational ecology in which the human is opened up to the immanent alien. I will also make a connection between these works and the early days of the mass medium of radio, conceived of as an 'alien' technology. In Lovecraft, horror is networked, tentacular, and, as I argue, resonates powerfully with the evolution of media.

Resonant evil

Fearful affect is routinely inculcated in contemporary Western societies. Brian Massumi has written of the social pervasion of 'mechanisms of fear production, with special attention to the role of the mass media' (Massumi, 1993, viii). These technologies are means by which power perpetuates itself, performing an affective capture of the materiality of the body. Sound, or more specifically noise, is an important aspect of apparatuses of capture. Steve Goodman describes, in particular, a sound/fear nexus, a sonic ecology of fear in which we are collectively controlled, kept on edge, by the cultivation of a chronic affect of dread (Goodman, 2010, 12). On the other hand, with Simon Reynolds (2004), we could counterpose to this dreadful domination-sound an interface of noise and horror in music such as Industrial which attempts to act upon the body in order to unleash unknown potentials (I have in mind here Throbbing Gristle's so-called 'metabolic music'). In these various approaches, we may conceive of noise in terms of epidemiology and affective contagion. A viral fear affect activated by sound-waves bypasses cognitive functions, prompting visceral, nervous and chemical reactions.

I will come back to the question of affect later, but for now I want to dwell upon the familiar notion that noise is something to be abjected. Noise occupies an invidious place or role in relation to the human. It promises mutations which are 'abhuman', to borrow the term of weird fiction author William Hope Hodgson (Hurley, 2004, 3–4). In fact, noise has been associated with a non-human, non-phenomenological model of existence in Nietzsche, Deleuze, Serres, and no doubt others, which revolves around the image of the ocean. Etymologically, noise ties back to nausea and revulsion, associated in turn with the nautical as, specifically, seasickness. Michel Serres conjures a vivid image of noise as a 'gray sea', the pandemoniac 'ground of the world' multiplicitously raging and flying at the trembling 'receiver of the flux' (Serres, 1995, 62, 63). He claims that 'noise is not a matter of phenomenology [...] it is a matter of being itself' (1995, 13). Noise 'lies under the cuttings of all phenomena, a proteus taking on any shape, the matter and flesh of manifestations' (1995, 14). With Nietzsche, we can consider ontological genesis from, and dissolution back into, the world in terms of a vibratory structure in which the sound of particular waves merges with the sea noise. Nietzsche hails the world as a 'monster of energy [...] a sea of forces flowing and rushing together [...]: this, my *Dionysian* world of the eternally self-creating, the eternally self-destroying, this mystery world of the twofold voluptuous delight, my "beyond good and evil" ' (Nietsche, 1968, §1067).

Oceanic, inhuman noise is given cultural expression in various kinds of music (see e.g. Toop, 1995), but it is also expressed in fiction. H. P. Lovecraft, my focus here, is a literary figure whose weird tales emerge from a lineage of noise-preoccupied horror fiction dating back, at least, to Edgar Allan Poe. In gothic stories such as 'The Fall of the House of Usher' and 'The Tell-Tale Heart', Poe exploits the phenomenology of audition. Thus, Roderick Usher, proprietor of the mansion of the story's title, was afflicted with a 'morbid condition of the auditory nerve which rendered all music intolerable to the sufferer, with the exception of certain effects of stringed instruments' (Poe, 1993, 145). The locus of uncanny horror here is phenomenological and it is psychological. The landmark tale by M. P. Shiel, 'The House of Sounds', originally written in 1896 and later published as 'Vaila', much admired by Lovecraft, marked a point of departure. 'Vaguely like, yet infinitely unlike' Poe's 'Usher', as Lovecraft put it (Lovecraft, 2005, 151), Shiel's tale of a house on a northerly island which stands at the centre of a system of violent oceanic cross-currents suggests contact with an inhuman universe, a 'Machine of Death, a baleful Vast. *Too* horrible to many is the running shriek of Being – they *cannot* bear the world' (2005, 235). As the protagonist puts it, 'I seemed to stand in the very throat of some yelling planet' (244). Here, noise is presented as radical, cosmic alterity. This very much presages Lovecraft's weird cosmic horror. His fervour for visual description notwithstanding, Lovecraft's weird is as much sonic as scopic. In his survey of weird tales, 'Supernatural Horror in Literature', he explicitly defined the weird in sonic terms, the 'one test' being an imagined 'contact with unknown spheres and powers; a subtle attitude of awed listening, as if for the beating of black wings or the scratching of outside shapes and entities on the known universe's utmost rim' (2005, 108). This scratching may also be heard much closer to home. Matt Lee has associated Lovecraft's weird with the 'radical alien nature of the Oceanic depths' and has drawn a connection between this and Deleuze's oceanic 'clamour of Being' (Lee, 2007, 73). The horror that is the great God Cthulhu, first appearing in the 1926 tale 'The Call of Cthulhu', exerts its pull from its ruined city beneath the ocean. The horror of Being is an alien, submarine voice.

There is a fundamental disavowal in Lovecraft's understanding of his aesthetic of the weird. He believes that humanity is trapped within a cage of immutable natural laws and his express wish is to imagine an escape from this cage, or at least, 'the illusion of some strange suspension or violation of the galling limitations of time, space, and natural law' (cited in Joshi, 2004, 79). Yet, at the same time, his desire to flee a pessimistic, mechanistic material universe is fused with a loathing of the alien materialisms he conjures up in his fiction. Lovecraft wrote that phenomena are only properly weird if they '*could not possibly happen*' (Joshi, 2004, 86), but of course his work was an expression precisely of the potentiality, the virtuality and unconscious of an already weird world. The horror is that the scratching from 'outside' is already inside, infecting, running rampant, warping and deforming human life. His disavowal is of the reality of the weird. For the fantasy writer Fritz Leiber, Lovecraft was horror fiction's Copernicus. In him, the locus of horror shifted from man to the black gulfs of the cosmos (Joshi, 2004, 125). I would say, rather, that the locus of Lovecraft's horror is the black cosmic gulf *within* the human. He did not believe in an outside, yet his fiction promised an altogether different kind of materialism than the one he consciously advocated (see e.g. Fisher's formulation of 'gothic materialism' in Fisher, 2001). It channelled the Dionysian, oceanic excess of the cosmos.

As Michel Houellebecq insists, Lovecraft, unlike Poe, had no need of psychologistic narrative. All his tales required were human sensoria to which he would offer new percepts, abominable sensations. Houellebecq says we should consider, in particular, the 'maniacal precision with which HPL arranges the *soundtrack* to his tales' (2008, 70), and it is on this soundtrack that I now focus in a little depth.

The polyglot abyss

S. T. Joshi argues that the hideous biology of monstrous beings, upon which Lovecraft is prone to lavish unstinting visual description, is not the most horrifying aspect of his tales. What conveys the intended sensation is the phenomenon of imitation. As Lovecraft himself commented, 'it is not wholesome to watch monstrous objects doing what one had known only human beings to do' (cited in Joshi, 1990, 200). This is particularly focused around the use of language – reading and writing, but most importantly, *speaking*. In Lovecraft, aliens compose letters, manipulate books, but it is their speech that is most fascinating, especially when it is imitative of the human. As he writes in 'The Call of Cthulhu': 'There are vocal qualities peculiar to men, and vocal qualities peculiar to beasts; and it is terrible to hear the one when the source should yield the other' (Joshi, 1990, 200). It is a vile imposture when the alien contaminates and mixes with the human, which we can quite obviously connect to Lovecraft's notorious revulsion towards miscegenation, or, as he would no doubt put it, 'mongrelization'. The impor- tance of race hatred in his fiction cannot be minimized. It reaches its height in his descriptions of a certain slum locale in Brooklyn, New York (a city in which he lived and loathed for a few years) in the story, 'The Horror at Red Hook'. Red Hook, populated by a complex racial mix, is a 'polyglot abyss', a 'babel of sound and filth' (Lovecraft, 1969a, 72, 73). Here, the horror is emphatically vocal: 'From this tangle of material and spiritual putrescence the blasphemies of an hundred dialects assail the sky' (1969a, 74). This infernal district gives issue to a contagion of shouting, drum-beating, singing, chanting, whispering hordes, underpinning which, Lovecraft persuades, there is some terrible cultic purpose.

Lovecraft spooks himself with mongrel, blasphemous becomings of the voice. In his tales, the voice swerves from signification as it is invaded by an alien resonance. Sense breaks down, words cannot be pronounced and names cannot be rendered. Astutely, Raymond Saint-Jean's 1998 Canadian TV film *Out of Mind: The Stories of H. P. Lovecraft*, makes one of its first scenes Lovecraft (played by Christopher Heyerdahl) wandering in the forest near to his home in Providence, Rhode Island, experimenting aloud with the pronunciation of the name of his alien god Cthulhu, coaxing and venturing the word for maximum effect. Something demonic enters speech, some vibe beyond the verbal, beyond language and, in fact, beyond audition. We are back to affect and asignifying vibration. The protagonist of 'The Call of Cthulhu' dreams Cthulhu's voice from below: 'a voice that was not a voice; a chaotic sensation which only fancy could transmute into sound, but which he attempted to render by the almost unpronounceable jumble of letters, "*Cthulhu fhtagn*"' (Lovecraft, 2002, 143). Transmitted via the body, this 'subterrene [*sic.*] voice or intelligence (shouts) monotonously in enigmatical sense-impacts uninscribable save as gibberish' (2002, 143–4). At the climax of 'The Dunwich Horror', Lovecraft describes a similar affective sonic event born of a 'speaking impulse':

> Without warning came those deep, cracked, raucous vocal sounds. [...] Not from any human throat were they born, for the organs of man can yield no such acoustic perversions. [...] It is almost erroneous to call them *sounds* at all, since so much of their ghastly, infra-bass timbre spoke to dim seats of consciousness and terror far subtler than the ear; yet one must do so, since their form was indisputably though vaguely that of half-articulate *words*. (Lovecraft, 1963, 112–13)

We could also consider another of Lovecraft's greatest accomplishments, 'The Whisperer in Darkness', written in 1930. The tale begins by pointedly rejecting spectacular effect: 'Bear in mind closely that I did not see any actual visual horror at the end' (2002, 200). In this tale, the Vermont floods of 1927 have washed down apparently non-human bodies from the New Hampshire hills. These corpses strongly resemble beings from the stars told of in Indian legends. The old legends mention the beings' attempts, communicating with 'buzzing voices' (Lovecraft, 2002, 203), to seduce humans into unsavoury alliances. This coincidence attracts the attention of Wilmarth, an academic folklore specialist from Arkham, Lovecraft's fictitious city in Massachusetts. He commences a correspondence with Akeley, a farmer living in a remote part of the affected area, since Akeley claims to have happened upon a conclave of the beings and their human allies, engaged in ritual, and to have taken the opportunity to make a phonograph recording. This documents the celebrants' insectile drone, a sound which exercises a hypnotic pull. The beings – as it transpires, representatives of the Mi-Go from Yuggoth (our Pluto) – are basically bee-voiced bat-winged prawns with antennae. They give off bad vibes, operating on an alien frequency. Mi-Go are composed of matter – a tissue structured like fungus – which vibrates at a different rate to anything humanly known, clashing inharmoniously with terrestrial vibrations. Their motive, once their stealthy coexistence with the New Hampshire farmers is exposed, is to invade and abduct. In this they are instructed by Nyarlathotep, the Crawling Chaos, Lovecraft's shape-changing messenger of the Old Ones, the 'gods' outside the known universe. Wilmarth, eventually travelling to meet Akeley in person, actually (and somewhat confusingly for the reader) encounters Nyarlathotep in Mi-Go form but disguised as Akeley. Masked Nyarlathotep represses his native buzzing in order to 'whisper' to Wilmarth in a simulacrum of human speech and tempt him into an alliance.

In this tale the insectile buzzing could be understood machinically along the lines of Parikka's notion of 'insect media' and his discussion of an 'ecological ontology' (Parikka, 2008, 341), in which:

> the figures of the insect functioned as a weird reality [...] where the familiar notions regarding perception and movement did not hold. Instead, in a parallel enterprise to the emergence of technical media that likewise challenged the phenomenological world of the human being, insects' capacities paved the way for experimental takes on folding with the world, of finding novel action-perception circuits.
>
> (Parikka, 2008, 355)

In the final section of this chapter I wish to draw out another dimension of Lovecraft's noise-horror. The affective sonic contagion – weird becomings and mongrelizations – by which Lovecraft characterizes his attempt to imagine a new vibratory materialism is, in 'The Whisperer in Darkness', writ large. However, I believe that, in the cosmic alienage of Nyarlathotep, a being inclined to imposture and in command of faculties of mind control and hypnosis, there are also other implications which connect up with the idea of insect media.

Cosmic radio

Nyarlathotep – appearing across a number of his writings – is one of Lovecraft's most enigmatic and fascinating creations because he is so variously drawn. He suggests self-differing multiplicity and Deleuzian powers of the false. He first appears in a 1920 prose poem based on a dream of Lovecraft's which has been interpreted by Joshi as a 'parable for the decline of the West' (Joshi, 1990, 226). In the dream, Nyarlathotep, here incarnated as an immortal Egyptian, is painted as an imposter and a charlatan, a travelling showman staging entertainments in which crowds are dazzled by eerie and alarming, sparking electrical instruments and phantasmagorical projections of images of world destruction. As the shows culminate, some force descends from the moon and ushers the audience into a 'sightless vortex of the unimaginable' (Lovecraft, 2002, 33). The piece concludes with a reference to the mindless music (disquietingly reminiscent of the ancient North African Sufi music associated with the Master Musicians of Joujouka and other collectives) with which Lovecraft typically associates the cracked rim of the universe: 'the muffled, maddening beating of drums, and thin, monotonous whine of blasphemous flutes [...] whereunto dance slowly, awkwardly, and absurdly the gigantic, tenebrous ultimate gods – the blind, voiceless, mindless gargoyles whose soul is Nyarlathotep' (2002, 33).

Some have made convincing connections between Nyarlathotep and Nikola Tesla, a strange figure from the occult and occulted history of modern electricity and wireless communication. Indeed, the paths of Tesla and Lovecraft may even have crossed at some point, since both were acquaintances of Hugo Gernsback, a key figure in magazine publishing in the fields of both modern electronics and science fiction. At the time of Lovecraft's dream, Tesla was notorious for his controversial performances of electric sorcery, in which his appearance – body 'traversed by a powerful electric current, vibrating at about a million times a second' (Tesla, cited in Seifer, 1998, 112) – seemingly approximated some Cthulhoid manifestation. In Tesla's own words:

One sees the experimenter standing on a big sheet of fierce, blinding flame, his whole body enveloped in a mass of phosphorescent streamers, like the tentacles of an octopus. Bundles of light stick out from his spine. As he stretches out his arms, roaring tongues of fire leap from his fingertips as myriads of minute projectiles are shot off from him with such velocities as to pass through the adjoining walls.

(Seifer, 1998, 142)

Given that Lovecraft's ambivalent desire was to escape the confines of natural law, Tesla's tentacular spectacle, this 'effulgent glory' (1998, 138), embodying the apocalyptic conjuration of unknown forces, will most certainly have appealed to the writer and appalled in equal measure. It even seems to be echoed in his 1919 story 'Beyond the Wall of Sleep', in which a 'cosmic radio' apparatus is imagined, facilitating telepathic communication: 'Chords, vibrations and harmonic ecstasies echoed passionately on every hand, while on my ravished sight burst the stupendous spectacle of ultimate beauty. Walls, columns and architraves of living fire blazed effulgently around the spot where I seemed to float in air' (Lovecraft, 1969b, 26).

The 'Lovecraft Event', to use Benjamin Noys' phrase (2007), is, I think, inseparable from a certain 'Media Event'. China Miéville has contextualized American weird fiction in the 1920s and 1930s as a response to the barbarism of the Great War, modern rationality in crisis as the comfort of the known is shattered by violence (2009, 513). However, perhaps the affective core of Lovecraft's major work (usually understood as his cosmic horror phase running from 'The Call of Cthulhu' in 1926 through to his death in 1935) was also formed by the babel-tongues of the modern as they were transmitted in the early days of broadcasting. Just as much as the barbarism of war, which Lovecraft did not actually experience at first hand, it is surely the 'barbarism' of commercial broadcasting, the new wireless traffic in media messages, that formed a more immediate context. The first US national radio network was launched in 1926 – the same year Lovecraft shrugged off the influence of the Poesque gothic and ushered in the new cosmic horror with his tale of Cthulhu – and by this time there were already voices of concern about the 'psychopathic' consequences of mass media, commercial radio perceived as a war against intelligence on the part of corporate power. Miéville suggests that weird fiction is an expression of the sublime; not a heavenly sublime, but the sublime as an alien, predatory, totalitarian threat (2009, 511). This totalitarian sublime may also be conceived of as a media sublime. The received social history of the mass media has occluded Tesla-related motifs of occult forces and interplanetary communication – Tesla believed his pioneering radio experiments in his Colorado lab had picked up regular impulses possibly emanating from Venus or Mars – but in the early twentieth century these were very prominent. Perhaps Lovecraft's most famous invention is his imaginary forbidden grimoire, the *Necronomicon*. In a short history of this volume, he declared that the original Arabic text, written by the mad Abdul Alhazred around AD 700, was entitled *Al Azif*, which names the nocturnal buzzing sound made by insects and associated with the 'howling of daemons' (Lovecraft, 2008, 173). Perhaps it is not too fanciful to imagine the radio set as the *Azif* in the living room, the great unmentioned, unnameable tinnitus that howls through his work. Invasive, tentacular and alien, radio may be conceived of as the whisperer in darkness, the 'soul-petrifying voice of an agency from beyond the wall of sleep' (Lovecraft, 1969b, 28).

Jeffrey Sconce has charted the anxious discourses emerging in the first three decades of radio. Initially, the new medium was fantastically conceived, and, in fact, legitimated by Edison's own beliefs, in terms of an 'aural "ghostland" ', vibrations transmitting the voices of the dead across the ether (Sconce, 2000, 67). Radio facilitated a communications revolution but it also opened up a vast, alienating gulf that rendered the universe uncanny (2000, 62). The oceanic metaphor was ubiquitous: 'not only did the metaphor of the "etheric ocean" encourage the idea that one could become "lost at sea", but it also implied that, as with the oceans of the earth, unknown creatures might stalk this electronic sea's invisible depths' (69). So radio was a 'nautical technology', as Sconce puts it, signals like 'ships in the night' of this sea of noise (70). However, the discourse gradually shifted from ghost-obsessed to alien-obsessed, precipitated by the inauguration of broadcasting. There was a shift from an oceanic model to a network model. Radio began to be conceived, in submissions to pulp magazines such as *Weird Tales*, for example, as a net or web in and through which people are captured and controlled:

> Founded on the new metaphor of a blanketing and inescapable sense of electronic presence, these tales were less a meditation on extraordinary, paranormal forms of communications than a lesson in the implicit horrors of the 'network' as a system for binding together a national audience, even against its own will.
>
> (Sconce, 2000, 109)

Radio was now less ethereal than tentacular. This imaginary chimes with recent work on the rich possibilities of the sonic for warfare and control in the contemporary. Steve Goodman (2010) has detailed how sound is deployed in media networks to modulate collective mood, to create a certain immersive affective ambience and capture in a state of distraction. The network horror chimes also with Matthew Fuller and Andrew Goffey's so-called 'evil media studies' in which it is suggested, drawing on the work of Isabelle Stengers and Phillipe Pignarre on 'capitalist sorcery', that 'practices maligned by the ascendancy of critical rationality, such as *hypnosis*, be treated far more seriously' (2009, 143). And it resonates with the 'contagion theory' of writers such as Nigel Thrift (2009), Jussi Parikka (2007) and Tony Sampson (2009), much of which recovers ideas on social imitation formulated in the nineteenth century by Gabriel Tarde in order to develop thinking on the viral transmission of affect.

David Punter is mistaken when he claims that Lovecraft is a dead-end, a phobic point of atrophy in the literature of terror (Punter, 1996, 45). Lovecraft's major work deals with the horror of modernity, its new indeterminacies and babels and the emergence of strange non-mechanistic materialisms. These tales engage with the terror and the ecstasy of unstoppable chaotic becomings, impostures and mongrel vibrations. With Noys, we can say that together they constitute 'a reactionary event that produces something new' (2007). From the contemporary perspective, we can deplore the sorcery of capital as affective regime but find in Lovecraft, against his consciously expressed intentions, a resource salvageable for the project of a weird ecology and a vibratory oceanic noise ontology. Sampson has discussed the transmission of affect in contemporary societies. One of the ways in which social power spreads is through the inconspicuous route of pleasant distractions and fantasies, a warm bath which seduces potential consumers and voters. He calls this 'viral love' (Sampson, 2010). We are somnambulistically carried away by an epidemic of feeling. Sampson conceives of this carrying away as akin to the operation of the Trojan Horse of myth. Destructive, mortifying influences stow away and disguise themselves as joyful, affirmative encounters. Beyond good and evil, the virus worms its code into the happy host bodies and promulgates a hidden, dominative agenda. In similar fashion, the viral *fear* with which Lovecraft's cosmic horror is replete may also be not quite what it seems. Considered as a Trojan Horse, the phobic reaction his work displays could be understood as camouflaging an escape route. In short, horror fiction may be employed to hack the network, just as Goodman describes resistant forms in the context of sonic culture, mobilizing affect via techniques of dissimulation.

More recently than Lovecraft, J. G. Ballard is another writer who has obsessively focused on the human bid to escape the confines of universal laws of time, space and nature, and who has also intimated monstrously ambivalent end-games. Is Ballard's positing of deviant logics which challenge social reality nihilistic reaction or immanent transcendence? His work is an extended prevarication: 'I think the whole of my fiction is poised on that balancing point. Sometimes it tilts one way, sometimes another' (cited in Baxter, 2008, 124). The protagonist of J. G. Ballard's short story, 'Track 12', is murdered by an acquaintance he has cuckolded. It is an unusual deed, a murder with microsonics. The cuckold, Sheringham, administers a poison which effectively drowns Maxted in his own body's fluids, seeing to it that the event of death is accompanied by the hugely amplified sound of an adulterous embrace:

Maxted had almost gone now, his fading identity a small featureless island nearly eroded by the waves beating across it.

'Maxted, can you hear the sea? Do you know where you're drowning?'

A succession of gigantic flaccid waves, each more lumbering and enveloping than the last, rode down upon them.

'In a kiss!' Sheringham screamed. 'A kiss!'

The island slipped away and slid into the molten shelf of the sea.

(Ballard, 2009, 71)

The weird oceanic horror rendered here makes love and fear indistinguishable, intimating ecstatic annihilation in a secret noise ontology. Lovecraft's mad music from the rim of the universe flows together with the furore sounding from Georges Bataille's *Mouth*. In the latter, the constipatory attitude of the human, 'magisterial look of the face with a *closed mouth*, as beautiful as a safe' is shattered (Bataille, 1985, 60). The head is joyfully thrown back, mouth blossoming like a flower, ejaculating screams, kisses, buzzes and drones, rending the human safe house with nature's explosive propagation.

These writers strain towards a weird ecology in which sonicity plays an important role. The oceanic, cosmic horror of Lovecraft's major works, which is also, I think, a network horror, may be linked to Gilles Deleuze and Félix Guattari's notion of a 'strange ecology' in which nature is conceived as a teeming, multitudinous space, a violent inhuman furore (see Goh, 2008). Deleuze and Guattari stress nature's contestation of the human and also its self-contestation. A relationship of mutual desire pertains in which experimental imitative alliances are sought in order to elicit new life, new contagious becomings. In this relationship, which I would extend to the media ecology, the human becomes the sorcerer, flying into the furore to capture the animal and to submit to capture: 'we become with the world. [...] We become universes' (cited in Goh, 2008, 209). In other words, we are at one with the whisperer in darkness, transmitter of world-shaking vibrations: 'Sorcerer, emissary, changeling, outsider...that hideous repressed buzzing.' (Lovecraft, 2002, 267).

6

The matter of numbers:

sound technologies and the experience of noise according to analogue and digital models

José Cláudio Siqueira Castanheira

Jean-Luc Nancy tells us that sounds, when reverberating in the various bodies that exist in their path, are endowed with significant references, producing different meanings. While resonating, sounds perceived as a 'presence' share the same space of references as sounds perceived as *logos*. There would be two dimensions in sounds: one that focuses on a certain sense to be understood, and another that is interested in the resonance of sounds itself, that is, in the way they spread in space and touch objects. To listen would be an attempt to reach a possible meaning of sounds or a meaning of things through their sounds, meanings that are not immediately accessible. But, in Nancy's words: 'perhaps it is necessary that sense not be content to make sense (or to be *logos*), but that it want also to resound' (Nancy, 2007, 6). There is a kind of meaning to be found in the very resonance of things.

Electronically synthesized sounds, which, in a first moment of audition, are not attached to any empirical object, would lack some of these significant references. According to Schaeffer, sounds from these electronic sources are not audible until they are *translated* by loudspeakers. They are *unheard* in their construction, *absent* from nature (Schaeffer, 1966, 420). They would induce a process of filling the gaps between sounds and objects from the relationships established between the mechanisms of perception and the sound itself. These mechanisms are thought of as fundamentally tied to a biological body and therefore sounds are manifested in relation to the physical conditions of sound sources, their existence in the environment, and technological aspects concerning those objects. Going through the spaces between bodies, sound acquires less 'pure' contours, retaining from the surroundings, from the apparatus of production and reproduction and even from our biologically shaped sensory apparatus, noises that bring sound closer and invest it with significance. The sampling of pre-existing sounds, involving electronic and/or digital technologies, may be viewed as a model different from that of sound synthesis. In spite of that, both processes are guided by a technical logic which uses electronic devices to meet its ends. Thus both 'pure' synthesized sounds, close to abstraction, and complex sounds, when digitized, maintain 'electronic' features.[1]

This chapter aims to demonstrate how this technicist logic subverts another, older one, which guided the very early relationship among natural sounds and their recordings. Noises were assumed to be a natural part of listening in analogue techniques of sound inscription and reproduction, despite the idea of a similarity between the original and the recording, claimed since Edison's phonograph records. Regardless of its constructed character, recorded sound strongly searched the perfection of fidelity to the original event. Noises were a part of the experience to be ignored, but still made their voice heard. In today's digital model, we perceive efficient strategies defining which part of the experience must necessarily prevail. The binary encoding of signal is presented both as a matrix and as a result of new ways of listening to a sonorous universe. How is noise absorbed in this new model? Is it still perceived as oppositional? How does it present itself in increasingly sophisticated technological mediation processes?

Generated sounds and sampled sounds

It is appropriate to make at least two distinctions regarding the nature of both electronically generated and sampled sounds, and the possible implications in our ways of apprehending them. One is about synthesized and non-synthesized sounds. It is undisputed that the use of pre-recorded sounds on different materials, after their original production, is as old as recording technology itself. Presumably due to the tacit assumption about the realistic properties of sound inscription, which Edison's phonograph (along with the other analogue technologies that followed it) cultivated, these sounds, removed from an original space and a time could not give vent to a greater creative potential. As recordings were thought of, mainly, as reproductions of reality, early technologies were not expected to encourage any kinds of editing features.

Some decades later, composers like Edgard Varèse, John Cage and, later, advocates of *musique concrète*, draw on these new technologies to give the sounds more expressive traits, assembling parts of different recordings into one work of sonic bricolage. Sometimes this could be in dialogue with traditional musical instruments or with new technological devices, as in some of Cage's pieces. The possibility of sampling by means of electronic apparatuses, as we understand it today, was, nevertheless, originated in this kind of disconnection between the sound and its characteristics as a sign. It no longer refers to a specific object, thus losing the semiotic duality of the signified/signifier relation:

> Sounds as sampled objects are no longer signs. The original reference has dissolved. They can be linked with many other visual or acoustic objects and then attain a new and perplexing symbolic quality. Detached from their 'here and now' they can, now in a sampled manner, be placed into different contexts.
>
> (Motte-Haber, 2002, 205)

In addition, according to Motte-Haber, sampled sound, which lacks a 'here and now', establishes a new contact with reality – a fragmented reality. The perception patterns are disrupted and the receiver must strive, at the moment of hearing the sounds, to situate him-herself in the world. The various possible meanings of these 'constellations of signs' challenge the very position of each one of us in the world. Each person should therefore build his or her own system of references, with the awareness that there is not only one system. In this sense, contemporary art (including in this generalizing term music, sonic art, different kinds of audiovisual production and many other current forms of expression) may best be experienced as an act of consciousness enacted through technologically mediated models as opposed to other more traditional practices such as concert music. A world filled with simulated events is uninterruptedly and technologically re-created through sampling. Space-time coordinates of this world dissolve easily, forcing us to constantly rebuild our references. Reality is a network of complex and variable signs. Thus, for Motte-Haber, the role of art is to 'create irritations and make a process of perception possible which is necessary for determining one's own subjective position' (Motte-Haber, 2002, 205).

However, this expansion of the sonic object's spectrum of meanings makes the space in which we move uncertain. There is an obvious difference between sonic matter which is cropped and enlarged, via sampling methods, and entirely synthetic sonic material, already distanced from the concrete world in its birth, that is, sounds which only come to life via electronic generation processes. At first, synthesized and 'real' recorded sounds seemed to maintain a huge distance between them. Even the term 'sound object' (Schaeffer, 1966) seems to have been coined not taking into account electronic sounds, which lack those morpho-typological properties that most interested Schaeffer.[2] The idea of spectral mass has never been very productive when dealing with some simple sounds like those of early synthesizers. Those sounds, made by the combination of simple sine waves, did not generate much interest in concrete music composers, probably because they could not obtain the same richness of type and form found in complex natural sounds, such as sounds produced by man, by industrialization, or by urban or natural environments. Schaeffer acknowledges the synthesis process, mostly still in development in the 1950s, as a way of producing new timbres, but, at the same time, makes it clear that it is a type of research that does not interest him:

> It is true that the mode of electronic composition has to, more than any other, meet a systematic spirit. And, reciprocally, that the use of electronic equipment has undoubtedly reinforced this tendency. It is also true that the problems in music composition have historically been the starting point for a musical research of another kind, claiming the experimental method. And, reciprocally, that the choice of a live and complex material, resistant to analysis, and of a mode of composition that could only be effected empirically and by successive approximations, may be characteristic of another type of spirit.
>
> (Schaeffer, 1966, 22)

Apparently, decades lived in contact with these technologies, and the cultural practices that were made possible by them, softened this genetic difference.

Analogue sounds and digital sounds

The second distinction is between analogue and digital sounds. This distinction raises a deeper concern about the recording, storage and playback processes of sampling. In a first analysis we can see a difference at the organizational level of the sonic material. The analogue process involves signal continuity, a movement of increase and decrease in air pressure that once captured and converted into electricity – in a transduction process – becomes a set of voltage variation. The signal to be stored and then played back again is converted into physical structures. These structures could be the grooves of a disc, the arrangement of metallic particles in a magnetic tape or other material structures. The nature of these material structures, both the disc topography or the arrangement of particles on the surface of the tape, is what will constrain sound in a reproduction process which reverses that of recording when read by the appropriate devices. In an analogue model, the processes of recording and reproduction are strongly determined by physical and chemical events. Of course, when we consider the mechanisms of listening there is also a biological dimension. When converted into electrical signals, inscribed on a surface or arranged as a magnetic field, this sound cannot be separated from the obstacles imposed by the environment. There is a determination of an external order that places limits on the forms that appear in these successive transformations of the original audio. Matter is a limiting force that adds its own characteristics, its 'noise', to recording. Noises are an integral and essential part of the analogue model.

In defining the musical code as something that mirrors and confirms social rules, Jacques Attali subsumes noise as a locus of power, as something which denies this organizing role. Within a traditional perspective, noise is regarded as an intruder in certain models of musical fruition. We may even consider different types of noise for different musical experiences. But it will always be inscribed into a system, and thus, in that way only, it may be understood as noise: 'A noise is a resonance that interferes with the audition of a message in the process of emission' (Attali, 2006, 26). All organized form assumes a level of disorganization. And so, for Attali, noise is of the order of death, questioning the role of a dominant code. It is the unexpected that must be abstracted, but that also inevitably conditions our perception of the object.

Noise, situated externally to codes of organization, can lead to a change of these codes. For a long time the technologies of recording and playback were guided by the idea of fidelity, ruling out the possibility of noise. In general, we are presented with a perspective of immediacy (Bolter and Grusin, 2000), namely that there would be a direct contact between the listener and the original sound emitter. New technologies provide new cognitive models that are presented as magical solutions to shorten this distance between the experience and the real world. The advent of the digital is no different in this respect. As in the case of earlier technologies, the myth of transparency remains.

Attali also says that noise, by unchanneling the sensations of hearing, thereby putting an end to certain meanings, creates others. It generates modifications in structuring codes. Noise would be a construction outside meaning but, at the same time, it would be the presence of all meanings, bringing new information and order within itself. The listener's imagination would be freed by this absence of meaning 'in pure noise or in the meaningless repetition of a message' (Attali, 2006, 33). New codes may appear, generating new kinds of organization. What constitutes noise for a certain order becomes the harmony of another.

Digital sound, unlike analogue, is built through a coding of portions of the original signal. It is worth stating that the process of transduction of an acoustic event (air vibration) into an electrical signal is still done in a manner similar to analogue recording. The digital sound still depends on the conversion of an electromagnetic dynamic into electricity. The difference lies in the storage procedure. And here there is a clear concern for the elimination of the material interferences of the recording process. The electric signal, which, supposedly, is what counts here, is subjected to a numerical coding. It is transformed into a binary string of zeros and ones, eliminating duplication and avoiding factors external to the digitized material. Thus digital sound, as with any other contemporary digital manifestation of communication, can be treated as information, as zeros and ones. This belief in the prevalence of the informational character of media as a result of the transition from writing for the technical media is visible in the work of authors such as Friedrich Kittler (1999) and Lev Manovich (2001).[3] New media, understood as involving computing technology, are therefore able to handle communication events in a homogenizing way. Kittler, responding to this generalized process of digitization, calls into question the very concept of media:

> The general digitization of channels and information erases the differences among individual media. Sound and image, voice and text are reduced to surface effects, known to consumers as interface. Sense and the senses turn into eyewash. Their media-produced glamor will survive for an interim as a by-product of strategic programs. Inside the computers themselves everything becomes a number: quantity without image, sound, or voice. And once optical fiber networks turn formerly distinct data flows into a

standardized series of digitized numbers, any medium can be translated into any other.

(Kittler, 1999, 1–2)

New technologies, having a numerical basis as a kind of alphabet devoid of symbolic mediation, turn away from those forms of mechanical inscription that emerged in the nineteenth and became dominant in the twentieth century. The need for an approximation of a textual character that guided previous media still clung, at that time, to those new apparatuses. The *élan* of closeness to the real that was attributed to those technologies made it difficult to reduce sound and moving images to a symbolic dimension of text. Those new aspects of media created possibilities of different approaches to some emerging audiovisual practices, although they did not exclude a traditional analysis of sound and image as if not tied to a material basis. For Lisa Gitelman, sound inscription technologies (as well as image technologies, represented by cinema) must be seen as products of textual practices, in a reciprocal manner, 'rather than just a causal agent of change' (Gitelman, 1999, 2). They were completely tied to the spirit of representation of that period.

It is worth noting that this *effect of the real* produced by artefacts like the phonograph or the cinematograph, analysed in accordance with the Peircean notion of index, may not have a necessary connection to a real object. The sort of similitude with the real world that acoustic or optical events can represent may be due instead to perception or memory processes. Thus a concert recording may resemble a previous experience that someone had but not specifically the moment and the place where the recording was made. An index can reveal traces of something that happened but not necessarily reproduce it. In recordings (as well as in films) we have the construction of a sort of narrative, where technology structures routines and codes of reality, enlarging the distance from the original sonic event; an event to which, in fact, we can never have direct access. Rodowick's (2007) approach to this question, regarding digital processes in film production, is somewhat different from having analogue images as indexes of real objects or events. For him, the continuity that could possibly exist between filmed objects and the stored data in digital devices is lost in its translation to a numerical code. This code will, later, necessarily mediate our experience of the digital images or sounds, as if there was no specificity between one and the other. This 'discontinuity between input and output' would be what differentiates analogue from digital images. So, in an effort to maintain a sort of 'perceptual realism' to which we have been accustomed to in classical cinema, digital films have to incorporate old codes from cinematographic language or specific aspects of analogue images, that may become, in a stylized manner, vintage accessories on digital post-production.

In spite of this, the proximity of sound and image inscription with real objects has been greatly valued as something that could only be reached by new technologies. Gitelman points out that ' "nature" has become one of Western culture's most powerful labels. Beginning after the mid-nineteenth century, products became particularly valued if they could be characterized as "real", "genuine", or "natural" ' (Gitelman, 1999, 153). In its action to register everything around it, independent of the subject's will, the gramophone is identified by Kittler as an approximation of the Lacanian category of the 'real'. He also associates films with the category of the 'imaginary' and the typewriter with the 'symbolic' dimension. The difference between the process of sound recording and the other two technologies of inscription used as examples by Kittler is that the real 'forms the waste or residue that neither the mirror of the imaginary nor the grid of the symbolic can catch: the physiological accidents and stochastic disorder of bodies' (Kittler, 1999, 15–16).

These accidents are the very components that the logical ordering of the digital tries to avoid. The imposition of a 'grid', a system of a mathematical nature that establishes what does and does not enter during the coding process, distances itself greatly from the analogue model, where these sound dimensions are not under strict control. In the analogue model, what remains registered is the result of a clash between a whole that is given and a material base that, due to its own physical limitations, will keep just a part of that whole. In every stage of this operation there are, of course, discarded elements, but this is more or less unpredictable. A saturation effect even occurs when a much larger signal than the media is prepared to endure is imposed. In analogue media, such flexibility, this agreement with the excess, may be used for aesthetic purposes. The distortion caused by the flattening of the sound-waves as the result of an excessive dynamic has been used as a hallmark of musical genres or for specific purposes in some of the special effects developed in audiovisual productions. As we enter digital domains, this signal overload cannot occur. It is technically impossible to achieve the same effect. When the signal exceeds the limit of 0 dB, there is a clipping – a cut in the digital recording. If the margin of error is excessive, in the place of a distorted sound, there is an inaccuracy of information. Analogue distortion is characterized by a signal that breaks a specific code, a sound that exceeds the limit. On the other hand, digital distortion is characterized by a non-sound. The solution to this is to digitally simulate the effects of analogue distortion. The waves are modelled to reproduce the flattening characteristic of an analogue procedure. Moreover, it is not uncommon to see this type of simulation routinely used in various contemporary media. Effects that simulate the wear of old films, the hisses and clicks from vinyl records, the yellowing of old photos, the narrow frequency band of the first recordings or of telephone lines have become part of a gallery of antique references in state-of-the-art equipment. They are analogue digital presets, a kind of high-tech nostalgia.

Binary code black box

In this way, noise becomes no longer the questioner of an old order, but is instead inserted into media as a component of a new order. It functions in the same mode of the usual sounds, obeys the same rules. There is no way to separate noise from (usable/desirable) sounds since, stylized or not, it will always be presented as part of the experience in any form or technology in which it arises. Noise is the proof of the mediation of bodies during the act of listening, whether of organic bodies or the bodies of machines. Besides this kind of limitation on the saturation of signals, digital sound has another peculiarity: it is made from regular takes of the electrical signal intensity values, encoded by A/D (analogue–digital) converters. This fragmentation of the signal by discrete nonlinear data raises questions about how much we lose by doing so, in the relationship between the real object and its recorded form and, crucially, about the ways perception models, which may also be seen as a construction, deal with processes of listening to this type of sound.

Some theorists insist on the fact that 'something' gets lost during this encoding process and that, however great the accuracy of the process, the linear character of 'natural' sounds, along a continuous segment of time, would demonstrate a difference in kind. This difference would prevent a perfect assimilation of the analogue signal by digital encryption. To think that a digitizing model, even the most advanced, can give us a faithful representation of reality would be like suggesting that the world itself could also be thought of as digital, made up of parts irreducible to smaller pieces that, together, compose all the objects around us. This idea is far from being unanimous: the greatest difference between the actual and the virtual would be, in this perspective, a kind of creative power of the actual that cannot be apprehended by fixed or static representations.

The sampling rate, which would be one of the parameters used to accomplish a realistic rendering of reality, is directly responsible for the frequency band available in the digitized sound. For example, the rate used commonly in CDs is of 44.1 kHz; that is to say that the analogue–digital converters effectuate this process of sampling at a speed of 44,100 times per second. This means that on a CD the highest frequency possible would be 22,050

Hz. The range of possible frequencies in that case covers or even exceeds our capacity of hearing, situated, in perfect conditions, between 20 and 20,000 Hz. Vinyl analogue playback, for example, not being tied to that type of procedure, could reach slightly higher levels (close to 25 kHz). In terms of bass frequencies, digital recording could even perform better than analogue.[4] Why, then, the quite common argument that digital sound does not offer a 'complete' experience? This is a fairly common view among vinyl defenders and CD detractors.

The question that arises is, perhaps, not really about being capable of listening to the subtleties of such sound differences, but is rather concerned with the different nature of the process of perception that is not just linked to the sonic environment, but also to a specific way of living guided by the latest technological processes. As Aden Evens puts it, in a somewhat conservative way, what gets lost in the digital is:

> a productive difference, a not-yet-determined, an ontological fuzziness inherent to actuality itself. Every particular difference left out of a digital representation can be incorporated in the next round, the next scan, the next interpolation, but difference as productive cannot be digitized.
>
> (Evens, 2005, 70-1)

Our real biological hearing capacity, especially in contemporary urban environments, is very distant from ideal values. When we admit that secondary frequencies, or those above and below a certain limit, are eliminated in the process of recording and reproduction, we must also admit that this occurs in both models – in the analogue and in the digital. Something is missed in one way or another. The difference may lie in the intentionality of how this loss is engendered from the programming of technical devices. Vilém Flusser argues that contemporary machines operate in the manner of black boxes from the perspective of *input* and *output*. All incoming signals are processed by a previously defined program. We are subject to a machinic logic producing the same effects, within the same repertoire, conditioning our own way of conceiving images and sounds. Apparatuses are made to think in a 'Cartesian' way. According to Flusser, computers 'reduce Cartesian concepts to just two: "0" and "1" – and "think" in *bits*, in a binary way, programming universes suited to this kind of thinking' (Flusser, 2002, 63–4). If the binary language of computers can really plan universes, as the author suggests, we might ask ourselves how much of our mental models subsist in that process, since we have created the initial programming. Perhaps the linearity of which we are so proud in our analogue universe can itself only be accessible through a partitioning of the world to be explored by our cognitive processes. Jonathan Sterne makes an analogy with magnetic tape where, in parallel to the continuous magnetic field generated by the polarization of metal particles, we have the very arrangement of these particles which is discontinuous. The argument of linearity as defining a 'real' environment shows some weaknesses and is not enough to measure the difference between analogue and digital.

Digital encoding and perception

According to psychoacoustics, the processing of signals coming from the auditory system by the brain takes place at a slower speed than that of sound propagation. We do not hear at the same time that sound occurs. This does not prevent us from having detailed information about the course of these sounds, from their attack to their decay. Nor do we hear in the same way or at the same time with each of our ears. It is mainly because the sound comes with time differences for each ear that we can detect, even if imprecisely, their source in space. Effects such as frequency masking – the non-perception of certain stimuli by the basilar membrane, situated in the cochlea – are responsible for the difference between the vibrations entering the auricular apparatus and those that are actually processed. Certain frequencies, depending on their height and intensity, can produce responses (undulations which travel through the membrane) that overlap and hide those produced by less intense frequencies in nearby areas. Observing this behaviour on the part of our physiology, we can come to the conclusion that our auditory perception is due both to external and internal factors and, especially, that there is no direct listening. The world we hear is not what is actually sounding. Or, perhaps, 'worlds' that sound are those we hear, subjectively. There is no single model of reality.

Sterne also reminds us that these processes of discarding and interferences that occur in the relationship between hearing and brain are also the basis for audio compression technologies present in formats such as mp3. The perceptual coding takes into account the physical-acoustic model of our hearing to determine which elements of the whole sound will be rejected. The idea is that only those details that would not be perceived anyway, given the characteristics of our biological apparatus, should be eliminated. Digital sound on account of a storage space economy, especially in compressed formats, proposes to provide a full experience of sound by giving us only a part of it. It allows our brains to fill in the remainder: 'The mp3 plays its listener. Built into mp3 is an attempt to mimic and, to some degree preempt, the embodied and unconscious dimensions of human perception in the noisy, mixed-media environments of everyday life' (Sterne, 2006b, 835).

The much-heralded argument of sound fidelity, of the correspondence between recorded and original sound, embraced from the beginning of recorded sound and important for the valuation of the digital today, in fact proves to be less determinant than it might seem at first. Assuming that what we hear in film, television and music is constructed from the moment we choose which microphone to use and in what position sounds will be captured to the more sophisticated processes of editing and mixing, the question of fidelity collapses. Although it is a term still very usually referred to, most of the technological advances in recording and reproduction areas do not necessarily take into account a true similarity with 'real' events. Very distant from the possible correlation with the 'real', the point which seems more important today is that of definition, the amount of sonic details offered in an audition experience. Technically speaking, the achievement of a broader frequency spectrum both in recording and reproduction is not a problem any more. It got closer to our biological capacity to hear (in fact, exceeded it). High sampling and quantization rates in digital models, as well as the near absence of noise from the mechanisms of reproduction, brought on the possibility of hearing minimal components in sound recordings. Accuracy, definition and precision are terms that would suit better some of the practices related to sounds nowadays. The 'silence of the loudspeakers', as put by Michel Chion (2007), reveals a hidden world of sounds. Now, much more of our attention is necessary to follow and discern abundant heteroclite elements in a soundtrack. That refinement seems to appear as the horizon of current sound technologies and at the same time to be able to work more intensively on our sensory involvement in complex acoustic ambiances. The increase of information within these new models of 'compact sound spaces' may lead, in addition, to a sort of perceptive disturbance, as Birger Langkjær (1997, 99) points out:

> The aesthetic use of high definition sound (including digital sound) has not necessarily led to more easily distinguishable sound space. Rather it seems that sound designers are inclined to fill in more sound detail, thus pushing sensorial awareness toward the edge of perception. This kind of extremely dense sound texture is often hard to separate for the ear, and represents what I call a compact sound space.

In the experience of contemporary film, features like multi-channel reproduction of sound or the use of very low frequencies can be picked out as examples of a non-realistic employment of sound. The excessive manipulation, the predilection for the extremes of the frequency band and the arbitrary distribution of certain sounds in the theatre space aim to produce a sensation that is more real than reality. Fidelity, in this case, is something very relative. We can, moreover, understand definition as a shortening of intervals between different sound samples. A 'greater slice' of the world. Thus, the conversion of discrete data would be closer to a linear ideal, in which no detail would be lost. Anyway, as we have seen, a greater definition won't lead necessarily to a greater fidelity.

The digital desires the analogue and its proximity to the empirical world. Analogue sound, due to its close relationship with the idea of continuous time, remains unattainable and evanescent. When we listen to a sound, it has passed. To log into zeros and ones is perhaps an update of Leon Scott's desire to ensure a lasting dimension of the sonorous whole, immobilized in time, like a written language.[5] The minimum data taken in the process of sampling is a way to fix something fleeting at a precise point in time. To illustrate this discussion, we could refer to Bergson's idea of a continuous multiplicity in which we should not isolate fixed moments of a totality, such as movement, thus losing the integrity of its duration. Time would present this homogeneous and continuous aspect that is related to consciousness. Space may be thought of as a discrete multiplicity, of intervals created between objects, of the world's externality. As Bergson says: 'now, externality is the distinguishing mark of things which occupy space, while states of consciousness are not essentially external to one another, and become so only by being spread out in time, regarded as a homogeneous medium' (Bergson, 2001, 99). This idea could be destabilized, if we thought of time itself, as do some physicists, as non-linear. Some theories would say that, just like energy and matter, 'time might come in discrete packets', consuming an increasing amount of energy when divided into ever smaller intervals (Pohlmann, 2005, 50). If that was so, maybe there would be no such difference, in terms of discrete or continuous data, between both models: the analogue and the digital. But that would have to be the subject of many diverse and unfinished discussions.

Conclusions

We can understand that, by becoming present to bodies in a non-symbolic form, noise, in analogue environments, emerges as something that is beyond what should be conventionally apprehended. It should not be there, impregnating, masking, even ruining, the enjoyment of a particular sound, but it certainly changes that sound and its meaning. The role of technology has always been to minimize these effects of noises on our experience, if we believe that there could be a unique and ideal experience of the 'real'. In consequence, we establish and reproduce practices modulated by a strong symbolic instance.

When we set sound experience through a language of another order – one might say meta-symbolic – we still start from the same idea that something should be taken and something must be excluded from that hearing. Now, it is not a case of ignoring unwanted noises in the act of listening, but simply not including them in the encoding process. Old analogue sounds of restored recordings acquire a classical status. They are now part of the experience of an ancient sonority. New digital devices abolished, at least in theory, analogue noise in current recordings. The digital project ignores the struggle of materials. Frictions, variations of electromagnetic field, converted into electrical signals, have given way to the precision of a code that will always be read in the same way. There is no distortion that has not previously been engendered. The error cannot be perceived by humans, only by the machine. As Manovich (2001) says, binary code is a language made for the machines to understand each other. Listening should be, by those precepts, strongly tied to a unique experience.

The perfection the digital assigns to itself is greater than the idea of fidelity in analogue models. It escapes from dilettantism, being imbued with efficiency and numerical obscurity. The imperfection of matter situates us face to face with uncertainty and the fluctuations of different sounds. The digital is intended to be ultimate, defining listening even before any sound reaches us. It is therefore beyond question.

PART TWO

Audiovisual noise practices

7

'As if from the sky':
divine and secular dramaturgies of noise

Benjamin Halligan

What now? [Pause.] *Words fail, there are times when even they fail.* [Turning a little towards WILLIE.] *Is that not so, Willie?* [Pause. Turning a little further.] *Is not that so, Willie, that even words fail, at times?* [Pause. Back front.] *What is one to do then, until they come again?* – Winnie, Act One, *Happy Days*

(BECKETT, 2006, 147)

This chapter concerns just such a question: what is to be done, until words – as forming a discourse that makes some sense of the world, and that shapes and articulates meanings to interpret it – are possible once again? It is in the moment *before* that possibility, an interregnum therefore between stretches of clarity, that words, suddenly insufficient, seem to fail. Such a moment typically 'defaults' to noise. But in the examples discussed below, noise does exist as simply denoting the lack of possible meaning or interpretation – as non-meaning or non-sense. Rather, noise here works to push beyond meaning and sense: to continue to articulate something even once words have failed or reached the limits of their expressive possibilities.

In the first instance, this lexical crisis occurs in respect to the unknowable nature of the divine. In the second instance, this chapter argues, such a lexical crisis persists even 'after' the divine, on into secular times. Looking to post-structuralist models of analysis, and Derrida's concept of the 'aporia' in particular, the noise to which the ineffable gives rise can be isolated and analysed. Indeed, noise would seem to liberate the text to move beyond the limited expressive possibilities of the words that fail, and breaks with and so modernizes dominant modes of discourse and thought. This tendency is examined in examples drawn from cinema, poetry and theatre.

Sound and vision

The aural is typically cast in a subservient position to the visual in cinema. Sound arrived belatedly, and then struggled to redefine the role of mere speech and incidental accompaniment that had fallen to the audio components of the film experience. While technology pushed the possibilities for the image, sound remained in a marginal place across the subsequent decades. It was a full half century beyond the first feature film presented as a 'talkie', *The Jazz Singer* (1927, Alan Crossland) that, Biskind notes, George Lucas brought about the junking of tinny PAs and the installation of Dolby stereo equipment for cinemas wishing to show *Star Wars* (1977) (Biskind, 1999, 335). Only the fear of jeopardizing future income finally exerted the need, as the Dolby company put it, to 'implement and staff a film sound programme' across many 'disparate segments of the film industry' (quoted in Sergi, 2004, 21).[1]

At this point, mere speech and incidental accompaniment were no longer sufficient. This *Star Wars*-centred 'expanded cinema', which by the late 1970s was anticipating and shaping the 'High Concept' cinema to come, countered the previous model of 'expanded cinema'. For Youngblood (1970), that expansion of cinema was countercultural, a waystation on the path to expanded consciousness. This new cinema of the early 1970s, he argued, was intrinsic to the happening and the psychedelic liquid light show, and was seen as only a beginning.[2] The late 1970s expansion was clearly merely industrial, in simple terms of greater box-office returns. But it would be ahistorical to see these two phases in dialectical terms. There was clearly a continuum of ideas developed or associated with the former phase of expansion, and now technologically enabled and accommodated. Enhanced sound was for enhanced experience – and Youngblood and Lucas shared the sense of cinema as experiential. But wonderment or envelopment or immersion – or 'tripping' – to what ends? There is undeniably a shift in the popular imagination of the future in these half-dozen years: from revolt and communalism to the new state forms of cosmic imperialism.[3] In terms of semiocapitalism (in respect of which Bifo hails 1977, the year of *Star Wars*, as a watershed moment; Berardi, 2009, 14–29), the imaginary was being reassigned, from countercultural spheres to the techno-militaristic. As Paul Virilio argues (1989), cinema soon came to function as a showcase for the new armoury, and indeed continues to develop hand-in-hand with it. Speech and incidental music, in this context, are bare essentials: noise, atmospherics, ambience and vibration are the primary colours of the soundscape. It is ironic that the catalyst for this – Dolby technology – was advertised at this time as a matter of 'noise reduction'. For Michel Chion, Dolby, 'a physical reaffirmation of sound', fully achieves 'a sort of aerodynamic aesthetic of sound' (Chion, 2009, 124–5), which became central to the cinema experience. He identifies 1975 as marking the 'return of the sensorial' in this regard (117–45).

This sensorial development was apparent, prior to *Star Wars*, in the disaster movies cycle: the moment at which a hi-tech cinema experience was sold, and an attempt at dramatic and sensory overload was made, so as to reinvigorate the most commercial wing of the medium, as if staging a counter-attack on the New Hollywood films of the 1970s. Thus the sonic battery of *Earthquake* (Mark Robson, 1974), rendered via the Sensurround system, reportedly (albeit in the sense of urban legend) caused nausea and induced nosebleeds in some audience members, and cracked cinema ceilings. Prior to this, sound was a matter for the foley artists, who were placed in a lowly position in the credit pecking order and were understood to be doing their job well when nobody noticed their contributions (shuffling stock sounds for doors opening, footfall, keys in locks and so forth): a technical endeavour. Now the 'sound designer' (as a parallel to the set designer), or those engaged in 'sound montage' (parallel to editors), rose rapidly through the credit ranks: now a creative figure, mediating between art and new audio technologies.

The Megasound system created by the Warner Bros company in the early 1980s was utilized to full effect, in 70mm, by two filmmakers known for a tendency to immerse their audiences in a sensory rendition of the worlds of their films. Ken Russell's *Altered States* (1980) placed the notion of the expansion of consciousness at the meeting point of religious ecstasy and scientific research – an endeavour that embodies exactly the Youngblood/Lucas tension. The film concerns a disillusioned Harvard scientist who, in the late 1970s, returns to his late 1960s experiments in altered consciousness but now armed with more powerful hallucinogenics. This time he seems to achieve the alteration of his physical form as well as his mind, and accesses a universal consciousness in both mind and body as well as, seemingly, a fifth dimension. The 'trip' sequences induced by these experiments were to be experienced more than viewed (and with the low-frequency rumblings and roarings to be felt as well as heard), and this was achieved via sound-scaping in Megasound as much as through liquid light show-like visuals. (Russell recalled that stoned UCLA students would wait in the cinema lobby to be called in by one of their number for the hallucinatory sequences: the 'dialogue' was of little interest to them [Russell, 1989, 187]).

As with *Altered States*, Michael Wadleigh's *Wolfen* (1981) also finds a dramatic trope entirely appropriate to the consciousness-raising concerns of this new sensorial cinema. This occurs via a dramatization of the notion that since the body is merely the expression of the soul, it is essentially unstable in its outward form and capable of shape-shifting. The film, which combines elements of horror and the techno-thriller, follows two New York detectives who investigate a series of murders that seem to be at the behest of big business or terrorist groupings. The murders are soon revealed as wolf attacks, at which point the one surviving detective begins to surmise that the wolves are literally itinerant, landless and disenfranchised Native American workers. So for Wadleigh, co-adapting Whitley Strieber's 1978 novel *The Wolfen*, Indian folklore becomes the access to expanded consciousness, whereas for Russell (drawing on Paddy Chayefsky's 1978 novel), it is attained via LSD use and sensory deprivation tanks.

Experientialism in *Wolfen* occurs via wolf-eye, point-of-view, long-take, travelling shots in solarized/psychedelic imagery as a thermal rendering of the blurred, moving surroundings. The image is degraded in this way, for these 'trip' sequences, and sound is upgraded – becoming a pre-eminent and heightened sense. Sound is the way of navigating and negotiating the ruins of the Bronx for the wolves. Here sound is dragged down several frequencies so that the points of registering an event, in terms of a sort of 'spectrum of cognition', seem both oblique and much expanded. Thus crashes and thumps leave static traces, the breathing seems deeper and closer as the wolf watches, or psychically visualizes, a protagonist making love, and the cavernous echoes of gunshots in an abandoned church overwhelm the initial crack of the bullet as discharged. Even spoken word is subjected to a Vocoder-like treatment, and so seems guttural, and emanates from the throats that are target to the wolves' attacks. In this way, noise reorganizes the world of the film, and begins to assert a dramatic, narrative and aesthetic dominance over the image.

But Russell and Wadleigh are the exceptions in their uses of sound at that time: typically, within the predominant schema of naturalism and realism, sound offers an aural verification, as a quality of the reportage ontology of the *mise-en-scène*. Gianluca Sergi makes the case that not only has critical and academic writing largely ignored film sound, leading to an 'image bias that is so predominant in most film theory and history' (Sergi, 2004, 9), but also that no satisfactory critical lexicon exists should attention be turned to sound. Consequently, basic questions – 'how to define sound' (Sergi, 2004, 6), for example – remain,[4] and the aural perspective on disaster movies is usually little more than a footnote in most critical writings on them. *Altered States* and *Wolfen*, which blended art and commercial appeal, and were hitched on the back of the disaster film cycle, occurred at roughly the point of the cycle that Feil identifies as 'the final downturn': the moment at which '[box office] disaster strikes disaster movies' of 1978 to 1980 (Feil, 2005, 19). High Concept cinema was more straightforward in aural terms: bangs for the explosions.

Seeing with ears, hearing with eyes

The confusions induced by this dramatic and sensory overload were typically offset by the disaster movie hero: in the 'classic' heroic mode, that larger-than-life figure, marshalling resources, improvising makeshift weapons, and corralling and leading the survivors. In the case of the on-screen presence and persona of Charlton Heston, this endeavour is seemingly part of a trajectory that includes Cecil B. DeMille's biblical heroes[5] with their WASP make-over of foundational Judaeo-Christian myths of disaster, exodus and civilization. The combination of individualism, individual vision and action rights the balance of social, political and civil upheaval unleashed by natural and technological disaster: new lines of command emerge, rematerializing old hierarchies of order in the midst of the upheaval. In these respects, the sensory overload may be seen to make critical, but not completely destabilize, the certainties and very materialism of the worlds that the films conjure. What is exceptional about the circumstances of disaster only ever becomes the exception that ultimately proves the rule, or rules, of law and order and the indestructibility of civil society. Most disaster movies grind to a halt at this conjunction. The God of crisis (a diabolical deity for secular times, one residing in the ecosphere or technosphere or, alternatively, heading-up non-Judaeo-Christian religions in the standard racist portrayals of non-WASPs) may demand that sacrifices are offered (in the deaths of Hollywood A-list stars), but these trials always result in the people being led to the promised land.

The testing itself, however, suggests a profound collective psychic dissatisfaction with existence in contemporary urban societies of the West. Erich Fromm, writing in 1974, diagnosed this 'new wave of destructive films' as

catering to the ever more rapidly increasing passion to destroy (necrophilia) [...] Necrophilia is the outcome of the increase of a certain socially
conditioned and shared pathology of cybernetic man [...] he has created a
lifeless world of total technicalization and bureaucratization in which man
becomes an appendage to the machine. (quoted in Feil, 2005, 11)

For Fromm, these imagined realms of death, as desired by the disaster movie
viewer (in which cities, aeroplanes, skyscrapers, ocean liners and so on
become imminent death-traps), and with the enforced reacquaintance with
morality on a massive scale, speak of the modern condition. Man, with his
characteristic fallibility and vulnerability, imagines himself as doomed by his
own Frankenstein-like creation: the encroaching technosphere, with scientific
advance merely a wilful charge into the valley of death. Fromm suggests
that this subjectivity, fed and nurtured by the disaster movie, is a form of
perversion which is centred on or displaced on to fetish objects: corpses.

Russell and Wadleigh attempted to push beyond this conjuncture, and
these restrictions of imagination (which could be termed, in a Manichean
way, civil society or barbarism), into uncertainty. The reorganizing of sense
and experience is seemingly in order to do so – so that the notion of
visualizing/'seeing' with ears, and the aesthetics and subjectivity of an aural
image, and audio scanning/'hearing' with eyes would seem to be in operation.
In this respect, film becomes, to borrow Chion's term, 'audio-vision'.[6] The
flaky contexts from which both films originate are merely a pretext: an excuse
for an entrée into 'expanded realms' of the mind, for experiential cinema. In
Altered States, a decade beyond the Berkeley riots, the hippies are now in
the laboratories they once occupied, running mind-expansion experiments
and revealing or summoning up Jungian archetypes and Darwin-esque
primal hordes from the human subconscious. In *Wolfen*, a decade beyond
Wadleigh's own *Woodstock* documentary (1970), a new counterculture
begins to emerge, a bridge between the 'wisdoms' of the living remnants of
Native American Indian subcultures and those of interplanetary messengers
(of Strieber's later concerns with UFO abductions and alien contact). Both
these narratives require a breaking with cognitive reality: to see and hear
'beyond' the everyday. And both may be said to represent a retreat from the
high tide of political activism of 1968 to a safer and more amenable ground
where the enemy is not the political economy and its state institutions but
merely, obscurely, spooky or theological, and conspiratorial rather than
ideological.[7]

In both cases conflicts with producers and studios resulted in the released
films, Wadleigh's in particular, being a far cry from the original intentions
of their directors. But in both cases these films were bound to fail on any

number of grounds. How could they not? The new visual and aural lexicons which the films assembled and offered in order to navigate these new worlds – solarized, psychedelic, superimposed blurs of imagery, plundering the semiotics and iconography of everything from Roman Catholic theology to monster B-movies – become the progressive elements of the films themselves. The films are merely experiential rather than philosophical; it was in the saying, not in what was to be said, that the films effectively functioned. The UCLA students that so bemused Russell were perhaps, after all, reacting in an appropriate or timely way to the cliché-ridden absurdity of *Altered States* – as Macbeth put it (Act V, Scene V): 'it is a tale/ […] full of sound and fury,/ Signifying nothing'.

And yet more dramaturgically rigorous applications of noise to the experiential have resulted in films that seem to detract from rather than expand the expected aural spectrum – in, for example, Elem Klimov's *Come and See* (1985), which aligns the experience of the *mise-en-scène* with hearing loss, or *Irreversible* (Gaspar Noé, 2002), which works to discomfort and unnerve the cinema audience. Where Russell and Wadleigh rupture, realign or even invert the standard relations between the aural and the visual, Klimov and Noé return their soundscapes to the historical supporting role – underlying and underlining the visual.

Dramatic crises

What is apparent in this overreach on the part of Russell and Wadleigh, for which sound and noise come to take on dramaturgical functions otherwise typically assigned to expositional dialogue, is the attempt to deliver some kind of 'primal scene' or fundamental meaning. The ambition is that of showing something of the origins of civilization and/or mankind for the secular or post-secular age, and sensorially realizing the same. These films do not have the luxury of summoning up gods (as with DeMille) or demons (as with William Friedkin's 1973 adaptation of William Peter Blatty's *The Exorcist*). The way in which Russell and Wadleigh and their collaborators then flunk their answers is beside the point.[8] Perhaps emboldened by their adherence to genre, and with the acceptance by the late 1970s of some of the ideals of the counter-culture that these films also embody, *Altered States* and *Wolfen* do not flinch or look away where other films and filmmakers would tentatively decline to pass comment. Or, put another way: the films bravely, or foolishly, avoid a complete negation of clear narrative meaning at moments of dramatic crisis.

Such dramatic crises are typically found at the point of confronting, to employ a Lacanian term, 'the big Other': the symbols, figures and orders of authority. Civilization is, as argued above, one such encounter. Heston's essential role may be said to be to re-establish the symbolic order at times of upheaval or crisis: to become or attain 'the big Other' in the wake of the big Other's sudden and alarming absence – connecting Heston's 'executive' actions in disaster movies to his appearing as Moses on Mount Sinai carrying The Ten Commandments, in DeMille's 1956 film of the same name. But a variety of other possible dramatic crises and their related Others present themselves.

The effect of coming up against such absolutes and imponderables is akin to the Angelic injunctive given to Lot prior to God's destruction of Sodom: not to look (Genesis 19: 17). And typically, in film, this occurs when the big Other is one that touches on foundational Judaeo-Christian myths: evolution and the prohibitions against incest (in Freud's terminology, 'totem and taboo'), and God and resurrection/afterlife. Invariably it is '*auteur* cinema', films of a poetic and philosophical bent, that tend to venture into such territories, or raise such existential questions, and so encounter or engender just such crises. In the examples that follow, all the films reach the point at which such questions are unavoidable, only to then enter into a state of avoiding clear answers while at the same time declining the possibility of withholding *any* answer. This difficult operation is mostly achieved through shunning the image and employing, or 'applying', noise instead. Indeed, God does not extend the injunction against listening too. In terms of film analysis, this application of noise may be identified as a return of the repressed: that marginalized and subdued component of film, the aural, steps into the breach at such critical moments, scrambling narrative meaning via its 'aerodynamic aesthetic of sound' (Chion, 2009, 124–5). The aural not only usurps the visual in terms of narrative import, but effectively censors the visual: screen-bound aesthetics that threaten to show too much, and so disobey the injunctive not to look, are – to use Chion's description – suddenly put into flight, and diffused into the auditorium, via the aural.

Such censorship can be achieved visually, and may be said to come into operation at such critical moments too. Bernardo Bertolucci's drama of Oedipal tensions, *La Luna* (1979), for example, opens with the protagonist as an infant, who then loses his mother's care and attention once she becomes distracted by the arrival of a mysterious male. A record is played on a turntable, and the mother and the male dance on the ledge of the veranda where the child plays, both seen in silhouette against the light of the sun reflecting off the sea. The male playfully waves a newly caught fish, and his fish-gutting knife, rhythmically at the mother, thrusting them between her legs – and this dance, very apparently a visual metaphor for sexual intercourse, is coded as a shot seen from the child's point of view. From this precise vantage point, and with the framing of this opening sequence as a distant or suppressed memory on the part of the child (introduced as an adolescent shortly afterwards), the film communicates the way in which the child's imagining of the parents copulating is both distressing (in that it denotes the loss of the mother for the child, and the phallic superiority, and knife-wielding, castrating potential of the father) and determining. He, crying, toddles into the house and, years later, his heroin addiction is presented as a seeming replacement for the similarly excessive sweetness of the affection of his mother – before the arrival of the male in this first scene, the mother feeds her child honey from her finger, on which he chokes.

The actual seeing of the act of copulation by the child, for Freud, was not necessary, since this 'primal scene' becomes effectively manifest in other ways: hearing, imagining hearing, and via displacement to metaphors such as this dance with its phallic stand-ins, and prohibitions flowing from the father's authority. Bertolucci adheres to this authority: he does not show the scene of intercourse, the 'primal scene', but, comically, the metaphors of its displacement. This is a kind of visual buffering on Bertolucci's part, a self-censorship, and it occurs again later in the film when the mother, learning of her son's addiction and trying to catch sight of his syringe-pierced underarms as they play a piano duet together, winds up fighting with him. The son uses physical authority to gain dominance over the mother, and at this stage his father, having suffered a fatal heart attack, is absent, and so the location of authority is now uncertain. This fight in itself would seem to be a displacement of sexual inclinations and such a reading does not require a Freudian basis to explain what is 'really' going on: 'light' incest does occur in the course of the film, and so the incest taboo is effectively broken. The evolving physical relationship, and the showing of the relationship, may therefore be said to be transgressive. And so for this fight Bertolucci again effectively censors himself: the camera tracks with the couple, aligning a large, open grand piano lid in parallax so that the view is blocked and, while the fight is heard, it can no longer be seen. In these moments Bertolucci declines to show the stand-in (fighting) for the unshowable (fucking) and so honours the word of the incest taboo if not its spirit. And yet Bertolucci never fails to show such intimations of the unshowable: the silhouetted dancing and the obscured fighting. In this, his dramaturgy mimics Freud's position on the imagining of the primal scene. In effect he allows the image to 'fail' rather than point his camera directly, and indecently, at the scene of all meaning. The following two examples, which both deal with resurrection (as part of the evolution of man, and as overcoming death) also consider climactic sequences in which the images, nevertheless, 'fail'.

The monolith of *2001: A Space Odyssey* (Stanley Kubrick, co-written with Arthur C. Clarke, 1968) functions in a way to simply defer, in the final analysis, clear meaning: blank and black, it resembles nothing so much as a censor's mark over offending images. The monolith is placed in a role that suggests a variety of possible interpretations of the narrative: both marking the geographical points of human evolution and as an agent of human evolution, or even the evolver, itself. So the monolith appears in the film at key moments of evolution – from prehistoric times (as primates learn to use weapons) to future times (the extension of war into space, in tandem with watershed moments in man's exploration of space). Such a role for the monolith is neither associated nor disassociated from the sense of the active presence of an external benefactor – God, or alien intelligence. Deleuze delineates the monolith precisely in respect to the themes of the film ('[t]he black stone of *2001* presides over both cosmic states and cerebral stages: it is the soul of the three bodies, earth, sun, and moon, but also the seed of the three brains, animal, human, machine') but still addresses the concluding image of the film – a human foetus in an amniotic sac, floating in space – in terms of the mysterious: a moment of 'the chance of entering into a new, incommensurable, unknown relation, which would convert death into a new life' (Deleuze, 1989, 205–6). For Youngblood the film, although deficient on a number of levels, is an aesthetic harbinger of the 'cosmic conscience' and achieves a didactic mass communication of 'the spiritualism in science' (Youngblood, 1970, 139). Eco, on the other hand, dismisses all such mystifications: 'the final images are kitsch (a lot of pseudo-philosophical vagueness in which anyone can put the allegory he wants), and the rest is discographic, music and sleeves' (Eco, 1986, 145).

Clear meaning remains a matter of conjecture in *2001*. The monolith marks and could even be said to police the limits of the horizon of explanation. Its unreadable blackness, its very blankness – in the final analysis – represents the failure or unwillingness to dramatize or show or fully explain. Readings can be projected, and all will pass without a comment. But this operation only occurs in terms of visualization; Kubrick's use of György Ligeti on the soundtrack, accompanying the monolith's appearances, may be said to dramatically and empathically underscore the moment of evolution, in a typically Hollywood (even crude DeMille) style, despite Ligeti's high avant-gardism – as Eco seems to indicate. Ligeti's myriad voices (of *Atmosphères*, *Lux Aeterna* and *Requiem*), Gregorian, choral and crescendoing, underscore the dramaturgical importance of such moments.[9] So while Kubrick and Clarke are happy to decline any clarity by ultimately evacuating meaning from the image, they retain control of the tenor of possible meanings via non-diegetic sound. The image is allowed to fail while the significance of the moment is shored up via the soundtrack. Despite the avant-gardist/Modernist trappings of *2001*, which come to the fore at such moments, the conception is little more than the voice of God (Heston) as emanating from the burning bush in *The Ten Commandments*.

Scorsese, drawing on Nikos Kazantzakis's 1960 novel for his 1988 film *The Last Temptation of Christ*, had less room for manoeuvre than Kubrick: the moment of transition is precise and locked into a biblical narrative that has no qualms about bringing characters back from the dead as final proof of divine intervention. As Christ dies on the cross the problem is clear: is this understood to be the end or not? Scorsese appends a 20-second psychedelic light show to the film at the point at which Christ (Willem Dafoe) closes his eyes. In part this sequence recalls the 'Star Gate' sequence of *2001*, in part the dying point-of-view shot of Larissa Shepitko's *The Ascent* (1976), but most particularly Scorsese's technique recalls Ingmar Bergman's, of *Persona* (1966). The celluloid itself is suddenly seen, in *Persona* and *Last Temptation*, as if detached from its sprockets and flapping wildly in front of the film projector's beam of light, as in a film run-out. It is as if the film has become damaged, or the projection apparatus, as if baulking at immense dramaturgical pressure, has ceased to project. Mixed into this, for Scorsese, would seem to be – from the general reddish hue (suggestive of sunlight seen through skin, and the eyelid skin of the bloodied visage of the protagonist), and seemingly subliminal shots of the eyelashes of closing eyelids – a literal point-of-view shot of the dying Christ. It would be enough to have the film 'revolt' over the fundamental questions now encountered (regarding the existence of God, the afterlife, resurrection and so forth), and so go no further in what is shown, and in so doing maintain the blindness of the faith required (faith being without evidence, and therefore a matter of belief rather than calculation). It may also be said that Scorsese suggests to the viewer, at this moment, that he times his film (in the sense of metres of celluloid) to run out as his protagonist's life terminates so as to cease to offer further comment. Film, a material medium, can only travel with Christ through his material existence, and cannot go further … if, indeed, there is a 'further'. Lars Von Trier's *Melancholia* (2011) ends in just such a way, unable to offer narrative beyond the end of the world.

But in reality Scorsese, unlike DeMille (who expresses no doubts at all), hedges his bets. Christ smiles and the closing light show merely suggests uplift, things after death, and a verification of Christ's happiness at, in his dying words, '[*sic*] [i]t is accomplished'. This sentiment is advanced not so much through the colour montage as the use of Peter Gabriel's non-specific ethnic voices and 'Western' drumming on the soundtrack, and then with a groove derived from a scale of what sounds like sampled church bells (as the closing credits are found waiting on the other side of the light show, against an orange background). It is as if this is the noise of all religious practices, distilled into a few seconds *and* finding common ground. Rather than offer precise meaning at this critical point of meaning, and rather than declining to offer meaning altogether, Scorsese fills the screen with vague meaningfulness, couched in a joyous tone via non-diegetic sound.

It is with such states of visual failure that the possibilities for and potentials of noise are opened up. In these states, in the above examples, noise would seem to be ushered in: noise as a new lexicon, to denote or explore or communicate what cannot be described both in terms of speech (verbalized) and in visual-dramatic terms (visualized). In terms of the interplay of suggested meanings and implied readings in the spaces of interpretation, the aural would seem to function as a dramaturgical 'solution', of sorts, to the insolvable. To fully function in this way (and Kubrick and Scorsese falter in these respects), the aural must first jettison the possibility of yielding clear dramatic readings. Or, to put this another way, the aural must attempt to neutralize any semiotics of sound. In this, then, the aural is – to paraphrase Dolby – 'reduced' to noise. Noise then marks abstraction, negation, crisis of dramaturgy, and the dramaturgical solution to that crisis.

Divine and secular aporia

To look away at the hand of God is a reflex that predates cinema to the extent that it could be said that visual cultures conflict with ancient injunctions against looking: at the sun (for fear of blindness), at the face of God or God's handiwork (as with Lot) and at images of saints or the Prophet (in Protestant and Muslim traditions). And the vista of what may be seen – the fallen world – is not one that, at any rate, is apt to yield divine manifestation, or its typical domain. To claim hard evidence of God in the everyday remained, even into the twentieth century, a blasphemous matter. The reverberation of this general position is apparent in conceptions of art at the dawn of modernity. After a visit to the South Kensington (now Victoria and Albert) Museum in 1882, Gerard Manley Hopkins wrote to his colleague Robert Bridges:

> In the arts of painting and sculpture I am, even when most I admire, always convinced of a great shortcoming: nothing has been done at all equal to what one can easily conceive being done. For instance for work to be perfect there ought to be a sense of beauty in the highest degree both in the artist and in the age, the style and keepings of which the artist employs. Now the keepings of the age in which for instance Raphael and [Michel]Angelo lived were rich, but unsatisfactory in the extreme. And they were both far from having a pure sense of beauty. Besides which they

have several other great shortcomings. But in poetry and perhaps in music *unbetterable* works have been produced
(quoted in Phillips, 2007, viii; emphasis in original)

The aural here (and, arguably, by extension, in the sonic subtexts of Hopkins's own poetry) is the 'unbetterable' way of circumnavigating or overcoming the fallen state of the world: of attaining artistic expression of divine worth in spite of the all-pervasive, infectious nature of this fallen state ('original sin'). Sound (music, poetry as spoken word; freeform, as existing in air) seems the way to access the 'pure sense of beauty' once the image (of and as found in the museum: canvases and sculptures – that is, fixed, tangible, materially extant images) has inevitably failed. Sound transcends the limitations of the visual imagination while adhering to the injunction against seeing. Indeed, in Judaeo-Christian traditions, hearing the voice of God on earth is not that unusual. Years earlier, when considering how his initial intention to be a painter had given way to that of becoming a priest, Hopkins voiced his doubts as to the – seemingly – moral dangers of the creation of images: 'the fact is that the higher and more attractive part of the art put a strain upon the passions which I [*sic*] shd. think it unsafe to encounter' (quoted in White, 1992, 159).

Hopkins's sentiment, and this injunction, translates readily into post-structuralist terms. Now it is the impossibility of revealing, to use Žižek's deployment of Lacan's term, 'the Real' – the hidden or unspoken truth of the matter, a truth that structures or finds a symbolic order or personification in the 'big Other'[10] – that results in this turning away. Turning away becomes a matter of deferring meaning: a rekindling of blind faith for the secular age – the truth will be revealed, but not at this moment, even as the truth is imminent to this moment. And the materially uncertain sphere of the aural (aerial, invisible) is better suited than that of the visual (visible, readable) to allow for such a deferral. In terms of brushing against 'the Real' – and promising to articulate what cannot actually be articulated – this aural preference, and the obliqueness of a dramaturgy of noise, effectively pre-empts, and so neutralizes, the inevitable failure.

What does not translate so readily as blind faith is an analogue of Hopkins's faith in transcendence. Mystery is necessarily upheld in the Victorian frame of theological thought: man, in his fallen state, is incapable of knowing, and cannot hope to know. Indeed, it is this position which gives rise to forms of religious practice that can ultimately only exist *as practice*, and familiar to Hopkins the Jesuit: the ritualism of the Oxford movement, for example. Hopkins the poet is merely tactical in respect of his dealings with such an assumption. He qualifies the protean, dizzying nature of the dappled (rather than pure or consistent) beauty of the natural world, in his 1877 poem 'Pied

Beauty', with respect to God's creation, with '(who knows how?)'. That micro-view, of and revealed in the 'fickle [and] freckled' wildlife, as much as the macro-view of 'The Wreck of the Deutschland' (1875–6), which posits divine order and ordering in the '[w]orld's strand [and the] sway of the sea', repeatedly abandons final explanation. Explanations cannot be known, merely isolated and beheld. Hopkins' respectful blind faith, in its post-structuralist extension or parallel, cannot be sustained. Blind faith now becomes the blind spot: an instance of aporia, the looking away at the moments of dramaturgical crises discussed above. Mystery is not replaced by revelation, but by the deferral of the anticipated and promised revelation. And it is the tone of this deferral (that is: the suggestions and intimations of the nature of the revelation) that, as with Deleuze and Eco, becomes a matter of debate or derision. Dramaturgically, then, sound comes to determine that tone – from bombastic and grandiose for Kubrick, and the use of the 'noise' of avant-garde forms of music, to the layered liturgies of noise for Scorsese – in the sequences discussed above.

In Derrida's description, such constant deferrals, making for such a halting state – forever encircling the point of unknowing, a 'barred passage' as he puts it (Derrida and Attridge, 1992, 399) – comes to represent the final discourse itself:

> the question of knowing what it means 'to experience the aporia', indeed to put into operation the aporia, remains. It is not necessarily a failure or a simple paralysis, the sterile negativity of the impasse. It is neither stopping at it nor overcoming it. [...] Let us ask: *what takes place, what comes to pass* with the aporia? (Derrida, 1993, 32; emphasis in original)

In a different context (roughly, the question of the possibility of one's own death, as the 'passage' of oneself from life to death – moving from the known to, as the anonymous Middle Ages mystical tract puts it, the 'Cloud of Unknowing'), Derrida writes, when he first encounters the possibility of aporia:

> the difficult or the impracticable, here the impossible, passage, the refused, denied, or prohibited passage, indeed the nonpassage, which can in fact be something else, the event of a coming of a future advent [événement de venue ou d'avenir], which no longer has the form of the movement that consists in passing, traversing, or transiting. It would be the 'coming to pass' of an event that would no longer have the form or the appearance of a *pas*: in sum, a coming without *pas*.
>
> (Derrida, 1993, 8)

The aporetic analysis is applied by Derrida and by subsequent post-structuralists, and with a characteristic looseness (breaking with the 'scientific' dogma of structuralism), to the fields of ethics, politics, law, and philosophy itself. The aporia highlights the point, or nodes, of the unqualified assumptions in such discourses, their blind faiths that persist so idiosyncratically into the secular age. In this way, aporetic analysis corrodes the total readings seemingly, or potentially, possible with structuralism (or earlier manifestations or versions of structuralism). The aporetic analysis prompts a search for the irreducible underpinnings of the argument, the area which remains in a state of being *unaccounted for* by or within or, finally, *as*, the parameters of the argument.

The aporia is quite other to the structuring thought that determines the text (the author, or dramaturg) – in Derridean terms, this person is a ghost to the live text, or the uncanny to the canny; the impossible, uninvited, undesired agent that then casts doubt upon the entire enterprise by 'explaining' what it all means (this is a trope typical of '*auteur* cinema'). This otherworld of the inexplicable is revealed through a close, textual examination of that which is, as often as not, in the text itself, fudged, circumnavigated, overlooked or dissolved into strategies of avoidance. In the aporetic analysis of Derrida's 'Aporias', the aporias multiply, auto-engender, so to speak, until a climax is reached; it is more apparent here than in Derrida's earlier writing that the aporia is not a minor or accidental appendage to the text – an oversight, or dramaturgical failure. It is, rather, the very condition that engulfs the text – that enables it, in the sense of allowing it to be created, and then provides a motor or conceptual foundation for that creation. The aporia is the very condition of the text. In this respect, an aporetic analysis allows for a radical rereading of the text – a '*negative form*' (Derrida, 1993, 19; emphasis in original) that splits the text asunder and reveals the workings of the conceptual foundation. Indeed, it may still be said, in relation to Sergi's and Chion's criticisms of the methodologies of film analysis discussed above, that noise itself remains the aporia of the disciplines of 'film studies'.

As an aside, the aporetic analysis is not a meta-criticism that, as with God's destruction of Sodom, levels all in its way. It is, rather, a way of enabling the challenges posed by the big Other or 'the Real' to be parlayed into artistic forms. The aporetic condition allows for the universal, archetypal and cosmic, and allows for a dealing with the fallen state of the world in artistic terms. In the video *A Portrait of the Artists as Young Men*, Gilbert and George perform as if for a currently non-existent audience – for that audience of the future who, one surmises, are intrigued, in the light of the anticipated successes of Gilbert and George (hence 'the artists'),[11] and now wish to see old footage of the pair. To the contemporary audience, their performance is barely fathomable: in medium shot they seem to act, or adopt, slow-motion movements, and seem unaware of each other, themselves, their immediate surroundings, and the raging thunderstorm heard on the soundtrack. The pair seem lobotomized, narcoleptic, in a trance or semi-comatosed. As with performance experiments at the time (the piece is dated 1970) conducted by the Zanzibar Group of filmmakers, the Living Theater, or Werner Schroeter, Gilbert and George seem to be living rather than performing roles under temporary conditions of artificially induced neurological impairment. The relatively lengthy duration of the performance (and its cheapness: blurry, black and white, committed to videotape rather than celluloid), and their quiescence throughout, induces unavoidable questions for the viewer: What is wrong with them? Don't they have something else to do, somewhere else to go? Why is no information forthcoming about them? Why am I watching this? But the title of the piece announces a deferment in terms of answers to these questions. They can be answered – or will no longer be in need of an answer – when these artists are no longer young men: in the anticipated (and seemingly dreadful) future to come where, one assumes, this will be seen as quite normal behaviour, the video itself will be seen as entertaining, or rich in the kind of information that cannot at present be extracted from it. In short, the key to *A Portrait of the Artists as Young Men* is that the aporia engulfs the text: the video merely looks to something that it cannot yet be.

The use of noise, as discussed above, finds a more certain role in the aporetic. Noise becomes the way of securing the moorings of the text even *in extremis*: resurrection, evolution, totem and taboo, civilization. The internal pressures that would split the text asunder are alleviated by the application of noise. Noise allows unqualified assumptions to be placed safely outside any stress testing that must inevitably arise at such moments. To use this 'negative form' of rereading, one could say that Kubrick's and Scorsese's films, discussed here, could only function on the understanding that their key questions are not to be absolutely answered. It is acknowledging this limit, and grappling with it, rather than (as with Russell and Wadleigh) attempting to overcome it, that positions noise in a privileged space – one that breaks with the processes of interpretation, and signals that breaking in the name of the impossibility of showing. Noise is a dramaturgical operation: for Hopkins, aural and auratic (in the sense of attaining a divine aura), in Derridean, post-structuralist terms, aural and aporetic.

Coda: 'As if from the sky'

In Chekhov's *The Cherry Orchard* (first performed at the Moscow Arts Theatre, 1904), the problematic truth of the world of the play gives rise to conditions of denial. Denial is apparent in both the dramatis personae and, by extension, more generally in the fictional off-stage (that is, educated Russian society of the end of the nineteenth century, as refracted in Chekhov's characters) and concerns the coming termination of this bourgeois lifestyle enjoyed by the happy (or, for Chekhov, unhappy) few. This shift will prove to be ideological, industrial and ecological. Chekhov suggests a number of melancholy metaphors for this state of affairs and places the cherry orchard itself (unkempt, unattended, abandoned, to soon be chopped down) as the central poetic image of the play. Mid-point during a conversation in Act Two (which seems to occur during a rest break on an evening stroll near the cherry orchard) an arresting stage direction, without explanation or further elaboration, is given:

Gayev. The sun has set, ladies and gentleman.
Trofimov. Yes.
Gayev (*softly, as if declaring*). O nature, wondrous nature! You shine with an everlasting radiance, beautiful and indifferent; you that we call Mother united within yourself existence and death; you give life and you destroy it…
Vatya (*imploringly*). Uncle!
Anya. You're doing it again!
[…]
Gayev. I am silent. I am silent.

They all sit lost in thought. Silence. All that can be heard is FIRS *muttering quietly. Suddenly there is a distant sound, as if from the sky: the sound of a breaking string – dying away, sad.*

Ranyevskaya. What was that?
Lopakhin. I don't know. Somewhere a long way off, in the mines, a winding cable has parted. But a long, long way off.
Gayev. Perhaps a bird of some sort … something like a heron.
Trofiov. Or some kind of owl.
Ranyevskaya (*shivers*). Horrible, I don't know why.

Pause.

Firs. It was the same before the troubles. The owl screeched, and the samovar moaned without stop.

(Chekhov, 1990, 33)

This interjecting noise, which Chekhov seems to decline to specify exactly or even locate ('as if' from the sky, and its echo seems of more concern),[12] lends itself to numerous interpretations. Lopakhin, Gayev and Trofiov are pragmatic and realistic – and yet these are the characters whose fates, and that of Tsarist Russia, are tied up with a failure to anticipate the coming revolution. Gayev's ode to nature locks human fates into its eternal cycles, implicitly undermining any reason or hope for decisive action to change the course of events. Nature, for Gayev, is a paradoxical process which occurs, at any rate, 'beyond' our simple understanding: nature is 'beautiful and indifferent' and 'existence and death'. It is a philosophical position of and for such landed gentry, conservationist and conservative. And yet Gayev's response to this outlandish and unusual noise utterance from nature is dismissive: the message will not be heeded.

The most historically accurate interpretation, albeit one of precognition, is offered by befuddled, muttering Firs, the 87-year-old house servant seemingly in the last hours of his life. The sound is a portent of disaster to come and in this respect Firs' comments recall Horatio's in *Hamlet*.[13] The breaking of the social and civil order that has coloured Firs' life (as with the emancipation of the serfs, which Firs here refers to as 'the troubles'), and that will sweep away these aesthetes and estate managers, and that will determine, in Lewin's phrase, the Soviet Century, is near. But to suggest any reading – ornithological or precognizant, on the part of Chekhov's fictional characters, or via pat critical explanations – is to reduce the defiantly inexplicable to the rational. And, via the mouth of Firs, Chekhov might just as well have been discounting the obvious interpretation (which would otherwise be in keeping with Chekhov's elegiac tone) while continuing to decline to clarify further himself – or finding himself unable to clarify further. The negation is precise: the sound represents that which occurs beyond the limits of verbal or visual perception. Thus the possibility of meaning is suspended, and this is denoted via noise.

The same equivocation is found in critical responses. For Braun (for whom 'there is nothing "symbolic" about the cherry orchard (or the breaking string, for that matter) in the sense of the universal, the transcendental or the ineffable' [2000, 115]) and Rayfield, additional materials (entirely inadmissible) are brought in to support Lopakhin's reaction (Braun, 2000, 115, 120n. 14; Rayfield, 1994, 74, 107).[14] Tulloch's structuralist analysis is open to wider interpretations: the sound is 'from the technological world these nursery people have ignored' (Tulloch, 1980, 202) and dramatically works to delineate the position of each character in terms of their concerns. When a tramp-like passer-by appears shortly afterwards, to whom Ranyevskaya gives some money, he 'emerg[es] as if out of the sound of the breaking string' (Tulloch,

1980, 194). Cross notes the difficulty of staging this moment and that, quoting Maurice Valency, the string that breaks is:

> the golden string that connected man with his father on earth and his father in heaven, the age-old bond that tied the present to the past [...] the symbol is broad; it would be folly to try to assign it a more precise meaning than the author chose to give it [...] its quality is not equivocal. Whatever of sadness remains unexpressed in *The Cherry Orchard*, this sound expresses.
>
> (Valency, quoted in Cross, 1969, 510)

The dramatic, thematic and conceptual importance of this moment is such that Valency's study of Chekhov is called 'The Breaking String' and his aesthete's florid analysis becomes positively Lacanian in its implications. The sound is a kind of 'surplus value' of the elegiac, which bursts beyond the materialist confines of naturalism and finally denotes rather than directly articulates, that which may not have then been clear but seemed apparent none the less.

Chekhov later repeats the sound, and solely to Firs, at the close of the play. The scene may be said to represent a last breath revelry for Firs who, forgotten by the others, is accidentally locked in the house. Here Chekhov remixes and recontextualizes the sound so as to verify Firs's analysis:

> *The stage is empty. There is the sound of all the doors being locked, and then of the carriages departing. It grows quiet. Through the silence comes the dull thudding of the axe. It sounds lonely and sad. Steps are heard.*
>
> *From the door on the right comes* FIRS. *He is dressed as always, in jacket and white waistcoat, with his feet in slippers. He is ill.*
>
> FIRS (*goes to the door and tries the handle*). Locked. They've gone. *(Sits down on the sofa.)* They've forgotten about me. Well, never mind. I'll just sit here for a bit. [...] (*Mutters something impossible to catch.*) My life's gone by, and it's just as it I'd never lived at all. (*Lies down.*) I'll lie down for a bit, then... No strength, have you? Nothing left. Nothing. ...Oh you ... sillybilly ... (*Lies motionless.*)
>
> *A sound is heard in the distance, as if from the sky – the sound of a string breaking, dying away, sad.*

Silence descends. And the only thing that can be heard, far away in the orchard, is the thudding of the axe.

CURTAIN.

The locking of doors, the unintelligible mutter, the noise from the sky, the thud of the axe and even Firs' stream-of-consciousness monologue, make for a soundscape that could be termed variations on the themes of *The Cherry Orchard.* Increasingly fragmentary words and sounds alone could be said to attempt to articulate 'the Real' of the drama rather than replace or stand in for it.

This emergent modernity of form in Chekhov, fired by his chafing at the limits of language (as with Hopkins), would not prove to be a resolvable crisis. Indeed, to chafe in this manner – to confront and test, to make critical, and then to begin to render language obsolete in meaning and function – would characterize strains in Absurdist theatre (to which Chekhov has a critically unresolved relationship). 'Words fail', as Winnie puts it in *Happy Days,* and yet Badiou finds in Samuel Beckett an imperative to speak none the less, or to make noise, that is autopoietic: the reflex to talk is one that is enacted in, or upon, '"the speaker" of *The Unnameable* [who], trapped in a jar at the entrance to a restaurant, is rendered immobile' (Badiou, 2003, 46). When words fail, noise rather than silence is the result for Beckett: blabber and gabbing, and then increasingly 'post-dramatic' garbling (as with *Not I*), or merely breathing (as with *Breath*).

Thus Beckett anticipates or signals, as Begam (1996) has it, 'the end of modernity', while Chekhov's modernity of form can be quite precisely located at the start of this cycle. Chekhov marks the start of the evolution from the notion of the ineffable to that of the Absurd, which is also the passage between the divine and the secular, and a passage which upholds and glosses the injunction to look away (from God, or the big Other), with noise.

8

Physical Spectatorship:
noise and rape in
Irreversible
Laura Wilson

When *Irreversible* (Gaspar Noé, 2002) was screened at the Cannes Film Festival in 2002, *Newsweek* magazine predicted that it would become the most 'walked-out-of' movie of 2003 (Ansen, 2003). In his article 'Style and Sensation' Tim Palmer places the film within the rubric *'cinéma du corps'* (Palmer, 2006): a group of films coming out of France that seek a more 'confrontational experience' (Palmer, 2006, 22) through explicit representations of sex, rape and bodily mutilation. This aggressive form of cinema that causes mass audience walk-outs is not constructed solely through graphic images however. Palmer points to a particular sound frequency used in *Irreversible* that causes an 'unease and, after prolonged exposure, physical nausea' (Palmer, 2006, 29). *Irreversible*'s electronic score was written by Thomas Bangalter of Daft Punk. Its atonal waves of abrasive sounds increase and decrease in intensity with no suggestion or promise of climax, thus inducing a suspended state of anxiety. Enhancing this state is the sound frequency to which Palmer refers. By running a DVD of the film through a frequency analyser I have ascertained that the particular frequency used in this film is between 27 and 28hz. Although some online sources mistakenly state that this frequency is infrasound, it is actually sub-bass. Infrasound is below human perception, i.e. below 20hz. The frequency used in *Irreversible* is a very low, barely perceptible, *audible* frequency. A frequency this low is known as sub-bass; human hearing generally ranges from 20hz to 20,000hz (20khz). Sub-bass frequencies and infrasound (frequencies that go below 20hz) are, as Palmer states, known to cause anxiety and nausea in those who hear them for a prolonged period of time. Through the use of this noise that could be best described as literally 'situating itself', or locating itself, within the body of the spectator, *Irreversible* is constructing what I will call a *physical spectatorship* that disrupts the dominance of the gaze and resists a reading of the representation of rape as pure spectacle.

It is arguable that *Irreversible* constructs a transgressive spectatorship through noise while its characters and narrative serve to reaffirm hetero-normative values of class, race and sexuality. This is a tactic of evasion that is expounded by theorist Will Higbee in his contribution on the film in Susan Hayward's book *French National Cinema*. His categories of evasion include the 'auteurist evasion', decontextualization of violence, and extreme images that 'render [...] the racist and homophobic discourses present ... as beyond the director's responsibility ... and as worryingly "out of control"' (Higbee, 2005, 326–7). I would add to this list a saturation of affect caused by the construction of a physical spectatorship that, although transgressive in its nature, draws attention away from the film's thematic workings that illuminate such racist, homophobic and class elitist discourses. There is much to be discussed here: What do I mean by physical spectatorship? How is it transgressive? What do I mean by affect? Through exploring possible answers to these questions I aim to argue that *Irreversible*, in its use of noise, disturbs the dominance of the visual to allow for a critical and resistant reading of its representation of rape.

The term 'physical spectatorship' is conceptual and it should be under-stood as a spectatorship that is *constituted by the film* to allow for a reading of a film that takes into consideration the spectator's *body*. As the spectator is popularly understood as a textual positioning, allowing it a physicality draws it dangerously close to being collapsed with such terms as viewer and audience. Indeed, Carl Plantinga, author of *Moving Viewers*, argues at the beginning of his book for a change in how the term *spectator* is used (Plantinga, 2009, 16–17). For Plantinga the spectator is always 'flesh and blood' and should be used interchangeably with terms such as viewer and audience, leaving the textual positioning previously known as spectatorship to be called simply positions and roles. Although the clarity and simplicity of this proposition is tempting, its limits are highlighted when Plantinga asserts that the positions and roles constructed by the text may be accepted or rejected by the spectator/viewer/audience. This suggests that the acceptance or rejection of 'positions' constructed by the text is both conscious and unprob-lematic. However, I argue that the spectatorship (and it *is* a spectatorship, not simply a 'position' to be allowed or discarded) constructed by *Irreversible* severely limits a spectator's/viewer's/audience's ability to consciously evade its affects. Plantinga states himself that an affect may be, although not necessarily, cognitively impenetrable (Plantinga, 2009, 29). A textual positioning is always a physical as well as an intellectual construction, hence the term physical spectatorship; separating the flesh-and-blood spectator from the fairly clinical-sounding textual roles or positions denies this. My thinking here is informed by the work of Christian Metz on spectatorship and Laura U. Marks on embodied visuality.

In her book *The Skin of the Film* Laura U. Marks describes an 'embodied visuality' (Marks, 2000, 151) that does not hold vision as master over the object it sees but rather 'yields to the thing seen, a vision that is not merely cognitive but acknowledges its location in the body' (Marks, 2000, 132). Her analysis of a scene in Shauna Beharry's *Seeing is Believing* (1991) where the camera 'looks closely' (Marks suggests that 'focus' is not the right word) over the folds of a sari that once belonged to Beharry's mother brings to her attention that her vision was being used 'as though it were a sense of touch' (Marks, 2000, 128). The disparity between the 'searching movements of the camera' that marks the object as present for the spectator and Beharry's 'wistful voice' that signals her own loss 'creates a poignant awareness of the missing sense of touch' (Marks, 2000, 129). The memory of Beharry's mother that is held within the folds of the sari relies on touch as well as sound and vision to be fully recalled. The distance Marks describes as existing between the audio and visual that reminds her of the missing sense of touch is bridged by the embodiment of the spectator, by locating what is seen *in* the body of the spectator.

For this to occur, of course, the body of the spectator must be present. In 'The imaginary signifier', Christian Metz suggests that the spectator is *not* present as anything other than an all-perceiving eye and ear. Metz argues, *pace* Freud, that the screen is a mirror akin to that of the 'mirror phase', where a child simultaneously perceives her or himself as a subject and object; that is, where he or she 'know[s] that objects exist, that he himself exists as a subject, that he becomes an object for others' (Metz, 2000, 215). However, Metz goes on to say that unlike 'the child in the mirror [that is: the spectator] cannot identify with himself as an object, but only with some objects which are there without him' (ibid.). The spectator is absent from the screen, situated on the side of the all-perceiving, and the mirror *and* screen effectively becomes 'clear glass' (ibid.). But in an embodied mode of spectatorship the spectator *is* perceived: she or he is perceived by her or himself. They are transformed from a subject which holds mastery over all that it sees, to a subject/object which is all that it feels. The 'great eye and ear' (Metz, 2000,

216) that signal the spectator as present for Metz are the organs of senses that can travel over distance. The sense of touch demands that the object be immediate to the perceiving subject. As the sense of touch missing from the screen arises from and is located in the body the spectator must be perceived as the object by her/his self.

The body of the spectator, now present as 'the great eye and ear' *and* perceived object, disturbs the idea of cinema as absent. Metz says of cinema: 'what unfolds there may, as before, be more or less fictional, but the unfolding itself is fictive: the actor, the "décor", the words one hears are all absent, everything is *recorded*' (Metz, 2000, 214; emphasis in original). Thus even a non-fictional film will still be fictional as the figures on screen are an illusion – 'mere shadows or reflections' (Rushton, 2002, 107–18). Yet when an embodied spectator can perceive her/his self it is no longer possible to make the claim 'I know I am perceiving something imaginary (and that is why its absurdities, even if they are extreme, do not seriously disturb me)' (Metz, 2000, 216). The unfolding of a text that creates a physical response in its spectator is not entirely fictive, absent or recorded. It engages the body of the spectator who is no longer cast as a 'pure act of perception ... a kind of transcendental subject, anterior to everything *there is*' (ibid.). If the perception is no longer entirely imaginary, then Metz's 'extreme absurdities' *do* have the power to disturb.

Can physical spectatorship be transgressive in its ability to collapse the senses of hearing and touch? Marks's notion of 'embodied visuality' (Marks, 2000, 151) may be used here to argue that the use of particular images *with* particular sounds creates a missing sense of touch that can be located in the body of the spectator. However, it is possible for noise alone, without any images, to create a physical sensation for the listener. *Irreversible* thus uses noise to its full potential by including a sub-bass frequency on its soundtrack of 27hz that is known for creating anxiety and nausea in those who hear it for prolonged periods of time. Although camera work is also used to this end (for the first hour of the film the camera repeatedly spins sickeningly out of control) I shall explore how the invasive nature of sound – that, as Storr notes, cannot be easily dispelled or located (Storr, 1992, 100–1) – is more effective than what is seen in creating such physical affects. However, *Irreversible* is also a visual text. Therefore it must be asked *how* was noise used in this film to create such an uncomfortable and sickening spectatorship when the presence of a nine-minute-long rape scene would presumably be sufficient?

This leads on to the final point of definition: what do I mean by 'affect'? I have already mentioned Plantinga's reading of affect as potentially cognitively impenetrable, an idea which may also be found in Matt Hill's definition of affect, in *The Pleasures of Horror*. For Hills an affect is a feeling that is 'cognitively impenetrable' as well, which he explains as 'not relat[ing] to clear objects framed by cognitive processes of evaluation; they are not "object directed"' but rather they are '"pure" physiological sensations' (Hills, 2005, 19, 26). The 27hz frequency used in *Irreversible* creates such object-less physiological sensations yet it is eventually accompanied by images of rape that *can* be cognitively processed to create 'feelings that have a cognitive knowledge component and a discriminable object' (Hills, 2005, 13). Hills calls these feelings emotions. Although a frequency of 27hz may produce uncomfortable affects in the listener, when used alongside images of rape an object is provided on to which may be placed the object-less affects of anxiety and nausea. Noé thus uses noise and rape to force the spectator into moving between affect and emotion, emotion that has a clear object and yet at the same time remains object-less. Although for some it may be difficult to imagine a more horrifying and emotive image than that of rape, I would argue that these feelings are intensified through the use of affect making the rape in *Irreversible* one of the most notorious and disturbing examples of its kind.

The use of the term *affect* here is influenced by the work of Elizabeth Cowie, Carl Plantinga and R. B. Zajonc. The commonality that runs through all their research is that affect is a bodily response. The variable component is the extent to which this involves cognition or 'mental work'. For Cowie affect is *the result* of 'a mental and (perhaps unconscious) process of thought' (Cowie, 2003, 30). In other words, cognition is needed to produce affect, even if affect may be detached from the original experience and/or object. Plantinga provides a different argument by stating that affect does not necessitate cognitive processes (Plantinga, 2009, 29), although it can sometimes arise from them. Zajonc, on the other hand, describes affect as '"pure" sensation', it is '"pure" sensory input' that is *not* cognition (Zajonc, 2004, 287). He goes further to make the claim that '[i]t is further possible that we can like something or be afraid of it before we know precisely what it is and perhaps even *without* knowing what it is' (Zajonc, 2004, 254). It is this final explanation of affect that clearly describes the experience of hearing a sub-bass frequency such as the one that is played throughout most of *Irreversible*. Yet images of violence and rape allow the pure bodily sensation to be cognitively processed and become what Plantinga calls a 'concern based construal' (emotion). Affect in *Irreversible* therefore comes to form part of an emotion, but initially exists solely as 'pure' sensation.

Whenever rape occurs in a film the questions that are typically voiced by cultural critics are the same that appear when any film with rape, violence, or even sex is released: Is this necessary? Is this gratuitous? Why did the film need to include this? Why do we need to watch this? What is being said, if anything, about the ethics of witnessing a representation of rape? Can we learn anything

from this? Can it tell us something about the significance of rape and its representations to Western culture? In her book *Watching Rape* Sarah Projansky
makes a persuasive argument, drawing on Laura Mulvey's foundational work on
visual pleasure (Mulvey, 2000, 238–48), which links rape with male control over
language and the gaze in Ridley Scott's *Thelma and Louise* (1991). Projansky
does this by producing a close textual analysis of camera movement, editing
and character acting, and argues that control over the gaze is subverted – albeit
ineffectually – with final clips of 'women looking at and being with women'
(Projansky, 2001, 132). To a certain extent then, the damage caused by looking
(as the gaze is linked to assault) is finally and momentarily relieved by looking.
At the end of the film women have a certain amount of control over the gaze,
although this is limited by the isolated shots of very short duration that restrict
their bodies and bind their gazes to a particularly short, and posthumous,
moment in time. The question remains: if the gaze is closely linked to sexual
assault, as Projansky argues, how can an analysis of the structures of the gaze
ever be sufficient in providing a reading of the film's rape?

In her book *Public Rape* Tanya Horeck asks the pertinent question 'can
looking cure the damage done by looking?' (Horeck, 2004, 97). In reference
to Projansky's analysis of *Thelma and Louise* the answer would be a very
tentative 'sort of, not really'. Yet the privileging of sight in this question
screams for attention to be paid to other senses in order to answer it: hearing
and touch in particular. According to Constance Classen the sense of hearing
has historically been second only to that of sight in its connection to an intellectual – therefore 'high' – status (Classen, 1998, 66). If this is true then why
has music, sound and noise been so frequently neglected in the study and
research of film? Analyses of the representation of rape in film, including
those cited by Horeck and Projansky, rarely if ever consider the impact which
sound has upon the film's spectatorship. Concern is almost always with
whose point of view is provided for the spectator, if the camera positioning
invites a voyeuristic spectatorship, and of course with just how graphic the
director has 'dared' to make the visual representation of rape. Could the
neglect that music, sound and noise in cinema have suffered be due partly
to the connection between hearing and feeling, sound and touch? If sight is
the 'highest' sense with hearing coming in a close second, touch is certainly
the 'lowest' sense being the most associated with the body and corporeality
(Classen, 1998, 66). The collapse of hearing into touch shifts music, sound,
and noise into the realm of the body rather than of the mind, irrationality
rather than reason, and physicality rather than intellectuality, leaving sight as
the sole indicator of rationality, culture, and intelligence.

In the simple yet evocative first sentence of *Color of Angels*, Classen
states that '[*sic*] Modern Western Culture is the culture of the eye' (Classen,

1998, 1). This culture is, as stated above, one of reason, of intellectuality, of the mind. Certain terms that are used by scholars in the study of film reflect this. For example, to 'read' a film suggests a detached study of the text that avoids any reference to its physicality (Plantinga, 2009, 3). In her book *Carnal Thoughts* Vivian Sobchack calls attention to the disparity between film critics and film scholars, stating that reviews will often focus on the physical act of watching a film whereas scholars will shift any meaning extracted from this process on to language (Sobchack, 2004, 57–8). Yet meaning extracted from an analysis that takes into account the body of the spectator is not, as Plantinga points out, separable from or parallel to the meaning gleaned from a study of the dialogue, narrative structure and visual styles. Instead they are intertwined, each having an effect on the other. Meaning taken from a construction of physical spectatorship may even contradict that taken from a detached reading and, further, misunderstanding the physical spectatorship (again according to Plantinga) may lead to a misunderstanding of the 'thematic workings of a film, and perhaps even … the story itself' (Plantinga, 2009, 4). I am not convinced of the extent to which a film may be 'misunderstood', or even how this would be measured or who has the final say, nor would I want to suggest that those who walked out of the theatre when *Irreversible* was screened at Cannes Film Festival in 2002 were in some way wrong to do so. However, I would suggest that the extreme variations of response to this film, and other films like it, may be indicative of the cracks within critical and scholarly discourse into which the body of the spectator has fallen.

Before I go on to a textual analysis of *Irreversible* in which I shall argue that noise is used to disturb the dominance of the visual so as to allow for a critical and resistant reading of its representation of rape, it is necessary to ask: what mode of spectatorship does the rape in *Irreversible* construct? When Horeck asks the same question the options given are either witness or voyeur: 'Are we bearing witness to a terrible crime or are we participating in shameful voyeuristic activity?' (Horeck, 2004, vi). This is a critical question not only because one position implies innocence and the other guilt, but also because each has a varying level of complicity and physicality. A voyeuristic position is a detached vantage point from which the spectator may spy on, in secret, a given object and potentially derive sexual gratification. Plantinga rejects the notion that *any* form of film viewing is voyeuristic due to its lack of secrecy (Plantinga, 2009, 23–5). However, I would argue that both the darkness of the cinema and the feelings of guilt and shame at being seen *looking at* (and potentially enjoying) a representation of rape, are voyeuristic.

During the rape in *Irreversible* there is a fixed camera position at ground level that frames the rape as if an unseen person were crouching and spying; this type of camera-work invites a reading of this kind. Interestingly, this may be a homage of sorts to Stanley Kubrick, who makes use of just such ground-level shots in *A Clockwork Orange* (1971) for a scene in which a homeless man is beaten by the main protagonist (also called Alex) and his followers. Further support for this connection may be said to come in the inclusion of a poster for Kubrick's *2001: A Space Odyssey* (1968) in the final scenes of *Irreversible*,[1] and the fact that both *A Clockwork Orange* and *Irreversible* make the use of sound (in the case of the former it is the use of the song *Singin' in the Rain* rather than sub-bass frequencies) intrinsic to the construction of their highly disturbing rape scenes. However, it is more often than not the camera work, and not the use of sound, that is of critical note. Both Horeck's analysis of *The Accused* (Jonathan Kaplan, 1998) (Horeck, 2004, 91–116), and Sarah Projansky's reading of *Thelma and Louise* (Projansky, 2001, 121–53), have suggested that the act of rape is strongly connected with the act of looking. More overtly, Yoko Ono and John Lennon's documentary *Rape* (1969), where a young woman is followed with a camera until she is reduced to tears, implies in no unsubtle terms that to be the object of the gaze is to be raped. The spectator position constructed as described above thus forces the spectator into complicity with the rape through the desire to control; although not actually involved with the act of rape, simply *looking*, as Horeck notes is suggested through *The Accused's* narrative, is bound to the law. Alternative spectator positions are offered by certain camera locations that disrupt voyeuristic gratification; for example, in Lukas Moodysson's *Lilya-4-Ever* (2002) when Lilya is forced into the sex-trade her encounters are filmed entirely from her point of view. However, the voyeuristic position *is* one that *Irreversible* constructs through dialogue and camera movement/positioning and yet, I argue, it is one that is disturbed by noise.

To witness a crime, unlike the above discussion of the voyeur, is not to be complicit with it; yet the term Horeck uses in reference to watching rape – 'bearing witness' – implies a certain amount of physicality. To witness something is to see it, to *bear* witness to it means to endure it, to go through it, to suffer it. In her article 'Carved in skin: bearing witness to self-harm', Jane Kilby argues that to bear witness to another person's acts of self-injury means to look at their own 'painful, if not aggressively compelling, desire to testify to their own traumas' (Kilby, 2001, 125). This is an answer to a question posited above of *how* the sound frequency of 27hz is used to create anxiety and nausea when visual images of rape would have been sufficient. As well as intensifying the emotions through affect, the sound frequency resonates in the body of the spectator therefore bringing the image or the object into her/his self – Marks calls this 'a form of visuality that yields to the thing seen' (Marks, 2000, 132). The representation of rape in *Irreversible* is a testament to the spectator's past, present,and future traumas. To bear witness to it is to witness one's own fragility and permeability – to bear witness to it is to witness one's own rape.

Although I argue that the noise created by a sound frequency of 27hz serves to collapse the senses and provide uncomfortable physical affects for the spectator, *Irreversible* attacks the senses in more ways than one. Palmer argues that the film approaches 'sensory overload, sheer aural chaos' (Palmer, 2006, 29). This chaos is intensified by, or created through, a narrative that resists placing each scene in context and camera movements that inhibit a temporal and spatial understanding of the film. *Irreversible* consists of 12 scenes, each shown in reverse order, beginning in a dark room where a man confesses to committing incest with his daughter and ending in bright sunlight where Alex (Monica Bellucci), the film's heroine, lies stretched out on the grass among happily playing children. As Higbee argues, while the reverse narrative decontextualizes the violence, it also serves to enhance it (Higbee, 2005, 326–7). Further, the spectator is denied any aid of character development to construct a positioning within the chaos. The movement of the camera that spins round on itself, seems to rove freely across walls and ceilings, and editing which moves swiftly and dizzyingly from long shots to close-ups, prevents the spectator from locating her or himself within the space of the film. From the very beginning the film is wilfully off-putting and lacks many of the techniques ordinarily utilized to make a film accessible for the spectator. Instead the spectator is bombarded with abstract images of filthy spaces, writhing bodies, and 'a queasy range of pulsing textures' (Palmer, 2006, 29) from a barely perceptible rumble to the desperate cries of [the club] Le Rectum's clientele. In other words the film seems to do all it can to repel the spectator.

After a seemingly determined effort to repel the spectator, the camera moves from a disembodied to a subjective positioning. As Alex walks through the city at night and descends into a subway tunnel the camera follows her at a close distance. The spectator becomes her stalker, only to be shifted to the role of a voyeur once her rapist, Le Tenia (meaning tapeworm), pushes Alex on to the concrete and the camera settles at a medium-long shot, at ground level. Such camera movement and positioning suggests both alignment with a potential attacker and sadistic voyeur respectively. Predictably the object of the camera/spectator's gaze is a female who is highly sexualized in a revealing white dress. *Irreversible* thus constructs what may be read as a sadistic voyeuristic spectatorship that, if male, upholds heteronormative structures of male/female, subject/object, activity/passivity. After 40 minutes of repelling the spectators, *Irreversible* positions them firmly within the text at the very moment of Alex's rape.

The voyeuristic camera positioning throughout the rape is subverted in two ways however. The first is through the return of the gaze, and the second is through the collapse of the senses of hearing and feeling that disrupts the dominance of the spectator's gaze. First, during the rape a figure appears in an extreme long shot walking into the tunnel. The figure is so far away it remains a blurred silhouette; however, it pauses momentarily, looking down the tunnel towards the rape and towards the camera/spectator before leaving. Horeck argues that images of rape always serve to make the spectator 'self-consciously aware of [their] position in relation to the text' (Horeck, 2004, vi). However, I would argue that in this instance it is this figure that does this more forcefully. The figure disrupts the secretive voyeuristic gaze by returning it; the rape is no longer private between rapist, victim, and spectator. It is thus made public and forces awareness on to the spectator. The figure reminds us that voyeurism is not just watching an act but *allowing the act to happen*. In this way *Irreversible* links the gaze with the act of rape and criticizes rape as a spectacle.

The film does not present rape as a spectacle to be merely viewed from a subjective positioning. The frequency of 27hz continues throughout the rape scene; as it is sub-bass it creates a barely perceptible noise that may be dismissed as background noise or the 'sonic presence' of everyday lives (Frith, 1996, 100). That it could be dismissed as background noise recalls Kim Cascone's analysis of David Lynch's work with sound: Lynch creates a 'viral contagion' that 'permanently infects the host body and alters our perceptual experience of life' (Cascone, 2003). By forcing a physical reaction in the spectator through this frequency, and one that finds its object not only in the body of the spectator but in the image of rape, *Irreversible* alters how the representation of rape is perceived in the film. It is experienced not only through sight and sound but through touch as well. It objectifies the spectator as she/he must perceive her/himself as the object of nausea, anxiety and rape.

A pertinent point of inquiry here, therefore, concerns just *how Irreversible* constructs a spectatorship that cannot be consciously evaded without the obvious choice of leaving the cinema. As stated above, one of the ways the film achieves this is through the use of a sound frequency of 27hz throughout a large portion of the film. In an article that explores the affective potential of low register sounds, Bruce Johnson cites the work of neuroscientist Joseph LeDoux (Johnson, 2008, 3-4). In an experiment that understood the auditory chain as Ear>Auditory Midbrain>Auditory Thalamus>Auditory Cortex, LeDoux found that the cortex 'evidently played no part in producing the symptoms of fear, so that the auditory stimulus does not have to proceed to the auditory cortex' (Johnson, 2008, 3-4). Essentially this means that sound can have a physiological affect on the body *before* it is cognitively processed. In spite of understandable reservations towards the assumption that sound may be physically experienced in a universal manner, as discussed above, these experiments at least support Johnson's claim that when analysing the interpretation of sound, physical processes should be given priority as '[t]he body sets limits on the interpretive range which is then made available for cultural mediation' (Johnson, 2008, 2).

There is one noise that is strikingly absent from this scene: the female cry. Although Alex does initially resist Le Tenia both physically and verbally, once the rape begins she is denied the ability to cry as her attacker covers her mouth with his fists. Considering that one of the pioneers of research into sound in cinema, Michel Chion, argues that cinema is a 'machine made in order to deliver a cry from the female voice' (Chion, 1999, 47), the absence of Alex's voice during her rape is significant. In her book *The Acoustic Mirror* Kaja Silverman argues that the female cry serves to displace 'all traces of corporeal excess and discursive impotence' (Silverman, 1988, 94) on to the female. Thus while the act of rape betrays the male's physical desires the female's scream takes on his physicality. However, in *Irreversible* Alex's screams are muffled by the rapist. Although the absence of the scream may be argued as significant, since it denies the transference of corporeal excess, the sound of Alex's pained moans forced out of her by the weight of the rapist along with the image of her body forced to the ground renders the actual scream unnecessary. Alex's noises, although not fulfilling the order of the cry, still convey an excess of corporeality.

So what does this nature of analysis offer in terms of perceptions of rape in film? I have argued that it forces the spectator to bear witness to the rape and allows for a textual positioning that aligns the spectator with the rape victim rather than with the attacker. I have also argued that it disrupts mastery over the image and subverts the dominance of seeing over hearing and touch. How does this contribute to the ethics of both creating and spectating representations of rape? How can one justify the necessity of including a representation of rape in a film? By returning to Horeck's questioning of the act of looking at the portrayal of rape, the possibility arises that the representation of rape has the potential to cure the damage done by rape. I have already argued that through the analysis of camera angles and points of view alone this particular potential is limited. Does physical spectatorship, and the use of noise, change this? Can it be argued that it has a reparative value that makes the representation of rape necessary? To answer these questions attention must be turned to the final scene.

The final scene shows Alex laid out on the grass under the sun. The shot frames her entire body, once beaten and bloody, now intact and clean. By providing an image of her clean and proper body this scene both articulates the horror of her assault and denies its reality. It acts as both an ominous reminder of what is to come and a final pay-off for the spectator who has been subjected to the previous images and noise of her rape. The sound frequency that contributed to this noise ceased some time before this scene and in its place plays Beethoven's Symphony No. 7 in A Major. The classical music is as soothing as the image of Alex's recovered body, yet its reparative value is disrupted by the final sound of helicopter blades, which is acousmatic (that is: there is no image to attach a source to this sound). The film is an ever-oscillating soundscape between nourishing music and devastating noise that reminds the spectator of the transience of Alex's peace and safety. Thus, through the reverse narrative and the shift from noise to music, Alex has escaped her assault, but these techniques cannot *end* assault, nor can they ever fully cure the damage done by rape. To borrow from Projansky's analysis of Thelma and Louise's suicide, Alex is 'caught on the precarious brink between death and life' (Projansky, 2001, 133) – between resistance to the assault and the inevitability of the assault. Physical spectatorship does not, and cannot, cure the damage done by rape. By studying rape's noise rather than just its image it becomes possible, however, to change the way in which such representations are experienced and perceived.

9

Cinematic tinnitus

Robert Walker

The use of hearing loss and tinnitus as cinematic devices has appealed to a wide variety of filmmakers. The impairment of a character's hearing has allowed cinema to explore 'subjective' or 'point-of-audition' sound in formally inventive ways. Whether portraying pain, confusion, dislocation, removal from temporal reality or simply withholding information, impaired hearing has proven to be a valuable formal and aesthetic tool in contemporary cinema. This throws up several propositions. The representation of tinnitus in cinema has established its own set of conventions but they need to be held up against accounts from sufferers. Cinema may potentially be the best-equipped art form to represent the condition, yet it has been remarkably slow in doing so. This may be more to do with the status of sound (as opposed to vision) within the form of cinema than questions of the representation of tinnitus. The representation of tinnitus offers us something unique in cinematic form, but needed a particular set of technical and cultural circumstances before such representations could come to the fore.

Definitions

Before we examine cinematic tinnitus, we should consider its definition as a pathological condition. Derived directly from the Latin 'tinnitus' meaning 'a ringing', tinnitus is broadly any sounds generated or perceived internal to the brain and ear. Michael O'Toole, a sufferer and writer on the topic, defines it as:

> sound inside the head not caused by anything outside it ... to describe

the sounds takes a little longer: they may resemble almost anything from a hissing to the roar of a jet engine. The commonest include metallic banging, whistling, drum beats, water running, electric drills, clock chimes and telephone bells.

(O'Toole, 1995, 1)

Nor is tinnitus restricted to people who hear: 'many people with acquired deafness complain of whistling, hissing or buzzing' (Critchley, 1983, 542). The medical causes of tinnitus are wide ranging, covering physical damage, psychological factors, infection and causes simply unknown. It is also difficult to treat. Michael O'Toole continues:

The inner ear, with the cochlea, reveals a vastly complicated world ... with nerve connections to the part of the brain dealing with hearing. Damage through injury or ageing can play havoc with these micro-complex auditory pathways and is strongly suspected of being a cause of tinnitus. It is even thought that when certain signals fail to travel correctly or at all, the brain interprets their absence as a signal in itself and perversely creates sounds from what should be silence.

(O'Toole, 1995, 4)

Tinnitus caused by an over-exposure to sound could be considered to be a reaction to noise, a response to an over-stimulation of the ear. Quite why the ear responds to noise by creating noise remains a mystery in the field of medicine, and it appears that most treatments are focused on the management of the condition and the minimizing of its intrusion into people's lives.

Written artistic descriptions

Tinnitus has proven to be a source of artistic inspiration for, among others, Francisco Goya, Vincent Van Gogh, Jonathan Swift and Salman Rushdie. William Worm, a character in Thomas Hardy's A Pair of Blue Eyes, described it thus: 'I've got such a noise in my head ... 'tis for all the world like people frying fish ... sometimes 'tisn't only fish, but rashers of bacon and onions. Ay, I can hear the fat pop and fizz as natural as life' (Hardy, 1877, 219).

In 1874 the Czech composer Bedřich Smetana wrote that a 'cruel fate' had overtaken him. He told of 'buzzing and tingling in my ears as if I were standing in a huge waterfall' (cited in O'Toole, 1995, 8). Before his last days in a Prague lunatic asylum the composer revealed his haunted state of mind:

That ringing in my head, that noise ... is the worst of all. Deafness would be a relatively tolerable condition if only all was quiet in my head. However, almost continuous internal noises which sometimes increase to a thunderous crashing torture me greatly. This inexplicable pandemonium is pierced by the shrieking of voices, from strident whistles to ghastly bawling, as though furies and demons were bearing down on me in a violent rage ... I begin to wonder what the end will be.

(cited in O'Toole, 1995, 8)

Evocative though this description may be, these words perhaps fall short as a means of accurately, rather than poetically, communicating sounds. Recorded sound and images, imperfect as they may be as modes of objective representation, do at least engage the relevant senses directly. In cinema we can hear an approximation of the sounds of tinnitus themselves, at the same time as seeing how this affects the sufferer physically which helps establish empathy and identification with the character.

Robert Slater and Mark Terry's *Tinnitus: A Guide for Sufferers and Professionals* is a medical textbook on the condition and suggests that the use of synthesizers may be one way of gathering data on the tonalities of tinnitus.

The synthesizer allows an almost unlimited variety of sounds to be used in attempting to find a match with the tinnitus. However, obtaining a reasonable match to a complex tinnitus can be a long process, possibly a matter of hours, even with an experienced operator of the synthesizer ... a finer class of categorization of tinnitus types may be possible with this technique and study of this data could be informative to the clinician.

(Slater and Terry, 1987, 82)

Apart from the appealing mental image of a Brian Eno-like doctor attempting to catalogue the condition through synthesizer recordings in a late 1980s sonic research lab, this does highlight the sense of frustration at how words alone cannot communicate a condition of the senses and perception that is so intimate to the sufferer. Michael O'Toole again:

It is even claimed by some sufferers that artistic expression, in writing, music or the visual arts, is the only adequate way of describing tinnitus to people without it. A drawing or painting of a tortured face silently pleading for quietness says more than the standard definitions found in medical dictionaries. A poem about what it feels like to lose silence forever is more eloquent than what the average doctor can say about a tinnitus patient. The colours of an oil painting depicting inner torment can vividly represent the perpetual frustrations of the sufferer artist. If it deserves any gratitude at all, tinnitus can be thanked for stimulating a wealth of art which enables many people to find liberating relaxation in a world of inner sounds which sometimes seem capable of engulfing them.

(O'Toole, 1995, 25–6)

Point-of-audition

The term 'point-of-audition' is used to refer to sound as heard by the character, and is directly analogous to the more familiar 'point-of-view'. In most examples of cinematic tinnitus, it is important that the viewer/listener be placed within a context where they share the auditory experience of a particular character as the condition is so internalized. Rick Altman defines it in the following way:

point-of-audition sound is identified by its volume, reverb level, and other characteristics as representing sound as it would be heard from a point within the diegesis, normally by a specific character or characters. In other words, point-of-audition sound always carries signs of its own fictional audition. As such, point-of-audition sound always has the effect of luring the listener into the diegesis not at the point of enunciation of the sound, but at the point of its audition.

(Altman, 1992, 60)

The silent era and cinematic silence

Many cinematic representations of tinnitus are coupled with a hearing loss or a reduction in the onscreen character's ability to hear sounds we might otherwise consider to be within their hearing range. This raises two close formal companions for cinematic tinnitus: the silent era, where the physical medium of film did not carry with it recorded sound, and the use of silent moments within otherwise 'sound' films.

Cinematic silence has been difficult to create and attain, just as true silence has proven elusive in the realm of direct experience. It was John Cage's hearing of sounds inside a supposedly soundless anechoic chamber in 1952 that left him sure of the impossibility of silence: medical reports on those who have become completely deaf after acquiring language suggest that tinnitus and sound often remain for them, just not from their environment.

I will use the term 'silent film' to refer to non-synchronous sound film; that is, a film without a mechanically or electronically synchronized pre-recorded soundtrack, though the word 'silent' is very problematic in that silent films were never silent. Silent films were almost always accompanied by music, live sound effects and sometimes even informal commentary – the reading aloud of intertitles for those who were illiterate.[1] Many film theorists have discussed the sound of silent cinema and the impact of the arrival of sound, such as Sergei Eisenstein (1928), Béla Balazs (1930), Rick Altman (2004) and Michel Chion (1999). Béla Balazs sums up the critical mood around the arrival of synchronous sound writing in 1930, which has proven to be an enduring interpretation.

> The silent film was on its way to acquiring a psychological subtlety, a creative power almost unprecedented in the arts. The technical invention of the sound film burst upon the scene, with catastrophic force. The rich culture of visual expression that I have been describing is now in grave danger. This as-yet undeveloped new technology has attached itself to a highly developed cinematic art, and has thrown it back to the most primitive stage. And it is inevitable that the standard of the content of film will decline in equal measure with the degeneration of its standards of expression.
>
> (Balazs, 1930, 183)

Béla Balazs' scepticism with regard to the newly arriving sound film is typical of leading theorists. Making concrete sound that was otherwise imagined by the viewer was seen as regressive. The image of a woman screaming in a silent film is also 'heard' (that is to say, imagined as a sound) by the viewers because they know it should be there. As Des O'Rawe puts it:

> In the silent film, the audience observed images of sound that were so strong, so convincing, that they forgot to remember that they were not hearing the sound of speech. The appreciation of sound was thus enhanced not simply by silence but by the secret revelation of the sources of sound, a revelation that was, according to Balazs, so powerful that it eliminated our need to hear and our desire to experience a synchronous relationship between a sound and its source.
>
> (O'Rawe, 2006, 398)

Perhaps so. But once the talkie arrived, we again discovered this need to relate an image and sound synchronously. The opening to Sergio Leone's

Once Upon a Time in The West (1968) achieves a sense of quiet and silence more pronounced than a silent film because we hear the tiny sound of a fly buzzing around – a technical silence might be mentally louder because we would imagine much more sound. Sound designer Gary Rydstrom comments:

> But the trick to making things quiet doesn't mean that you don't play any sounds at all. When things are quiet in a movie, it means that you're hearing details you wouldn't normally hear. If you're trying to build up tension out in the woods before a dinosaur shows up, you have everything get really quiet, then you hear leaves hitting the electric fence, or you hear certain birds, or you hear animals way in the distance, or you hear winds whipping around. It's sort of a hyperawareness, like a drug state. Suddenly everything is incredibly sharp and detailed, but low-level. Those moments are tense.
>
> (quoted in Kenny, 2000, 63)

Whether the viewer/listener's imagination is preferable to the filmmaker's recording of sound is perhaps as debatable as the suggestion that radio is superior to television because the pictures are better. Des O'Rawe also suggests: 'the sound film … is the only art form capable of producing silence' (O'Rawe, 2006, 398).

Following this logic, the sound film has the ability to take away what was once there and make plain its absence. Stanley Kubrick's use of technical silence during key moments of the fatal spacewalk in *2001: A Space Odyssey* (1968) is a prime example. Only with the arrival of the talkie were the terms 'mute cinema' or 'silent cinema' created. The talkie rewrote its predecessor's sound aesthetic as one robbed of the human voice, or simply unable to hear it. Michel Chion describes it thus:

> On the contrary, [silent] film characters were quite chatty. … By the constant movement of their lips, their gestures that told of entire speeches whose intertitles communicated to us only the most abridged versions. So it's not that the film's characters were mute, but rather that the film was deaf to them.
>
> (Chion, 1999, 8)

The silent film was perhaps not formally equipped to represent hearing loss or tinnitus, but when a sound film uses this state we are able to briefly travel back to silent cinema, where images are free to associate unrestricted by the need for synchronicity. Mike Figgis' *Leaving Las Vegas* (1995), a sound film, uses total silence to suggest and underline alcoholic oblivion. Ben (Nicholas

Cage) is intentionally drinking himself to death and we see him reach the night's climax as he downs the end of a bottle of whisky in one go in a strip bar. The musical score peaks as Ben finishes the bottle and the film's soundtrack cuts to complete silence as he screams in pain and rants to himself in his car. The climax of his evening is nothingness, an absence, a black hole where he cannot feel. But this is most definitely not point-of-audition sound, because we neither see the world through his eyes nor receive a direct narrative explanation, leaving the silence as a poetic third-person perspective, not a physical phenomenon for the character.

These moments of non-synchronicity allow the talkie to become silent once again, destroying the assumption that films are one or the other – silent films have sound, and sound films have silence. And scenes of tinnitus and hearing loss form a linkage back to the 'lost' silent cinema.

The Dolby effect

It would take a significant change in cinema sound quality, brought about by Dolby noise reduction technologies of the early 1970s, to actually allow tinnitus to really be possible as a sound effect in film.[2]

What Dolby noise reduction did, along with improving the quality of replay for the cinema audience, was to allow filmmakers the ability to mix a much larger number of tracks during post-production. Prior to that, films would typically comprise a small number of dialogue tracks, some sound effects and music which would necessarily be duplicated across several generations for the purposes of editing, mixing and exhibition. For example, the film's original location dialogue tapes would be copied to magnetic film for editing, then replayed through the mixing console and re-recorded to the final soundtrack master. The soundtrack master would then go through several duplications before arriving at a release print used for public exhibition. Each stage in this process would add a small amount of hiss. Multiply this by the number of tracks and you have a lot of cumulative hiss induced by the analogue magnetic recording processes of the era. The effective limit to the number of these mixable tracks prior to the use of noise-reduction technology was in the single digits: mix more than, say, eight tracks together to create your final soundtrack and the cumulative tape hiss from each individual track would render the final soundtrack too noisy for exhibition. However, by using noise reduction at every stage of the post-production sound process, you could blend many more tracks without fear of losing the audience's attention under a thick patina of hiss. This was a major factor in the blossoming of sonically inventive cinema in the 1970s.

Another effect of the Dolby revolution was the abolition of the Academy
Curve (Figure 9.1).[3]

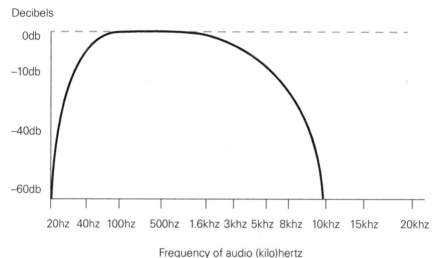

Decibels

0db

−10db

−40db

−60db

20hz 40hz 100hz   500hz 1.6khz 3khz 5khz 8khz   10khz 15khz   20khz

Frequency of audio (kilo)hertz

(not to scale)

Figure 9.1 The 1938 Academy Curve for cinema sound replay

The Academy Curve was an equalization[4] used in cinemas, agreed upon in
1938 (and used widely until the late 1970s) as a means of reducing hiss and
noise on early sound films and preventing distortion. The early synchronous
sound films used an optical method of storing the audio on the film print
which was not very high fidelity. To combat the problem of hiss, cracks and
pops evident on these prints the Academy of Motion Pictures proposed a
corrective remedy for cinemas to filter out some of the offending noise. One
very pertinent aspect of the Academy Curve was that it heavily filtered high
frequencies beginning at 5khz, and virtually eliminated anything higher than
8khz. This also happens to be the frequency range of most tinnitus effects
– thus making them almost technically impossible prior to 1975. Dolby's
noise-reduction techniques meant that the savage filtration of the earlier
Academy Curve was now largely obsolete, the Academy Curve being steadily
replaced in cinema replay systems by the X-Curve (Figure 9.2).

The X-Curve is still used today and allows a much more even frequency
response. Its introduction gradually phased out the use of the previous
Academy Curve and made high frequencies really usable within film sound.
Only after the improvements in film soundtrack technology from the late
1970s would audiences be able to accurately distinguish the intentional noise
of a tinnitus effect from poor system performance. There would be little point

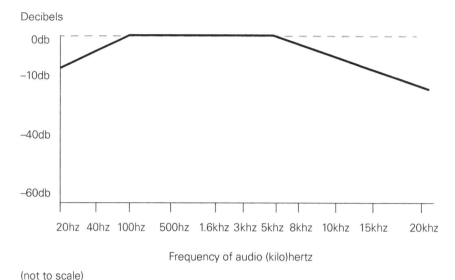

Figure 9.2 The X-Curve for cinema sound replay

in adding subtle sonic interferences to a film soundtrack if these interferences were indistinguishable from the medium itself or completely inaudible because a cinema could not reproduce them.

Explaining the transformation

Tinnitus and hearing loss offer cinema a route into the usurping of a third-person camera point-of-view in the shift to a subjective point-of-view. This could be termed a 'subjective transformation'. This describes moments in film where a shift to direct representation of a particular character's point-of-view occurs. Kathryn Bigelow's *Strange Days* (1995) represents the world of a virtual reality headset through subjective transformation – we see and hear the world through the wearer's eyes and ears. Tinnitus is often represented as subjective transformation, and like other formal transformations usually requires dramatic justification to retain the suspension of disbelief.

James Mangold's *Copland* (1997) does this by presaging its climactic scene of hearing loss. Freddie (Sylvester Stallone) is listening to an LP and as he does this, the familiar tinnitus whine bridges an edit into a flashback sequence of him rescuing a girl from a car and his hearing being damaged as a result. The narrative uses the fact that the character is actively listening (to the LP) to make us aware of his sense of hearing as active and not simply a passive receptor. Later, the fact that he is already deaf in one ear is underlined when Freddie's mechanical alarm clock can be seen rattling away to wake him up and we do not hear the alarm until he lifts his fully functioning ear off the pillow. Later, when he is asked, 'you know you can get this on CD ... in stereo?' he replies, 'It wouldn't matter to me.'

In the climactic gun battle, Freddie has a gunshot go off next to his fully functioning ear, and blood trickles out just to underline that his hearing is damaged. The film has already instilled dramatic and aesthetic precedents for what happens in this scene. The images intercut slow and normal motion, and the presence of tinnitus on the soundtrack offers a degree of unity between these two visual techniques by replacing the viewer/listener's need for fully synchronized sound. The actual tinnitus sound is very high-pitched, loud and also changes in volume, accompanied by some abstract fragments of electronic sound. It is not pleasant to listen to (unless the listener derives masochistic pleasure from intensely piercing frequencies) and, by inducing an unpleasant sensation, allows the viewer/listener to partially experience Freddie's current state – he is in pain, confused, and his judgement is impaired.

Elem Klimov's *Come and See* (1985) also uses a blood trickle from Florya (Aleksey Kravchenko), the main character's nose, but relies on the sound mix itself to instigate the formal shift to impaired hearing. Set in Belorussia during the Second World War, two children are caught in an airborne assault by German troops. After an initial bombardment, the explosions gradually become more muted in tone, the earth scattering but no longer making any sound, the German machine guns silently splintering the trees into destruction as the tinnitus ring starts to dominate the soundtrack. Florya's voice has an internalized tonality (that is to say, recorded close up and without ambient or reflected sound accompanying the direct sound of the voice) and the voices of the German soldiers are processed as being distant, scrambled and abstracted. The aesthetic is not purely reductive – we hear a sound montage of German marching soldiers, and German music through a gramophone, both of which are harsh and piercing, fusing the political and the sensory in Florya's experience of the moment.

What this allows the film to do is to go into a sound aesthetic that is removed from realistic representation, and so enter a more expressive world of Florya's point-of-audition. The tinnitus has become a trigger, a route into another cinematic form, and wrench in the characters' lives (the German attack also separates them from their comrades in the resistance). The musical score gradually becomes dominant and the sound mix selects and foregrounds different sounds from shot to shot, ignoring any sense of temporal continuity. As Florya and Glasha (Olga Mironova) frolic through the forest as a rain shower descends, their voices are not heard (though they can be seen speaking to each other) but the miniscule sound of droplets of water sprinkling on leaves is heard. As Glasha dances, Florya imagines a musical accompaniment when there is none for them to hear, yet her footsteps are silent. The effect is closer to silent cinema, the missing sounds imagined by the character, or us. The sound aesthetic of conventional narrative sound cinema is sidelined by the tinnitus effect, taking us to a sound space where the filmmaker can explore the possibilities of timbre and selective perception.

In both *Copland* and *Come and See*, the sound we hear is point-of-audition, but the images are not point-of-view. We hear the world through the character's ears, but we do not see the world through their eyes. The subjective transformation has taken place only in an auditory sense, not the visual sense, but has relied on narrative visual clues to make it possible. This is a purely cinematic or televisual possibility, the division of our senses between two physically impossible points-of-view/audition. Only through careful contextualization of narrative information is this possible as a formal shift.

Alienation

Michael O'Toole suggests that tinnitus can cause major shifts in temperament and mood with subsequent social effects:

> Worst of all, perhaps, is the overwhelming feeling of social isolation which sufferers may encounter. The sounds can build a barrier between the person hearing them and the rest of society. This leads to introspection which strengthens the disinclination to reach out to non-sufferers.
>
> (O'Toole, 1995, 5)

Michael Dowse's *It's All Gone Pete Tong* (2004) uses this unfortunate side effect of hearing loss as part of its narrative – we see the effects this has on Frankie Wilde (Paul Kaye) as he gradually loses his ability to hear, his social connections, his marriage, his music, and everything that he previously held dear. The deterioration is represented by subjective sound perspectives of muffled voices, ringing and the sound of him trying to clear his ears of non-existent blockages. This pattern of behaviour reaches its zenith when he violently wrecks his recording studio, and then turns up the volume on the mixing desk well into the red without a sound being heard. The poignancy of this is underlined by total silence – that rare thing in cinema.

Matthew Saville's *Noise* (2007) is about a Melbourne policeman, Constable Graham McGahan (Brendan Cowell), who is assigned to light duties after being diagnosed with tinnitus while a serial killer is loose in the city. The film delights in the aesthetic variety offered by noise, exploring both the textural possibilities of environmental noise and a multitude of point-of-audition tinnitus sounds which only Constable McGahan experiences. The policeman's tinnitus is by turns a plot device, motivating conflict between him and his sergeant, a way of obscuring the sound of other characters' movements and also a depiction of the pain which the condition causes. A particularly moving scene shows Constable McGahan switching on every possible sound-generating device in his house to try to dull the noises in his head, with the cacophony he creates allowing us to really understand the effect this is having on him as a person. *Noise* presents us with a study of the condition which takes the viewer/listener away from the convention of the high-pitched ringing and adds a more varied selection of tonalities, as well as a depiction of the social effects the condition has for long-term sufferers.

In the opening scene to Alfonso Cuaron's *Children of Men* (2006), Theo Faron, played by Clive Owen, gets an attack of tinnitus after a bomb explodes nearby. This allows Theo to seem disconnected from the world he lives in – as his colleagues grieve over the death of the youngest living person, his lack of concern is emphasized by his tinnitus and slight deafness muffling the sound of the world around him. In narrative terms, his character arc is from an apathetic disillusionment to reluctant hero and eventual saviour, and the tinnitus is an important part in underlining his initial detachment from society.

Contrast and dynamics

Klimov's *Come and See* has been widely cited as an influence on Steven Spielberg's *Saving Private Ryan* (1998), which also uses hearing loss in the two major battles, at the start and towards the end of the film. Sound designer Gary Rydstrom, who worked on the film, comments:

> Spielberg ... knows the importance of contrast: he built into the scene 'hooks' that we could use to give a scene, that could have been unrelenting, moments of contrast .... The [idea] was the Tom Hanks character would be shell-shocked and lose hearing. We would go into a point-of-view, into the Tom Hanks character, and the natural sounds of battle would drop away. We were left with what I tried to make into a sort of listening to a sea-shell kind of roar, all the realistic sounds drifted away, dropped away, and it gave us another point-of-view on battle. So now we

are seeing images without having realistic sounds go with them and that becomes a different take on it. We can see a man carrying his arm but we are not hearing the reality of it, and we take that in very differently than we were earlier on. He was shifting the perspective that way and making use of these stylistic techniques to offer us the possibility of contrast in the sound, which was really brilliant.

(cited in Sergi, 2004, 178–9)

In the film there is no direct reference to hearing loss, and because of this the use of a cinematic hearing-loss effect does seem to be a little incongruous – as though it has been done purely for this contrast in volume, to give the listener's ears a rest from the cacophony of battle. It comes across as the filmmaker making a stylistic decision rather than the character experiencing a condition, similar to the third-person sound perspective in *Leaving Las Vegas*. That is not to diminish the impact of the moment, but to suggest that, used in this way, the effect is not an outright attempt at a representation of a character's state of mind or sensory experience. Bryan Singer's *Valkyrie* (2008) is another example of a filmmaker using the state of hearing loss as a respite from an overwhelming battle sequence.

There is another important function of the tinnitus effect which is to withhold information from characters or the viewer/listener. The use of the tinnitus effect in the climactic gun battle in *Copland* allows characters to literally spring from nowhere, their arrival not pre-empted by their footsteps or body movements as might be expected as they attempt to shoot Freddie by surprise. Language is only visible as mouths moving, not audible, so removing any ability to negotiate – Freddie's assailants may be telling him to put the gun down, but he cannot hear them.

Jacques Audiard's *Read My Lips* (2001) is about Carla (Emmanuelle Devos), a partially deaf woman who can lip-read, and her relationship with Paul, who is a petty criminal given a work placement alongside her. The film quickly establishes the narrative as being from Carla's perspective by using 'point-of-audition' sound rather than 'point-of-view' vision. An early scene features Carla putting on a hearing aid. As she attempts to adjust and fit the device, we hear highly amplified clicks and scrapes synchronous with her physical manipulations. Once the device is fitted, we move from what was an almost silent background ambience to the more conventional hum of the office in which she is sitting. Visual framing is important here: the hearing aid is in extreme close-up, and using shallow depth of field to exclude the visual sense of anything other than the hearing aid and Carla's ear. This leaves no doubt in the viewer/listener's mind as to the cause of the amplified and close-up sound and allows the film to then move to Carla's point-of-audition when required by using the film's own established convention of the hearing aid.

In scenes reminiscent of Alfred Hitchcock's *Rear Window* (1954), the film uses the main character's deafness as a way to shut her out from key information made clear to the viewer/listener, and her ability to lip-read as a way for her to gain extra knowledge without hearing. The film's tense denouement relies on a conversation between her and Paul with her reading his lips, but the viewer cannot understand their dialogue unless we are able to lip-read French. This creates considerable dramatic tension, and although not a formal muting of the voice as in the silent era, it is a very deft combination of obscured sound in service of the narrative.

Cinematic tinnitus introduces a sound which has no direct visual representation, has only start and end points in terms of synchronicity and has no parallels in naturally occurring acoustic sound. The sound of cinematic tinnitus is most commonly much closer to a violin or synthesizer. In most cases it could be considered diegetic in that it is part of the story world, although not heard by more than one character. Tinnitus allows transition between various states in terms of point-of-view/audition and opens up creative possibilities in sound which the third-person perspective cannot permit in otherwise conventional dramatic form.

But are cinematic hearing loss and tinnitus better equipped than any other medium to represent the conditions to which they purport? Certainly, the linkage between occasional moments of tinnitus I have experienced and what we hear in these films seems to have a degree of verisimilitude, more so than any other form of communication. But how could I possibly speak for anyone else? The interface between thought and of language, whether written, spoken or signed, is problematic in describing the ways in which hearing effects can sound to the individual. Although creatively rich, poetic, poignant and artistic, tinnitus and hearing loss are no more or less cinematic constructs than any other technique. Their ultimate intangibility is perhaps what brings them closer in essence to an emotion rather than a physical presence and, by that virtue, they are better suited to artistic expression than empirical definition or quantification. The gap between direct experience and representation is creatively rich in the use of tinnitus in cinema.

10

Sshhh

Daniel Cookney

*There is no such thing as an empty space or an empty time.
There is always something to see, something to hear. In fact, try
as we may to make a silence, we cannot.*

(CAGE, 1961, 8)

A heavy bass line is my kind of silence.

(RASCAL AND VAN HELDEN, 2009)

This chapter documents a process undertaken by the author in summer 2010. Submitted as part of the University of Salford's MA Communication Design programme, the study resulted in a practice-based outcome – a compact disc of audio recordings housed within an illustrated book – that aimed to capitalize on a grey area located somewhere between noise and silence.

The Cagean fascination with background noise was key to this exploration, given how it has largely been derived through its ability to communicate while avoiding some contrived message aimed directly at the receiver. Unlike music, the random chatter and clatter of life in motion refuted the composer's creative agenda with any unclaimed aural turbulence being an approximation of Barthes' 'death of the author'. However, that accompanying birth of the listener was only really facilitated when an individual chose actively to meditate on these supposedly low-impact sounds. In general, these *were* ignored and often shifted away from concepts of 'noise' and back to a similarly ill-defined 'silence': a phenomenon that was noted as consistently mutating in tandem with those developments in noise perception.

Avoiding sonic politics, it *was* possible to define silence. The agreed thresholds of perceivable sound have located this nothingness outside of the range between 20 hertz to 20 kilohertz. And, even while within that particular range there may lie 'a whole cartography of sonic force' (Goodman, 2010, 9), much of what *could* register on this scale of perception simply failed to do so: among us, it had little actual impact. While all of this supposed emptiness was, as Cage might have suggested, completely full, the almost involuntary self-filtering of everyday noise from an individual's sonic environment, as well as selecting these spaces based on personal preference, had – it was argued – resulted in an anomaly of relative or subjective silence that remained impossible to map.

In addition, the impact of 'silence subjectivity' had the ability to affect audio content that was not designed to be ignored. The physicality of modern bass music, for example, was observed as rendered practically inert by modern listening practices. The fact that, via an already sonically compromised MP3 file, a track by Rusko or Skream could have its split stereo signal half-listened to through either 'R' or 'L' while a youth iPod audience supposedly retained one ear for further sensory stimulation. Witnessed within an inner-city classroom, there was a repeated process of 'select + deselect' with what was now only *arguably* described as 'the listener' capable of constructing an individual and hierarchical sonic backdrop. Challenged about its appropriateness within a learning environment, arguments were put forward that this background sound aided concentration. This development may have recounted Dizzee Rascal's assertion that a heavy bass line *could* be a kind of silence: a low end rumble seeming to register as a base-level zero on that scale of personal disruption. It was far from the 'hypodermic model' of musical effects as described by Stuessy. If anything, the kind of described listening experience in such a media-rich society was in complete contrast to that 'direct, unfettered freeway straight into the mind' (Walser, 1993, 141).

Here the potentially potent was reduced to little more than the oft-ignored 'muzak': the piped background melodies described by Kraftwerk as both 'sound pollution' (Bussy, 1993, 121) and 'a sort of valium' (Bizot, 1991, cited in Bussy, 1993, 153) and 'akin to castration' and 'the embalming fluid of earthly boredom' according to Attali and Schafer respectively (cited in Milner, 2010, 200). There is, however, a distinction to be made: whereas the observed personally constructed contexts in the classroom were democratic, muzak was more likely prescribed as an oppressive output that has relied on a definition of the listener as passive: a compliant, even impotent, inhabitant of a predetermined acoustic space. Subsequently derided as 'an emollient music ... which numbs the listener in order to promote uniformity and placidity' (Gilbert and Pearson, 1999, 129), muzak's supposedly innocuous 'easy listening' strains have been enforced to help eradicate these more random personal expressions of sound: exercising control over silence – particularly in spaces such as lifts and shopping malls – while presumably avoiding the assumed awkwardness that could be attributed to our placement in the sonically barren. But, while affecting wherever it has been introduced, muzak could also be a sound-bed for a quiet revolution through everyday non-compliance. In Russolo's 'families of noises' it may be the whispers, murmurs, mumbling, muttering and gurgling that attempt to *only just* be heard amidst the predetermined sounds; those incidental sounds that Cage may have lamented when bemoaning music's perfectness and its inability to describe 'the fallibility of humans' (Milner, 2010, 198). 'Sounds that reflect our reality while also critiquing it', as Attali would prefer (Milner, 2010, 200). Yet such is the power of muzak that only brief bursts of this low-level acoustic anarchy usually transpired before the well-mannered instrumental suppressed the outbreak, and compliance inevitably resumed.

There was, in addition, a further kinship between the listening processes of 'deselection' with ambient music. Brian Eno – the pioneer of this supposedly 'background' form – described a utilitarian soundscape that was able to 'accommodate many levels of listening attention without enforcing one in particular ... as ignorable as it is interesting' (Eno, quoted in Toop, 2001, 9). Considering it a benign if 'garbage' art form, he also praised muzak for its 'generous humility' (Frith and Horne, 1987, 170). While aware of their respective limitations, the functional properties of both muzak and ambient music prompted the questioning of the sounds within other shared environments. However, an initial exploration suggested that public spaces which had traditionally been recognized for dictating oppressive sonic codes had noticeably become more democratic in recent times.

Libraries, as a particularly notable example, were once observed as spaces for scholars that attempted to maintain absolute silence. However, they have since evolved to become more welcoming organizations aimed at the wider population. These more relaxed variations have then come to allow the various personal disruptions and disturbances that their respective visitors bring. Sonically, these have then been redefined as synergistic spaces that have been thankfully devoid of the risible passive-aggressive politeness of muzak or some new age-y *Music for Libraries*. But, of late, they had become far less likely to be sonically enslaved to the clichéd 'sshhh'-wielding librarian. Subsequently – and particularly in response to the question raised elsewhere in this volume regarding how noise or lack of noise is commodified – the role of the library and its relationship to the concept of subjective silence was

Figure 10.1 Aerial view of the British Library at St Pancras © British Library Board

one that typified the changing nature of sonic environments. Investigating this further, the British Library at St Pancras, London, emerged as especially interesting in its relationship to both silence and noise (Figure 10.1).

While created in 1973 as a legal deposit for all books published in the United Kingdom and Northern Ireland, the building on Euston Road has been the British Library's primary location since 1997. The depository's opening followed Colin St John's 35 difficult years working towards its construction. Its setbacks (culminating in what the architect described as his '30-year war') included major budget implications while the build process was also stalled by British governmental changes. Its large piazza – now containing sculptures by Anthony Gormley and Eduardo Paolozzi (but once a contentious part of the scheme when originally proposed for a Bloomsbury site) – set the library back from the London traffic. Stylistically, the architecture is influenced, in part, by Scandinavian modernism and, in other places, by more traditional Victorian brickwork. Internally the British Library at St Pancras is dominated by an airy foyer that quickly replaces the noise and chaos of Euston Road with its own, very personal acoustic environment. As with many public spaces, the hard materials used in its construction and the open-plan design do little to control the cacophony of its human traffic. On the contrary, St John's scheme may be seen as a purposeful part of the reimagining of the library as a space that relies on the 'buzz' of its users. For Russolo, it could have the potential for providing many of the instruments for his futurist orchestra – although just stopping short of delivering 'explosions' or 'death-rattles'. A concession to 'silence' in a more traditional form could be represented in the organization's noted King's Library (Figure 10.1).

Figure 10.2 Kings Library, the British Library at St Pancras © British Library Board

Here, within a four-storey glazed tower found centrally placed within the main building, manuscripts dating from between 1763 and 1820 are contained. Unlike the main collection, the contents of this vast smoked glass coffin appear to be static historic documents that are sheltered reverentially from the activities associated with twenty-first-century existence. Presumably climate controlled, there is a sense that the view from its shelves is also muted: shielded – unlike visitors – from the adjacent laptop tapping and café culture. And, while books in domestic environs have been placed into alcoves to absorb the sounds of noisy neighbours, these antiques are spared that task. These know only of silence.

Beyond the library's initial and most public of spaces, further reading rooms have been devised according to discipline. It is in these spaces that visitors can find a more traditional observance of the quiet study area (Figure 10.3).

Figure 10.3 Reading room at the British Library at St Pancras © British Library Board

Access to both the rooms and the vast collected materials is strictly controlled. Here the hushed adoration of that combined literary endeavour is apparent and, in places, almost monastic.

This, however, represented just one 'library'. Due to the sheer breadth of individual spaces described by the term, it was quite possible to complete a study of these spaces that would be solely concerned with typology. Interestingly this could 'classify the classified': then highlighting a direct relationship between subject and methodology while providing an index of related environments that examines their acoustic effects. Initially, while leaning towards this taxonomy aspect, other libraries in France, Denmark and Sweden were documented by the author. Each of these recorded spaces provided very individual data that only further demonstrated the changing nature of these organizations. Malmö's Stadsbiblioteket, as one example,

Figure 10.4 Stadsbiblioteket, Malmö by Daniel Cookney

was a clean and contemporary 'family-friendly' establishment equipped with such devices as under-floor conveyor belts capable of taking returned books to waiting staff (Figure 10.4).

Beneath thick glass panels, hardbacks zoomed quietly beneath the feet of visitors. Providing those necessary and predetermined quiet spaces, supposedly secluded yet ultimately visible work units were stacked on top of each other in the vast atrium-style hall. The arrangement of these single-person pods appeared to mirror the bookshelves. Copenhagen's Black Diamond was equally cavernous but, while an extension to a more established library in the Danish capital, the strikingly modern building had also developed a reputation for playing host to music concerts (Figure 10.5). Recognition for its role in these performances may, for many, eclipse its activities as a study resource and lender of books. It had certainly affected its footfall.

Figure 10.5 Black Diamond library, Copenhagen by Karsten Bundgaard+ © The Royal Library, Copenhagen, Denmark

However, within all of these explored environments, the book remained an iconic format; but only inasmuch as iTunes had used a logo featuring a CD long after its associated hardware had helped disassemble the signifi- cance of physical media. The monetizing parts of the organization – such as gift shops and the various catering options – were representative of the changing nature of the library: where non-borrowers were utilizing the space as they wished with their actions noted as further altering that acoustic environment.

One way that was identified as being able to draw attention to these oft-ignored changes was through the kinds of practices associated with 'found sound' recording artists like Matthew Herbert, Matmos, Scanner and Akufen. Each of these electronic mavericks had gained a reputation for intricate projects which reworked everyday audio into new, musical compositions that challenged traditional notations of musicianship, instrumentation and the romantic concept of the author. Herbert's project *One Pig* (2011), for example, had already caused debate during its production. The outlined process involved recording the noises made within a pig's life cycle including its slaughter – although Herbert did encounter some difficulties finding an abattoir and attending vet willing to allow the recording of this act. After being condemned by PETA (People for the Ethical Treatment of Animals) as 'cruelty as entertainment' and prompting a Facebook campaign to prevent the completed project's release in October 2011, the sample manipulator issued a statement explaining that the subject of his work was born on a farm that raises animals for consumption. Herbert pointed out that his project would not interfere in any way with these events but also made a case for the right to draw attention to just how meat is produced. Subsequently this work had become less about 'entertainment' and more about challenging ideas: 'life in the context of an otherwise anonymous food chain' (Anon, 2011) versus the arguably hypocritical squeamishness that can develop when faced with the truth about the product sold in supermarkets.

Less contentiously, the German Ostgut Ton label released the 2010 *Fünf* compilation featuring music crafted from field recordings made inside two Berlin clubs: Berghain and the Panorama Bar. Seemingly informed by the tradition of *musique concrète*, the concept and original recordings were devised by the producer Emika. These files were catalogued in a four-gigabyte library of sounds that were, in turn, made available to Ostgut Ton artists and other remixers as part of the label's five-year anniversary. Instigated by DJ conversations that highlighted the influence of the respective areas on their club sets, the recordings included capturing the sounds made by lighting, refrigerated rooms and ventilation systems before being reassembled as a series of largely techno-oriented outputs.

There was a comparison here to the philosophy behind the seminal *4'33"* composition. Cage's three-part music movement that the performers were instructed *not* to play essentially prompted any assembled audience to focus instead on the sounds emanating from a specific environment. LaBelle looked at this process while describing a 'presence through absence' (LaBelle, 2006, 173) and, here, the importance that *wasn't* placed on performance is turned towards the Cage-loved 'activity of sound' – background noise, only perhaps more so given how the *Fünf* project actually brought that noise to the fore.

While field recordings similarly captured the sonic activity in the studied library spaces, their manipulation was eventually seen as unnecessary in order to draw attention to their existence. The British Library's gift shop was instrumental in this decision, given how compact disc-formatted recordings of rainforests and birdsong were found to be on sale. The suggestion of the appropriation of a sonic environment within a completely different space even hinted at further, more relevant marketable opportunities for these raw recordings. If the British Library had come to represent both a considerable amount of collated intellectual ambition and a productive space to study, the sounds – or that even more abstract suggestion of 'ambience' – could be perceived as a transferable distillation of those qualities. In principle, these recordings had the potential to be viewed as having the power to transform the most intellectually redundant spaces. Essentially, this involved the assigning of socially produced rather than materially based values that, in art terms, perhaps reached its zenith with Marcel Duchamp's *50cc of Paris Air*: an 'empty' small glass ampoule originally purchased from a Parisian pharmacist in 1919. The library recordings could also be argued as being in the vein of this 'readymade', given how the reappropriation of sound severed the traditional ties between the original producer and recognized author of the work. However, with this in mind, there was also an underlying issue when first attempting to acoustically catalogue these spaces: Should the field recordings attempt to completely avoid sonically impacting on the environment? Or should any activity within that public space naturally equate with participation in what should be a democratic, collaborative soundtrack?

When seeking permission from the British Library to make the recordings, guidance was given to ensure that the process should not interrupt any of the everyday practices within the building. The pragmatic approach – especially when not wishing to influence the modification of visitors' behaviour (and, especially, the associated sounds) – was to discretely document the space in a way that almost denied the existence of the process, thereby limiting the impact on those activities that were routinely involved in the space. In addition, unlike Herbert, Ostgut Ton *et al.*, the avoidance of further processing the raw recordings was also tied to the author's own practice-based work: design rather than acoustics or music. Instead, accompanying the audio content, a series of complementary visual works was planned that would aim to pictorially describe and communicate the various acoustic effects.

The decision to concentrate solely on the British Library, coupled with the research that defined sounds as purely linked to their environment, made that one space completely integral to the form and content of any deliverables. As part of this, the organization's 'brand guidelines' had ramifications. Within the British Library's communication manifesto, the emphasis on 'knowledge' – its advancement and experiencing of – was related to a series of words such as 'discover' and 'explore'. The potential to challenge traditional ideas of the library was also confirmed with the assertion that the British Library should be communicated externally as 'bold', 'contemporary' and 'dynamic'. The British Library's architecture had already embodied these themes although not without some criticism. Some observers had found difficulty in the juxtaposition between its weighty tradition (relating largely to that mass of held literary work) and the more abstract aspects of the building. But its seeming irreverence for sentimentality then found itself mirrored in the design and layout for Roger Stonehouse and Gerhard Stromberg's book, *The Architecture of the British Library at St Pancras* (2004) and further weighted this study towards a practice-based outcome with an unashamedly modern aesthetic.

Stonehouse and Stromberg's publication, however, was a largely photographic exploration of the space that appeared to be predominantly interested in the structure of the building itself. Subsequently this documenting of the organization had avoided human interruption or interaction. Each image had a 'stillness' that was generated by monochromatic depictions of lifeless, perhaps even 'cold', environments. These *were* ultimately silent. And the images were seemingly unrecognizable from how the space works in reality

Figure 10.6 Detail from *The Sounds of the British Library* by Daniel Cookney

for a number of reasons. First, that layer of background noise – from phone conversations, footsteps or machinery – was not represented. Instead, the pictures boasted a clarity seemingly straight out of the modernist lifestyle pages of *Wallpaper magazine. Further to this, each one featured a visually unobstructed view while, in situ, a visitor would more likely be given intermittent glances of Colin St John's interior between the constant movement of library users. From this grew an idea to visually emulate Cage's work that used sound (or, perhaps more accurately, a lack of sound) to also direct attention back to the environment. The devising of the collected images to accompany the recordings involved the concept based around them communicating the kinds of visual disruption and to provide metaphors for how sound existed within the spaces. In addition, it was decided to avoid imagery that might attribute those sounds to a particular cause. Subsequently, like Stonehouse and Stromberg's offering, the completed project does not contain people, yet still highlights the disruption of the space (Figure 10.6).

John Cage's *4'33"* not only provided part of the theoretical framework regarding background noise and silence, environments and authorship. The name of the work also influenced the titles of the individual audio tracks on the compact disc. All of the field recordings were therefore defined by their

Figure 10.7 Detail from *The Sounds of the British Library* by Daniel Cookney

length in minutes and seconds: an indexing that, it was surmised, would not predetermine an audience's response to the sound. The time codes arguably offered the kind of objectivity that was hoped might also take place through encountering the package's more abstract visual elements.

Furthermore – taking inspiration from the 'found sound' artists – some of the images from Stonehouse and Stromberg's book were used within the project in a reworked format. Changes and variations in scanning resolution, for example, were intended as an indication of the varying degrees of perceived disruption using the secondary images. Other uses of this material included the importing of further elements to suggest physical layers of sound while more dominant geometric additions were a reaction to more ominous pockets of sonic activity or the refraction of sound (Figure 10.7).

The grids for these were, in turn, influenced by the axonometric and isometric projections of St John's architectural proposals and suggested an angular form of sound representation that, again, were very much tied to their environment. The culmination of the project was preoccupied with the interaction between style and content. The completed book was constructed using traditional bookbinding methods in tandem with the specialist mainte-nance that continues in order to preserve the library's volumes (Figure 10.8).

Figure 10.8 Detail from *The Sounds of the British Library* by Daniel Cookney

As a nod to the building's interior, a mix of contemporary irreverence and neo-classicism dominated the book's aesthetic (and perhaps found some kinship in early work by Peter Saville). Intended to visually represent a shorthand for the way in which the organization currently works, the publication also tried to define a style that could work for some viewers on that irreverent level. Yet it *could* still suggest a weightier, respectful approximation when read by a different audience. The book, titled *The Sounds of the British Library*, may be judged as something that captured the ambience of the British Library while also allowing for its appraisal as a mere design-led curiosity. To tackle this, it was beleived that a solution should not lean too strongly one way or the other: it would not be presented as a truly ironic gesture, nor as a 'lofty' product. The use of book cloth was essential for this as, alongside strong typography, it highlighted a simple fusion of the new and the established. Text, throughout, was represented through the humanist Syntax typeface – as used in all British Library communication. The various pages explored alternative ways to present those data alongside the recordings in a way that could be used almost as a meditative product supposedly imbibed with this knowledge-steeped environment. Inspiration was also taken from Mike Cina's visceral sleeve designs for American record label Ghostly International: a series that had given an abstract form to recordings and appeared, most importantly, to enhance the experience of those audio products.

This visualization process could have taken a number of alternative paths given the visual documentation of sound's extensive history. While acknowledged mainly for its concern with artistic reinterpretations of music, it can be traced back through Isaac Newton's colour music wheel of 1704 and the even older practice of creating notational manuscripts. Initial research within this particular investigation had naturally catalogued many of the traditional and contemporary ways in which sound had been given a visual form; but what was argued from the outset was that all sound visualizations are simply interpretations.

However, one difficulty that was encountered when considering this visual interpretation of sound was how to define a boundary. Even when solely considering 'music' (what we may view as noise's more politely and purposefully arranged counterpart) it had become necessary to agree on parameters. Otherwise it was possible to argue – quite convincingly – that dance has been but a visual display of music. Certainly, a literature review as part of this research project that involved seemingly specific phenomena like synaesthesia uncovered commentators who were prepared to divert into discussion of Busby Berkeley's choreography. That is despite there being no evidence that Berkeley was even a synaesthete. And while the kaleidoscopic spectacles generated through his Hollywood routines could present an almost irresistible urge to find some relationship to the geometry that might emerge through cymatics (i.e. the study of visible sound vibrations that can result in curious repeat patterns), it was essential for this study to avoid trying to investigate and, most importantly, *link* each visual interpretation of sound. So, while synaesthesia may have triggered what may be described as something close to a 'natural' (or, at least, *involuntary*) visualization of sound, the resulting information that came through this cross-sensory confusion was known to vary significantly among those with the condition. As a result, any correlation between audible and visible appeared to be unique and defined by the configuring of the individual's synapses. Cymatics, on the other hand, may have been argued as giving physical form to the effects of sound yet these too tended to be produced via the intervention of man-made equipment. Similarly, everything from music notation to technology offered different ways to 'see' sound but these were just individual systems employed to map specific elements: to compare one sound's relationship to another. Like language, these were just constructed codes and, as such, it was up to the individual to judge their relevance and value.

Figure 10.9 Detail from *The Sounds of the British Library* by Daniel Cookney

Considering onomatopoeia as an alternative embodiment of sound, one work within the finished book/compact disc package attempted to phonetically transcribe a recording from the British Library's cloakroom (Figure 10.9).

Usually more evident in the work of Roy Lichtenstein – whose 'Whaam!' and 'Blam!' re-enact the static explosion of the comic book for the often silent gallery space – this page prepared a visual/aural partnership that is perhaps most agreed upon: that which related to linguistics. Relatedly, while looking at musical notation and attempting to define that initial boundary, Birkhoff's 'Polygonal Forms' were of interest. Largely viewed as unfit for their original purpose as music notation, the various forms were perceived by the mathematician as being able to perform a similar task to the shapes within psychologist Wolfgang Köhler's infamous Bouba-Kiki Effect of 1929. While perception alters how any proposed image may be read, the Bouba-Kiki had defined such forms as having inherent meaning with its contrasting shapes indicating the sharp and staccato or more flowing and legato.

The works of Oskar Fischinger, The Whitney Brothers, Wassily Kandinsky and others were also investigated, but these provided few individual exchanges between an aural and visual stimulus that could actually be easily transferred: all of these works appeared to bridge sight and sound by appointing somewhat arbitrary exchange values. Viewing an additional selection of visual material also assisted with the consideration of whether a visual accompaniment to music was just that – an *accompaniment to* – or was, in fact, something with more of a symbiotic relationship: perhaps where a singular sensory effect was actually heightened by the other. Synaesthesia research had suggested that memory can be enhanced by cross-sensory interplay. This was not ignored – especially when considering the highlighting of background sound with the addition of visual metaphors. This was, in turn, also considered with regard to the value of 'the experience' within the development of the marketable product.

Exploring silence's relative or interpretive understanding, while attempting to visually mimic background noise, also involved the rejection of a number of rudimentary considerations. Of the basic interpretations that were ruled out during the very early stages of the project, general whiteness was considered to be too clean to really illustrate what was a generally confused or messy breed of silence. However, in conclusion, this process did prompt a future recommendation for visual material that could attempt to discuss that more 'absolute' silence. References have suggested that this phenomenon could be construed as being representative of everything from peace to spirituality, hostility to death. The latter, it was noted, could also be illustrated by the Japanese ideophone of 'shiin': a word that conjures 'absolute silence' *and* 'death'. That similarity between 'shiin' and our own 'sshhh' may not be quite so coincidental, either. Especially, invoking Cage and Attali, we should review the subsequent absence of sound urged by the utterance as 'sshhh' as documenting the absence of life.

11

Thunder and lightning:
noise, aesthetics and audio-visual avant-garde practice
Rob Gawthrop

Head[1]

This chapter starts from the premise that noise is not an art form but is positioned within (or outside) an aesthetic/anti-aesthetic dialectic. The presence of noise has rarely been absent of meaning or without affect. Culturally the deployment or reception of noise may be deliberate or incidental but its perception cannot be separated from its context or from the memory of experience. Such experience includes the visual, spatial and conceptual within cultural and socio-political contexts.

Noise here is considered in relation to specific twentieth-century avant-garde artistic practices (up until *circa* 1968). Avant-garde in this respect is considered as any politically advanced or progressive cultural practice. This includes avant-garde and underground cinema, experimental film, music and performance. When considered in relation to contemporary aesthetics and postmodern theory, avant-garde cinema in particular has produced many notable works that raise questions about our experience of music and noise, what it is and how it can be articulated.

Thunder and Lightning

Thunder and lightning name and identify the aural and visual phenomena of an electrical discharge to earth from charged particles in the sky. The connection between time and distance and the perceptual difference in speed between light and sound is recognized even in childhood. Pierre Schaeffer recuperated the term *acousmatic* from Pythagoras's use of the Greek 'acousma': what is heard (Pythagoras gave his lectures from behind a screen so that his physical presence would not cause distraction). Schaeffer used 'acousmatic' to describe the separation of a sound from its source, not as temporal separation as with thunder and lightning, but to deny its source.

A storm is one of the noisiest natural occurrences that can be experienced and, at night, there is the most extreme contrast between light and dark – not unlike a flash frame in film. Electric storms occur through forces over which we have no control. Thunder had generally been considered to be a manifestation of gods in myths and stories. Aristotle is believed to have given the earliest material reason for such storms and, after Isaac Newton and the Enlightenment, theologies and myths that previously explained causes of thunder have been rendered obsolete or reduced to metaphor. The extreme loudness of thunder and the intensity of the flashes of light are nevertheless evidence of forces of nature that can instil fear. The possibilities of being struck by lightning, spontaneous combustion, flight of animals, flood, the smell of ozone and attendant phenomena such as hair standing on end become very real. Through depiction, with the sense of danger removed, storms become spectacle and enter the domain of the sublime (and its association with awe, terror and veneration)[2] and, through implication, the aesthetics of noise.

Most artworks concerning lightning are representational but Walter De Maria's *Lightning Field* is an exception, since it is:

a work of Land Art situated in a remote area of the high desert of western New Mexico. It is comprised of 400 polished stainless steel poles installed in a grid array measuring one mile by one kilometre. The poles – two inches in diameter and averaging 20 feet and 7½ inches in height – are spaced 220 feet apart and have solid pointed tips that define a horizontal plane. A sculpture to be walked in as well as viewed, *The Lightning Field* is intended to be experienced over an extended period of time. A full experience of *The Lightning Field* does not depend upon the occurrence of lightning, and visitors are encouraged to spend as much time as possible in the field, especially during sunset and sunrise.

(Dia Art, 2011, n.p.)

Most people only experience this work through photographic documentation and those who have visited the site are unlikely to have done so during an electric storm. Stan Brakhage's *Fire of Waters* (1965) is a 16mm film of mainly black frames with glimpses of a street, houses and windows lit and exposed by lightning. Thunder is absent; instead there is a buzzing sound, possibly faulty neon lighting. Crackles similar to the end of a scratched record lead to the sound of magnetic tape rapidly speeding up, ending with yelping sounds. In this, rather than resorting to aural depiction, Brakhage uses a more subtle use of noise in his attempt at (as Jacques Rancière would say) 'representing the unrepresentable' (Rancière, 2009, 126–7). Henri-Georges Clouzot used silence to depict the explosion of a tanker of nitro-glycerine (and the death of its drivers) in *Wages of Fear* (1953) by showing a cigarette paper blowing off a dashboard with a plume of smoke appearing in the distance. The explosion is louder in the imagination than it ever could be through a loudspeaker.

What?

The cultural use of noise is as old as the cultures that have produced it. Researchers connected with the *Acoustics and Music of British Prehistory Research Cluster*[3] have found that cave paintings (including those with clusters of red dots, stencilled hands and similar) found in many locations across the globe refer to echoes and resonant frequencies. As Reznikoff proposed in 'On the Sound Dimension of Prehistoric Painted Caves and Rocks', suppositions can be made that in prehistoric times audio-visual events took place. These would have integrated the acoustic properties of the cave, marks on the walls and the flickering light from flames illuminating the spaces (Reznikoff, 1995, 542). The performer and drummer Paul Burwell spoke of people enjoying a 'good noise' when referring to fireworks or explosions (see Toop, 2007, 10). Indeed firecrackers, squibs, rattles, sistrums, bull-roarers, clapping, pipes, shawms, vocal whoops, growls and roars from all over the planet have contributed to atonal pleasures. Many instruments developed as aural imitators of animals, thunder, wind and the sea. Trap drummers in nineteenth-century Music Hall added similar sound effects and calls to performances as do foley artists in film and radio (simulating acoustically so-called realistic sounds). Physical labour, such as the pounding of grain, chopping wood or grape treading, produced noises incidental to the work songs that often accompanied or were integral to such tasks. Norm Cohen in *Worksongs: A demonstration collection of examples* proposes '"worksong" to identify an item that is actually sung during the work process' as distinct from '"occupational songs"' (Cohen, 1993, 333). Continuous noise occurs only from a limited range of sources in the natural environment such as the effect of the wind or movement of water. The amplitude of these sounds is not without affect, since when loud or increasing they can be powerful and instil fear, while sounds that are quiet or decreasing can be calming or impart a sense of tranquillity.

The European Renaissance's recuperation of Greek classicism included Pythagoras's 'Music of the Spheres'. His belief was that spatial and musical harmony was directly connected through the mystical properties of number and that the universe was in harmony. Similarly, Renaissance culture celebrated and strove to promote ideas of Arcadia – a mythical time when people and nature lived in harmony – through paintings, architecture, poetry and music. Implicit are notions of a higher order, separate from the grubbiness of everyday life. The Industrial Revolution produced a shift from the rural to the urban. The noise of machinery and the cacophony of the streets filled all waking hours. The factory owners, aspiring to aristocracy, acquired land, built gardens, listened to classical music inside their palatial houses and underwrote colonial expansion. The distinction between the music of power (in the home and the concert hall) and the noise of the populous (in the fields and in the streets) became explicit.

The Italian Futurist Luigi Russolo articulated the potential for the inclusion of noise within music in his 'Art of Noises' of 1913 (Russolo, 2004, 10–14). He cannot however be easily dissociated from the fascism of Filippo Marinetti whose earlier *Manifesto of Futurism* of 1909 proclaimed the glorification of war, patriotism, destruction of museums, libraries and academies,and espoused a virulent anti-feminism (Marinetti, 1992, 147–8). This is in sharp contrast to the Russian avant-garde that drew from the noise of labour and was demonstrated in Arseny Avraamov's *Symphony of the Sirens* of 1922 (Cutler, 2008, 19, and CD track 01). An event that involved the citizens of the Soviet city of Baku (now in Azerbaijan), where factory hooters, ships' horns and steam whistles were conducted with flags from factory roofs – a celebration of the revolution with the noises of the city at work, putting into effect the avant-garde manifestos of the Russian Futurists and Constructivists.

The development of the phonograph and the cinematograph enabled sounds and images to be reproduced, constructed and replayed. Apart from attempts to synchronize the two, sound and image were recorded separately and were generally kept apart. Culturally, film screenings were events and sound recordings were products. This separation continued with most film screenings being accompanied by live music, effects and narration while records were sold in shops. The early sound films were largely of the all-singing, all-dancing variety, constructed entirely in the studio. An exception at the time (along with the introductory section of Eisenstein and Alexandrov's 1930 film *Romance Sentimentale*) was Dziga Vertov's *Enthusiasm*, also 1930). Against all technical advice, the cumbersome recording equipment was transported across the Donbas basin to record on the railways, in the mines, steelworks and farms. This was not so much to produce a naturalistic representation as to construct an audio-visual symphony to celebrate labour and accelerate the five-year plan. The use of diegetic and non-diegetic sound and the play between noise, signification and music was, and still is, revolutionary.

Pierre Schaeffer defined *sonorous objects* as 'sounds independent of any causal reference' (Schaeffer, 2004, 79). It was not so much the separation of a sound from its source (acousmatic) but the very denial of its source that he proposed. This broke with the Western notation system 'in which phenomena are signified as values of pitch (A440), harmony (thirds, fifths, octaves), duration (whole notes, half note rests, dotted quarter notes) and rhythmic organization (3/4, 4/4, 6/8)' (Kim-Cohen, 2009, 40). Schaeffer's intention was for *musique concréte* to only signify itself and as such would conform to the extreme Romantic formalism that has characterized classical music (see Dyson, 2009, 56–8; Kim-Cohen, 2009, 12). Walter Ruttman's *Weekend* film for radio or 'blind cinema' of 1930 operated in the opposite direction. In this work, as with Vertov's experiments, the sounds used did not deny their source, despite their separation or disjuncture, and were probably the first use of aural collage.

The diverse range of approaches to cinema narrowed as narrative and the 'talkies' became dominant. Experimental, non-literary and sensory forms became increasingly marginal. As 'any art perception involves a conscious or unconscious deciphering operation', as Bourdieu argues (1993, 215), it is inevitable and obvious that dominant cultural forms will have a dominating effect and understanding becomes predetermined. Anything other than these forms becomes *different*. Some avant-garde cinematic practices, as well as opposing narrative and naturalism, also explored relationships between sound and image in ways that have hardly been recognized until comparatively recently, which will be explored later in this chapter.

Earlier criticism and theory has been largely ocular-centric or literary. Postmodernity identified (or produced) a shift away from production and autonomy of art to its reception and context. Rancière referred to aesthetics as 'a mode of articulation between forms of action, production, perception and thought. This general definition extends aesthetics beyond the strict realm of art to include the conceptual coordinates and modes of visibility operative in the political domain' (Rancière, 2004, 82). From this perspective, avant-garde films and events will be described and scrutinized in relation to how mediation and context has contributed to the experience of them.

In addition, consideration is given to the affect of visual information on the listening experience and how noise becomes music.

Thinking experience

What happens when something is encountered? This something may be an event, object, artwork or any kind of phenomena. The experience of this will be temporal and sensible (perceptible), prompting a range of modes of seeing and listening (and also feeling, moving, tasting and smelling), informed by previous experience from memory and prior knowledge. Phenomena can be ignored, reacted to or considered. This is dependent upon consciousness and degrees of decisiveness. Salomé Voegelin's Introduction to her book *Listening to Sound and Silence* outlines the problems of language in under-standing the experience of sound:

> Critical discourse does badly in dealing with sound as it assumes and insists on the gap between that which it describes and its description – it is the very opposite of sound, which is always the heard, immersive and present. Its language relegates the sonic into a position of attribute: sound is loud, clear, silent or noisy, it is fast or slow but never is it the noun under consideration. Instead it is sublimated to a visual referent, which mutes its particularity.
>
> (Voegelin, 2010, xiv)

The English language (and probably most modern European languages) is dominated by the visual with few exceptions, such as onomatopoeic words and names of specific sounds. What is seen is named (the noun), and tends to be objectified, while what we hear is denoted by the action (the verb) that produces it.

> Scholars who argue that this model is the cultural result of the visualism produced by literacy, and therefore not applicable to non-literate societies, offer another sensory paradigm for understanding the cosmologies of such societies: that of aurality, expressed in the term 'oral/aural culture'. Rather than being structured by sight, oral cultures are said to be animated by sound.
>
> (Classen, 1993, 121)

What is of concern here relates to time and how it is experienced. 'Cultural Studies', when informed by semiology, has tended to identify time through moments that can be named, described and combined within a narrative construct. In his novel *The Third Policeman*, Flann O'Brien satirizes a perceptual lack of understanding through a fictitious academic called de Selby:

> Human existence de Selby has defined as 'a succession of static experiences each infinitely brief', a conception which he is thought to have arrived at from examining some old cinematograph films which belonged probably to his nephew [...]. These are evidently the same films which he mentions in *Golden Hours* as having 'a strong repetitive element' and as being 'tedious'. Apparently he had examined them patiently picture by picture and imagined that they would be screened in the same way, failing at that time to grasp the principle of the cinematograph.
>
> (O'Brien, 1974, 44)

De Selby could have misread written music in a similar way, since when approaching normative music (music that is defined by pitch, tonality, harmony and rhythm) a *symbolic* notation system is used. This system reduces temporality to moments connected within a predefined system. The composer Steve Reich, in his 1965 essay 'Music as a Gradual Process', articulated an alternative to this (Reich, 2004, 304–6). This alternative has more in common with the majority of musics outside of the Western dominant tradition where duration, repetition and memory become integral to experience. In listening, in order to understand what it is that is being heard when there is no immediate referent, a process of comparison takes place and the listener 'refers to his memory of this type of sound, a memory resynthesized from data that are not solely acoustical, and that is itself influenced by films' (Chion, 1990, 108). As the technologies of sound recording and playback have developed it has become increasingly difficult to identify sounds heard, their provenance, their reproduction (heard through loudspeakers or headphones) or the difference between them. Listening has to contend with aural simulacra.

In *One Hundred Years of Solitude*, Marquez writes: 'The world was so recent that many things lacked names, and in order to indicate them it was necessary to point' (Marquez, 1973, 1). This act of indicating goes beyond the idea of naming. Louis Althusser described the ideological function as 'interpellation of the subject' and used the example of someone responding to being hailed in the street by a policeman (Althusser, 2002, 117–18). This moment of recognition constructed the person into a subject. When Marcel Duchamp put a bottle-rack into a gallery he did not just make a gesture about art, he enabled the bottle-rack to be approached in ways other than its originally intended function. These examples demonstrate through intentionality that when someone or something is interpellated, pointed at, positioned, framed or called, the process is both ideological *and* aesthetic. Dziga Vertov in 1924 anticipated this in relation to cinema: 'if we want to understand clearly the effect of films on the audience, we have first to agree about two things: 1. What audience? 2. What effect upon the audience are we talking about?' (quoted in LeGrice, 2001, 46). And Adolf Hitler reportedly said in 1938: 'without the loudspeaker we would never have conquered Germany' (quoted in Attali, 1985, 87). This positioning of an audience as a single mass of subjects has antecedents in classical times:

> Epidaurus was built in 330–320 BC [...]. The building is the expression of an age that saw the flourishing of mathematics, the influence of Pythagorean science and acoustics. It has remarkable acoustics for speech intelligibility, solo or unison chanting and for solo musical instruments. Rather than rising out of a single factor it is the cumulative effect of many refinements that contribute to its acoustic excellence. It can accommodate 14,000 people.
>
> (Vovolisr, 2003, 78)

The simultaneous focus on the singular and dominant (one voice, solo instrument, intelligibility) and the silencing of the (noisy and unintelligible) masses, demonstrates the ideological relationships between power, sound and technology. Andy Warhol in *Kitchen* disrupted narrative conventions by having dialogue rendered silent by the noise of grinding coffee for a long time. It could be said that the concert hall, lecture theatre and cinema are spaces where the effect is of transmitting one message to a silenced, totalized audience. This effect is simulated and dispersed through transmission into homes and workplaces through television and the internet. Sound is transduced, travelling at the speed of light '... *a speed of light* which now illuminates extension and duration with a new daylight, since it seems agreed that speed causes time to expand at the moment when it shrinks space' (Virilio, 2000, 37; emphasis in original).

Noise and picture

Experience is multisensory and sound will always be present though not always audibly. However, the see-able and the listenable do not usually have any direct connection with each other except when the source of a sound is seen or anticipated. This is reversed in performative situations, and cinema in particular. Sound will always be in juxtaposition with image and their relationship demands attention consciously or unconsciously. In narrative cinema, normative music tends to be used and accepted as an emotional reinforcement and as a temporal locating device. The diegetic and non-diegetic use of sound/music is considered in relation to pictorial space. Noise (when not acting as a signifier) confronts both the image and the viewer/listener but is unlikely to be recognized as music. Returning to Chion, we find that he refers to 'so called realistic sound' in relation to the intelligible and the construction of narrative (diegesis) (Chion, 1990, 108). In this sense noise is not intelligible but sensible. We have memories of experience and those experiences include film. Our memories do not necessarily distinguish between the lived and the mediated, and therefore it may be said that memories are mediated. In this respect noise is not neutral and is itself informed by memory and context. To repeat: to identify noise, or make noise conscious – in performance, recordings, soundtracks or events – brings it within an aesthetic regime. At this point the issue of music comes to the fore, and Douglas Kahn, in *In the Spirit of Fluxus*, outlines a problem in this respect:

> To musicalize sound is just fine from a musical perspective, but from the standpoint of an artistic practice of sound, in which *all* the material attributes of a sound, including the materiality of its signification are taken into account, musicalization is a reductive operation, a limited response to the potential of the material.
>
> (Kahn, 1983, 103; emphasis in original)

To return to Vertov and *Enthusiasm* we find that the film attempts a reflexivity by depicting the cinema auditorium, screen and audience. The film also shows cameras, recording equipment, an editing bench, microphones and loudspeakers, showing the new (as was) film technology as the means of production. Sounds and images of factory whistles, steam horns and sirens occur synchronously but are separated later in the film – the steam whistle sounds occurring at the same time as when, on the screen, cinema audiences arrive, workers walk to work and pit-head winding gear operates. The long sections of the film where this disjunction of sound and image occurs can be experienced in three ways:

1 Recognition of sounds remembered from earlier sequences of the film.

2 The meaning that is produced from these sounds in their relation to the imagery occurring both simultaneously and separately.

3 As music, in the sense that the sounds are abstracted, have an autonomy and are part of an aesthetic regime.

These correspond closely to Michel Chion's 'Three Listening Modes': 'causal' ('cause or source of the sound'); 'semantic' ('meaning of sound'), and 'reduced', where 'the sound itself may be described formally (spectral analysis, pitch etc.) or imitated' (Chion, 1990, 25–34). These modes however do not account for the emotional impact of such listening. The fact that these three listening experiences in *Enthusiasm* are in flux with each other produces more complex sets of relations. These relations cannot be separated from the viewer/listener as subject, and to quote Bourdieu:

> One may therefore distinguish, through abstraction, two extremes and opposite forms of aesthetic pleasure, separated by all the indeterminate degrees, the enjoyment which accompanies aesthetic perception reduced to simple *aesthesis*, and the *delight* procured by scholarly savouring, presupposing, as a necessary but insufficient condition, adequate deciphering [...] when the beholder's aesthetic intention is identified with the objective intention of the work (which must not be indentified with the artist's intention).
>
> (Bourdieu, 1993, 220; emphasis in original)

Rancière discusses 'mimesis' as the correspondence between 'aisthesis' as sense perceptible and 'poiesis' as making/creating: 'It is a delimitation of spaces and times, of the visible and the invisible, of speech and noise, that simultaneously determines the place and the stakes of politics as a form of experience' (Rancière, 2004, 13). *Enthusiasm* also includes speech and so presents a dialectic between the perceptible and the intelligible – mimesis and diegesis.

Artwar[4]

> Purge the world of bourgeois sickness, 'intellectual', professional and commercialized culture, PURGE the world of dead art, imitation, artificial art, abstract art, illusionist art, mathematical art, – PURGE THE WORLD OF 'EUROPEANISM'!
>
> (Maciunas in Higgins, 2002, 28; emphasis in original)

Two important aspects of Fluxus are as follows.

1   *The event*: this also corresponds to Dick Higgins' (1966) concept
    of '*The Intermedia*' (Armstrong and Rothfuss, 1993, 172–3) which

emphasizes the dialectic between different media. The event is dependent upon contexts of how it is presented, where it is presented and how it is identified. Cage's *4'33"* (1952) was originally dependent on the concert hall, the performer in evening dress and the grand piano. These were necessary components of the event at the time: 'The musicality inherent in the Event, then, while critiquing mainstream Western epistemology, also deconstructs the reification, totalization and reductionism of secondary knowledge formations (the disciplines of art history, musicology, philosophy and literature for example)' (Higgins, 2002, 55).

2 *The incidental*: where the occurrence of sound is *incidental* to the actions implied or instructed in the *score*. For example, George Brecht's instruction for *Solo For Violin, Viola Or Contrabass* (1962) consists of one word ('polishing'), where the performance that takes place is of an instrument being polished until it is clean, and the duration of the work and sound/noises produced (music) is determined by the task undertaken. This is literally the music of manual labour. The incidental has also been accommodated in free improvisation when extraneous or accidental noises and interruptions became incorporated into the performance.

The event gives identification or focus and the incidental is what happens at the same time. In respect of noise, this conforms simultaneously to its definition *and* places it within an aesthetic regime. George Brecht's *Drip Music* (1959) identifies and contextualizes itself as music by its title. The performance of this work is only dependent upon the identification of the event taking place. La Monte Young's Fluxus scores differed since the performed work was essentially durational and consequently promoted *listening*. His *Poem for Tables Chairs Benches etc.* (1960) requires the tables, etc. to be dragged across a floor so that the sounds should be as constant and as continuous as possible. *Arabic Numeral (Any Integer) to H. F.* (1960) (more commonly known as *X for Henry Flynt*) requires the performer to play an unspecified sound, or group of sounds, regularly (every one to two seconds) and as many times as the performer determines. It is the duration of these works that enables a shift of perception from gesture and noise to musicality through the time of its performance.

The destructiveness of work – as with Nam June Paik's *One for Violin Solo* (1962) for which a violin is slowly lifted up above the head, held still for a long time and then crashed down on a table – became primarily performative and related more to the destruction of bourgeois culture, as proposed in

Maciunas' text above, than to the sound produced. Noises of destruction also figure in Gustav Metzger's first manifesto 'Auto-Destructive Art':

Auto-destructive art is primarily a form of public art for industrial societies. Self-destructive painting, sculpture and construction is a total unity of idea, site, form, colour, method and timing of the disintegrative process. Auto-destructive art can be created with natural forces, traditional art techniques and technological techniques. The amplified sound of the auto-destructive process can be an element of the total conception.

(Metzger, 1965 [1959], n.p.)

The Destruction in Art Symposium (DIAS), in which Metzger was a key figure and co-organizer, took place in London in 1966. This programme of talks, exhibitions and performances included many artists, poets and scientists, most of whom were connected to or part of the emerging underground countercultures. The filmmaker and artist Jeff Keen also attended. His work, though closely aligned to American underground film, had more in common with English beatniks and the end-of-the-pier entertainments of amusement arcades and waxworks, as found in Brighton. Keen's film screenings also took the form of events, since described as 'Expanded Cinema', that took place between the mid-1960s to the mid-1980s. These made use of disused shops, halls, galleries and cinemas, and used multiple projection (16mm, 8mm and slides), newspaper screens, dolls, blowlamps, spray paint, live tableaux and nudity. The sounds of the live actions, the whirring of projectors, the deliberate use of megaphones, radios, instruments, toys and amplifiers, contributed to the noise of the events together with the accompanying soundtracks coming from the films themselves. Like Fluxus, there was also an acceptance of the incidental. Films may finish and run off while the projector continues projecting – the end flapping repetitively, equipment would be allowed to malfunction, and soundtracks might end before the pictures. With such unpredictability no event could be the same twice. Individual films were also made for screening in cinematic environments and most of this work has since been reconfigured so as to be released on DVD. Although the live context has gone, the availability of this work digitally has afforded an opportunity to scrutinize the use of noise in Keen's work and, in particular, four films made around 1967 to 1970.

Marvo Movie is a frantic stop-frame animation of American comics and trash literature, live action re-enactments, melting dolls and rubbish dumps. The sound is entirely vocal, made in an afternoon with Annea Lockwood and Bob Cobbing (also included in DIAS). The voices are whispery, semi-rhythmic, simultaneous, sometimes distorted (through overloaded cheap mics and megaphones) and generally unintelligible. This accumulation of indistinguishable voices and noises forms a collective utterance of breath and saliva in an undecipherable language. For *Meatdaze*, Keen comments, 'we took a war film, cut out the words and let the sound run on' (Keen in Fisher, 2009, 22):

> He tried to create a full cinema programme all in one film. He divided it into six sections, of which three main parts can be discerned: rapid animations (the cartoons of the programme), naked people at play (the supporting feature) and finally a collage of action and superimposition (the main feature).
>
> (Blaker and Giles, 2011, 216)

The sound, as indicated, is constructed from a Hollywood war film and runs continuously throughout the six sections. In addition to aircraft engines, gunfire and explosions there are 'dramatic' snatches of music, repeated periodically. The experience of the sound changes and fluctuates between the referencing of war movies, the signification of war and the pleasure of arrhythmic percussion. Sounds and images only connect conceptually and dynamically (the film comprises mainly single frames). Scene 5 is different and could almost be considered as an intermission rather than a supporting feature. It is set in a living room with Jeff Keen sculptures and found objects replacing conventional ornaments, and there's a TV on in the background. A naked woman with a painted white face is posing in the foreground and a naked man and woman chase each other round and round laughing. The man has a large, useless soft gun in place of a penis. The woman in the foreground is disinterested. The explosions carry on. Unlike the other sections there is complete disjunction between sound and image producing reflexivity on the part of the viewer/listener.

White Lite consists of glimpses of Jeff Keen characters overlaid on to images from Booth's (Victorian) Museum of Natural History. These are unclear as they are in black and white negative, scratched, marked with holes and bleached. The sound consists of hisses, clicks and thumps produced by the scratches passing through the sound area of the projector. The pre-title and title ('Meet the Anti-matter Man and the Bride of the Atom in White Lite'), and the inter-title ('The Chemical Wedding') allude to Cold War and post-apocalyptic B-movies while some imagery appears to connect detective stories with Duchamp (a nude descending a staircase). At the same time we are not allowed to forget the materiality of the film through the scratchiness of the sound and picture.

Rayday Film is a collage of white noise, analogue electronics and distorted voices that run alongside a number of semi-connected episodes, including stop-frame actions on a rubbish tip, the beach and in the street, and scenes of burning, stencil graffiti, melting toys, a roster of Keen characters (such as Dr Gaz, Motler and Vulvana) dressed up, pixilated, scratched and painted. Halfway through there is an image of a romantic kiss with a caption in a heart that reads 'the end'. Other captions are relevant: 'If this is a copy where is the original?', 'Kill the word, don't let the word kill you', 'How right Motler was to kill the word' and 'Deep War Hurtz-z-z sez Dr Gaz' (stencilled on a beer advertisement hoarding). It ends on a short piece, 'Above the Waves Beneath the Sea', which is a red-tinted frame superimposed on a magenta-tinted image of the sea and beach which gets scratched and fades to black. The sound continues for a while and then just stops. This last scene figured frequently in *Rayday* performances, often using several projectors with loops. These were often left running with nothing else happening: no great finale, no closure, no end.

The forms of noise that may be identified in these films are: incidental, functional, dissonant, cacophonous, of specific signification, and combinations of all frequencies. Unwanted (incidental) sounds such as passing traffic, seagulls or audience interruptions occurred when screenings took place in public spaces, empty shops or seafront arches.

Tail[5]

I experienced the works cited in this chapter at various times, and in different conditions and formats: I first saw *Enthusiasm* on 35mm in the Paris Cinémathèque in the late 1970s; Jeff Keen's films, in their multiple expanded forms, at a variety of locations in England between the mid-1970s and 1980s; Fluxus performances on written and photographic documentation, re-enactments and videos including UbuWeb and YouTube. La Monte Young's *Poem for Tables Chairs Benches etc.* was from an unauthorized four-CD La Monte Young compilation (no information included except track listings). My recent experience of these works (16mm screenings, DVD, CD) was made by viewings and listenings through the gauze of memory.

At Autograph[6] in Oxford (2011) Stephen Cornford performed Young's *X for Henry Flynt* (*Arabic Numeral (Any Integer) to H. F.*) using his forearms on the piano keyboard while a performance of *Poem for Tables Chairs Benches etc.* commenced in another part of the building, some distance away. The respective furniture was dragged and scraped ever closer, increasing in amplitude, to the ongoing *X for Henry Flynt* performance. The two works, as performed at the same time, were eventually in the same room. This posed an interesting problem regarding intentionality of listening and unwanted noise, not to mention the compromising of the original compositions. Samuel Rogers raised a similar issue, in his Masters dissertation, in his consideration of John Tilbury and Sebastian Lexer's performance of John Cage's *Electronic Music for Piano* (1964, 39). This is a piece that utilized microphones to seek out sounds in the immediate environment which are then processed using electronics and piano, and incorporated Cage's *Music for Piano 4–84*:

> [Since] the recording seems to invite one to listen to one's environment, John Tilbury asked the audience to turn off their phones before this performance, which one cannot ignore with regard to a performance of Cage's work. This, to me, suggests an attempt to isolate the content of the realization, much in the way one can in a studio or with a recording. Moreover, it suggests an aesthetic decision, that there are particular sounds that *are* a disturbance, perhaps others that are less so – such as traffic noise, for example, which in this instance was also unavoidable. I feel that this last point is key here – the individual makes a choice whether to leave their phone on during a performance, whereas the mass of people driving vehicles do not.
>
> (Rogers, 2010, 20; emphasis in original)

This demonstrates that performers of improvised and indeterminate musics are not immune from making judgements about what sounds (or actions) are acceptable and what are not. Most of these decisions will be predetermined by the space the work is to be performed in (a concert hall designed to exclude all extraneous noises, for example) and by the parameters of its genre or discipline (many improvisers will avoid rhythm and an excessive dynamic range will be difficult to record).

The guitarist and improviser Derek Bailey used the term 'non-idiomatic improvisation' to distinguish it from improvisation within idioms or genres of music (such as jazz, flamenco or raga). Inevitably, through reproduction, such music became recognizable and in the process became idiomatic. The premise made at the start of this chapter (that 'noise is not an art form but is positioned within (or outside) an aesthetic/anti-aesthetic dialectic') is also confounded by reproduction. So how can performances or events be experienced, without subjective predetermination and as if for the first time? Approaches to answering this begin with acknowledging experience as sensory, contextual and durational, as well as recognizing the complexities inherent in noise (particularly in its relationship with everyday life). The emergence of noise in relation to post-disciplinary practice and a resistance to its reification makes possible a recuperation of avant-garde as a politicized aesthetic force.

Electric storms do not reproduce themselves.

12

Sound manifesto:
Lee Ranaldo's notes for Robert Smithson
Felicity J. Colman

If we listen to sound, pure noise with no visuals, and then accompany the noise with the site, ideas and information from which the noise arises, we can make a correlation between form and expression, content and sound. But before we know anything about content, what do we hear? What is immanent to the sound? This question is problematic, and sounds tells us that. Any type of intentionality that we may want to inscribe on to the sound refrain frames an expressed content. Content and its meanings aside, all we have is the movement of ideas. Listening to sound is part of the process of making the sound. This processual movement creates the work.[1] It is a movement where an idea of something, somewhat intuited, makes the sound, and by description of that process becomes joined to a sound aesthetic.

I am listening to track one of musician Lee Ranaldo's fifth solo album, *Amarillo Ramp (for Robert Smithson)* (recorded 1994 NYC, effects Lisbon 1995). It is Sunday morning, the sun is shining through the windows of the house I am living in and, as the dust particles are illuminated and that solar colour permeates the room and fades out the 1960s wallpaper, my world becomes the busy activity of Ranaldo's sound effects. The track has a durational time span that links it to a slow walk and contemplation of the sculpture it is named after, *The Amarillo Ramp* (1973, idea by artist Robert Smithson, finished posthumously by Nancy Holt, Richard Serra and Tony

Shafrazi), which is an incomplete circular ramp – it is built from the red earth inside a cattle ranch in Tecovas Lake, Amarillo, Texas (Hobbs, 1981, 51).[2] The track is on the experimental side of Ranaldo's playing, as it approaches the purity of noise able to be achieved by a guitar sound, one that is less concerned with melodic or recognizable notes and sequential rhythms, but one that creates asymmetrical waves of noise by layering soundtracks and manipulating effects. The music that Ranaldo makes here is not *musique concrète*; he is not replicating the form of the artwork.[3] Ranaldo has produced sound work by engaging Smithson's work – and the experience of that work – in a number of ways, creating an acoustic ecology of and for Smithson. One of many such tracks, *Amarillo Ramp (for Robert Smithson)* is a requiem. Smithson died on this site in Texas, in a light plane that crashed while the sculptural site was being surveyed – along with his photographer, and the pilot of the plane. So while I listen to the 32 minutes and 21 seconds of this track, I am not transported to Texas to walk the ramp, but am audited to contemplate the solar dust. As the sun shifts behind a cloud and the light in the room fades, Ranaldo's guitar noise echoes itself, a hollow sound that disappears into the electronic ether and the moment of pure isolation evaporates and becomes something else. 'My' singular moment is (again) revealed to me as illusory, limited by my sensorial capacities, and created only by the syntheses of things, catalysed for consciousness by noise waves. The track surpasses its recorded moment and offers itself as art that describes existence absolutely. But for my neighbours it is just noise from next door.

While art is often defined by its form and aesthetic organization, it does not follow that the morphology of noise, sounds and music is 'formless'. Rather, this is something other than visually defined form. The terms we use to describe art exist only within recognizable economic and cultural conventions; the principals of 'form', 'medium' and its generic 'expression' or 'representation' fluctuate according to technologically determined platforms. Sound is neither form, nor formless thing, nor an 'excess'; rather, noise, sounds and music provide an intuition and a registration of the ontology of things, whether considered as events that not only convey the affective power of an event, but which direct other bodies (dust particles, consciousness) to further concepts and information about that event, as a position in and of consciousness. How does the affective encounter of sound and body of the auditor create an acousmatic ecology? I engage the term *affective* in the Spinozist inflection, where the encounter of two or more bodies has produced, and continues to produce, specific changes in the constitution of each, thereby productive of a dynamic ecology.

Smithson and Ranaldo

[O]n the way out in the car K. asked what was the intent of this piece; i didn't quite know how to answer this question simply. the answer is for me bound up in everything i feel smithson was and stood for, strived for, plus my own vision of his vision on top of that. i felt that the visit to the site was so important, the main focus of my involvement with the piece right now. to replace the image from some catalogue repro with the experience of the real thing. that was my immediate goal. the cult of experience, unquestioning. reproductions, useful reference tools possibly, are an abhorrent substitute for the art itself. Let's not reduce the spirit of art to one of cataloguing images for a slide show or yet another article.

(Ranaldo, 1985)

Ranaldo's type of noise music draws its form up and out of Smithson's land works and concepts. Situated in the broader spectrum of end-of-the-twentieth century artists, Ranaldo's style of work engages modes of 1960s technology time; of satellites and radars, of still analogue productions of the registration of a daily materiality, white-noise electronic feedback sound, plus an overlaying narration of the awareness of the historical nature of his craft (the musical histories he draws upon by guitar styles, collaborative projects, underground and commercial work) and the processual forms that music can make. It is in this processual focus, the praxis of making work, that Ranaldo finds synergy with Smithson. Ranaldo has written about his experiences of visiting Smithson sites, and his obsession with the dead artist's work. Ranaldo does collaborative work with a number of artists and artists' projects including Christian Marclay, Leah Singer (Singer and Ranaldo, 2010) and, during gigs, screens the film work of Stan Brakhage. However, it is Smithson's oeuvre that provides a fetishistic and generative impulse for some key sounds in Ranaldo's work over the years.

Acknowledged as one of the iconic artists of the twentieth century, the work of American artist Robert Smithson (1938–73) is catalytic for many art forms arising at the end of the twentieth century owing to the methods of artistic practice with which his work engages. Smithson is often classified as a 'land' artist (Tiberghein, 1995). However, as Ron Graziani has argued, Smithson is more accurately described as a producer of known 'earthworks', in reference to the economic determinations of what constitute art made in and by earth, land and 'landscape' (Graziani, 2004, 4–5). As well as *Amarillo Ramp*, Smithson's other key artwork in the United States is *Spiral Jetty* (1970), made at the site of an abandoned oil mine in the Great Salt Lake, Utah (Figure 12.1). Parallel works to *Spiral Jetty* exist at the site Ranaldo describes visiting:

Figure 12.1 Spiral Jetty, Utah, 2005. Photo: F. J. Colman

a disused Green Lake Quarry in Emmen, in the far north of the Netherlands, with two earthworks: *Spiral Hill* (1970) and *Broken Circle* (1970).

Smithson investigated the situation and framing of auto-productive works, whose potential is only realized through duration. Time in all of its forms (geological, biological, physical, cultural) must be allowed to pass for the work to produce its entropic form. This is the defining quality of art, its immanent quality of the continuum of the idea even as the medium mutates and decays.

Historically positioned in musicology as part of the post-punk movement (Cogan, 2006, 212), and best known for his work as part of the group Sonic Youth, Ranaldo's music is classified in terms of the history of noise music of the twentieth century.[4] Sonic Youth is typically discussed, in musicological terms, in the context of histories of no wave, the post-punk New York avant-garde approach to instrument modification, the timbre of sounds, and the history of the underground figures that were involved in that scene (cf. Reynolds, 2006; Moore and Coley, 2008; Browne, 2009). However, there remains more to be thought through, in terms of a philosophy of the noise art that this generation opened. The New York art (including music) scenes of the 1960s and 1970s exploded the boundaries of their disciplinary fields, not only shifting the types of aesthetic forms recognized as art, but refocusing attention upon the affective, and thus political dimensions of these practices. Experimentation and modification of forms facilitate new work. To produce his sounds Ranaldo uses specific types of guitars: modified Fender Jazzmasters (which have long necks and thus longer scale ranges) with audible inserts such as Telemaster pick-ups, and Tonemaster heads to alter the sound.[5] Ranaldo's noise moves through a post-punk a-musicality to the creation of rhythmic and sometime harmonious noise. He engages dissonant and atonal noise in random and repetitive indeterminate sound patterns, where distortion and feedback foreground the machinic sound of the guitar. That different technologies contribute to the structural platform of work is apparent. The platforms for Ranaldo's influences are transdisciplinary (art, film, photography, literature, cross-cultural), and his use of the guitar medium creates the sounds that link all things into connected feedback. However, it is through that medium's engagement with and contribution to a very specific body of process art where Ranaldo's music makes noise an aesthetic producer of territory: where the content and the structure of the noise is drawn out of the methodology of process and performs as durational art.

The territorial aspects of Ranaldo's sounds on *Amarillo Ramp (for Robert Smithson)* are not surprising, since Sonic Youth have always displayed an awareness and interest in charting responses to a sonic environment or situation. Sonic Youth songs are busy with noise plateaux, vocals, guitars, drums forming moments and waves of intensive noise that weave with sound effects, background electronic and machinic tone, hums and incessant beats. They build and peak, fall back and fade, creating layers of electronic noise. You can hear this acoustic ecology on all their albums, in noise, music and lyrics ranging from *Daydream Nation* (1988) ('Teenage Riot' lyrics include 'it took a teenage riot to get me out of bed ...'), the turn of the Republican decade reflected by the fuck-you attitude in *Goo* (1990) and *Dirty* (1992), the quiet nostalgia of neighbourhoods in *NYC Ghosts & Flowers* (2000) and the subjective places of personal experiences in *The Eternal* (2009).

In addition to his work with Sonic Youth, the solo sound which Ranaldo produces is not just about historical times, or offering additions to place. Ranaldo's sound details material resonances of forms that other physical and cognitive sensorial encounters with things do not provide. While we could critique the overall musical experience offered by Ranaldo in response to Smithson and his type of art, as being too cosseted by the New York City art worlds, perhaps too limited, or too restricted to those privileged worlds, this type of criticism would be to miss the point of this type of practice. As successful as King Tubby's music is in detailing the movement of the distinctive sound of steel drums over the forms that comprise Jamaican island life (Sarig, 1998, 212), the conditions of New York emerge in the sounds of Sonic Youth. Descriptions of the aesthetics of plastic art forms (painting, sculpture) often focus on events surrounding the construction of that form. Music, noise and sound also configure notional ideas of abstracted places, and provide acoustic histories of temporal situations. It is the notionality of noise that Ranaldo offers in his work on Smithson, although both state that they want to exceed the way in which a named notion 'fixes' the experience of the art (Ranaldo, 1985; Smithson, *A Heap of Language*, 1966). The musical track frames the 'affective notion' of the experience, as art, and stretches, as it unavoidably configures, the received cultural context of the sound aesthetic.

Interweaving the affective places of Smithson's artworks *Broken Circle/ Spiral Hill* and *Amarillo Ramp* (1973), Ranaldo made noise notebooks that work as attuned soundscapes: noise portals, material sound-capture machines, and travel diaries of the band. In his tracks *Broken Circle/Spiral Hill EP* (1994), *Amarillo Ramp (For Robert Smithson)* and *Non-Site #3, Notebook* (1997), the noise that Ranaldo produces makes temporal syntheses of acoustic places, modulating Ranaldo and the listener into the various narratives of Smithsonesque landscapes and experiences of temporal free-fall. Ranaldo responds musically to the landscape of Smithson's making, in addition to the sites and durational experience of finding these often hard-to-find art forms. As well as writing lyrics that account for his personal and physical response to Smithson's work, Ranaldo has also published, in text and in film collage, accounts of his journeys to visit Smithson's work. These notes situate the acoustic production within a field of an artistic philosophical reflexive practice, one that engages what appear to be the familiar tropes of phenomenology but in fact offer something far less deterministic. Ranaldo makes different noises that invoke not only the social and material histories of Smithson's specific geographical sites, but also offer a mode of noise philosophy. There have been musicians that make work by responding to weather situations – 'Sum-mmer-time, and tha livin' is eaa-sy' (of Gershwin and Heyward's 'Summertime') – but Ranaldo's type of musical response to an art form as a *component* of Smithson's affective art offers some core insights and methods.[6] In his response to Smithson's work, Ranaldo thus delineates an arena for a philosophy of art as noise affect and a sound manifesto.

Sound manifestos

Pierre Schaeffer defined sounds as sound objects, describing how sound recordings create 'new phenomena to observe' and 'new conditions of obser- vation' (2004, 81). Schaeffer takes what we can term a post-phenomenological approach, since it attempts to separate the sound affect from its media platform. If I listen to Ranaldo's tracks on a media player rather than watch him play his guitar live, Schaeffer's theory is, in parts, accurate. Where 'something' is perceivable, it is 'acousmatic' – that is, the noises one hears without seeing the cause, but which function as 'sonorous communication' (Schaeffer, 2004, 77). But Ranaldo, like Smithson, forces us to hear the technological platform of their work, whether chunks of dirt or guitar strings and amplifier. The medium is acknowledged within the event of the art. The self-consciousness offers a critical inflection into the intentionality of the work. Communication is not objective and quantifiable but affective and multiple. With multiple sound objects, the acousmatic noise creates its own world, perhaps described more accurately as the creation of an 'acoustic ecology': a whole world sounded out (see Schafer, 1980). But recognition of these ecologies is reliant upon direction out of the habitual, ordinary knowledge of things towards the affective dimensions. Following Smithson's prose in his essay on *The Spiral Jetty* (see Flam, 1996), Ranaldo accounts for a point of recognition of the affect of the work:

> [I] want to stand in front of the physical work and decide for myself. if painting loses that, it has lost everything. those who would rather read texts w repros that look at the real and decide for themselves have long ago missed the point. to see it in the real landscape of a backwoods abandoned dutch quarry, in emmen, merely a small dot on the map of holland, nowhere incarnate from the viewpt of 57th st., 2000+ miles away, in another universe. i could offer no verbal abstractions that held up in the light of simply being there, standing on that grassy hillside looking out and down at it. it became a 'place' at last, no longer a notion. that was enough.
>
> (Ranaldo, 1985)

Describing the auditory experience of sound – the sounds and noises of your/other bodies walking to a gig, walking to *see something, to hear something, to be something/where*, is asking: *what happens when things in the world produce new forms for experience?* As Ranaldo notes above, '[I] could offer no verbal abstractions that held up'. In answering *in sound form*, through the creation of noise, music, acoustic duration, an after-phenomenological sound position is delineated. The question of how to epistemologically 'represent' things, abstract 'simply being there', through art, and to then 'see' things through art, has been dispelled and critiqued for centuries by artists of all kinds who are aware of the bounded capacity of the forms created. In describing art forms as recording machines that move bodies through durational moments, the vital velocity of movement is highlighted. Air particles are productive of sound and some organic creatures have the sensorial facility to be responsive to those vibrations and their variations. Artists who ensure that their methods for determining forms through acousmatic practices of recording and describing provide elements for how a science of noise produces other arts, creating a record of the resonance of ephemeral vibrations, variations, pressures and moments of consciousness of such elemental reactions.

Listening to the different types of sound, noises and melodic phrases that Ranaldo's work has produced from his encounter with Smithson's work, I am aware of a range of nuanced affects with which both artists engage. The supreme affective power of noise and music is to be able to move consciousness elsewhere, in multiple, dynamic and not always pleasant or intuitive movements. The affective movements generated by noise are sensory, intellectual, cognitive, structured and free form. Some affects rely upon the technological platform that produce them – the type of guitar, string picking and strumming, sound effects, amplifiers, recording devices. Some affects are generated from other event platforms, such as encounters with other artists, other melodies, other noise, different performances, different albums, and through the affective encounter with Smithson's art work.

The affect of Smithson's crystal worlds

The writer J. G. Ballard describes Smithson's *Spiral Jetty* not as an artwork but a time machine (Ballard, 2000). However, the language of the abstraction and manipulation of historical chronology used to evaluate a visual image and its products is of little use for describing sound, in both its contemporaneous form and its potential. Walking in Robert Smithson's *Spiral Jetty* in the Great Salt Lake, or climbing around the *Spiral Hill* in Emmen and seeing his gallery-installed *non-sites* provides a certain sense of a material art 'experience', as I have argued elsewhere (see Colman, 2006). The experience of materiality means different things and causes different affects for different bodies. In response to the concept of Smithson's materiality, and the actual physical noises that materiality produces in its temporal existence, Ranaldo creates new sound conditions and harnesses old ones, enabling others to audit the forms of Smithson's works. If we take Ranaldo's perspective of an articulation of the sound affect of these forms, then the representational calculative terms of 'time and space' become redundant, and other terms are required to describe the affective reverberations of things.

In his work, Smithson drew out multiple layers of art-historical politics and aesthetic classifications, and the terms of economic mediality of the artist's craft: what it means to make art and to have an art practice. The reception of Smithson's work positions him in the art-historical category of conceptual art, with its re-examination of the overworked terms of network and boundaries, with their inferences of the artist as 'bricoleur' (Lévi-Strauss, 1966, 16–22; Shapiro, 1997, 180). Of course, Smithson treated his art practice as a component of the physical world, with forms contributing to the movement of biological, geomorphic and iconic formations across time. While such terms actualize a number of aesthetic precincts of art practices, across all chronological times, they have been shown to be problematic as global, universalizing concepts for thinking, and they gloss the specificity of sensorial responses. Smithson's site-specific earthworks provide a techno-logical platform for noise. At the earthworks there is noise made from landscapes that have lost their social constructions (farmers' land/oil-drilling site/disused quarry/public sculpture) but which have entered the perceptual abstract histories of famous art forms. The fame of the artist is undone by the materiality of the experience of the work – in this case noise. A rhythm, beat, melody or noise affects different bodies in different ways. At the *Spiral Jetty* in the Great Salt Lake in Utah, I was focused by the salt crystal crunch that constituted the work. What these works force you to become aware of is the noise of processual thinking; of the creation of pure matter – there are no 'objects or things', just ideas made from affective noises that come from and define the territory, and the limitations of one's body in traversing the noise.

When visiting the *Spiral Hill* in Emmen, the isolation from the habits and routines of life enables a certain type of asceticism to be accessed. This, I would argue, is different from the uncritical position of a phenomenology of perception that presents experience as knowledge or epiphany. Rather, an acknowledgement of the limits and limitlessness enabled by an ascetic territory (such as noise) enables the performance of events (effects) as ideas (affects). This is an artistic strategy that was well rehearsed by Smithson's historical era (Lippard, 1973) – and we see this played out in events staged by artists aware of their practice. Artists' films are the medium typically used in order to convey the broader registers that have informed one or a series of gallery works. Intensities of materiality and of experience are given greater scope in film and sound. For example, Smithson's film *Spiral Jetty* (1970) is an art form that seeks to describe how life is immanent, molecular in nature, and dependent upon the sun. The film draws attention to how consciousness is focused through the technological platforms given by the (sounds of) a helicopter, the (movements of) the camera frame, the soundtracks, the editing – all these aspects provide evidence for the dissolution of the uncritical self, which is Smithson's quest.[7]

Ranaldo's work contributes to Smithson's type of living art, by opening another body of and for that art. In accessing the synthesis of temporality that an idea has brought together in time, through various syntheses of noise and music that a song creates, Ranaldo's music produces notional noise, but with the intent of creating musicality not representative of 'The Spiral Hill' or 'The Amarillo Ramp', but of the affective range of those art ideas. It follows that Ranaldo's work, after Smithson, importantly corrects the thinking and classification of artwork: not as a fixed 'form' but rather something that is dynamic and not bound to its form or site of production. Artworks – inclusive of all media (music, sculpture, crafts, technological media) – produce meaning through their very immanent existence that is not reliant upon form but upon the duration of their ideas. How to discuss and critique the 'life of forms in art' is, as Henri Focillon discussed, a 'luxuriant' practice: wide ranging and subjective (Focillon, 1989, 32).

What is sound philosophy?

In different media forms the sound will audit and convey aspects of the condition of the ecology it vibrates. Musicology describes how the sounds of industry provided a platform for the types of noise, music and melody produced. But there remains a perhaps unresolvable civic attitude towards what political position that aestheticization then holds. To give something a structure provides an ordering narrative out of even a chaotic and random structure, or the uncertainty of a social situation. The structure feeds back into the idea, which in turn informs the form, and the sound territory is produced, and content is normalized through repetition and feedback. One becomes attuned to hearing matching situations or conditions. Music and noise and sound in this way can provide the structural forms and format for creative impulses and reactive forms.

In addition to this feedback territory, parts (if not all) of the sound refrain are detached from their habitualized process and join up with other noises/ sounds, and create something entirely different. The sounds of a screen text, a piece of music, industrial noises, aside from spoken dialogue, are frequently acousmatic, framing for the auditor the molecular (to use Guattari's term [1984, 28]), and solar (Smithson, *Spiral Jetty*) dimensions of life. Noises and sounds can also become autonomous in their detachment of the expressive content (of experiences, of materials) from their energy-inducing formal points of resonance (the site, the experience, the anticipation and so on). I am not advocating a return to some form of phenomenological quest for the 'origin' of a transcendent moment of creation of 'the sound'. However, within any discussion of noise, both components of participation *plus* autonomy have to be considered. It often comes down to that awful realization that repressive social conditions are productive of creative movements which create new things out of the forced cracks in given culture. The underground requires its normative ground to exist in order to reorient the audition of things.[8]

As one of the core sensorial modes required for cognitive and psychological mapping of an event to occur, sound and the audition of sound provides information about the world – but not just information in the Turing sense of a coding and decoding of semiotically defined materiality from distortion to comprehension.[9] Art is often the manifesto component of the artist's practice of framing audition, but perhaps it remains for the musician to be able to extend and detail the affective sound elements of the work of art, or indeed of an event, a place or an idea. Making (sound) art in response to a location, or another art form, is a common enough practice, and work like Ranaldo's forces consideration of the ways that are used to describe noise, sound and music. New work is not only responsive, but alters the symbiogenetic dimension of the initial form.

For Ranaldo, Smithson's work lies in its place, in a process of decay, and of existing within and towards that process. The music that Ranaldo produces after the encounter or encounters with Smithson provides access to other dimensions of the work's autopoietic potential of durational production.[10] The sound, like the art, is never finished. Sound's different affective dimensions form its sound manifestos. The noise refrain creates the territory, just as imagery maps out a narrative territory. The noise creates the world we audit. The meaning of the work is in the moment when process is created.

PART THREE

Noise, ethics and politics

13

Anti-self:
experience-less noise[1]
GegenSichKollektiv

Noise exacerbates the rift between knowing and feeling by splitting experience, forcing conception against sensation. Some recent philosophers have evinced an interest in subjectless experiences; I am rather more interested in experience-less subjects. Another name for this would be 'nemocentrism' (a term coined by neurophilosopher Thomas Metzinger): the objectification of experience would generate self-less subjects that understand themselves to be no-one and no-where. This casts an interesting new light on the possibility of a 'communist' subjectivity.

BRASSIER, 2009

There is a growing emphasis in contemporary capitalism on individual experiences in production and consumption. In a given context, when we experience our living labour being realized, the potential of our subjectivity, of our intellectual and affective capacity, we feel empowered. We feel that we can be, and that we are, a constituent part of the context that we are in. We don't have an overview outside of the situation: we are inside it. This feeling of self-empowerment is used by capitalism in its creation of a framework whereby a valorization of whatever activity that occurs within can be realized at different points and moments. While we gain unique experiences, momentarily feeling happy about ourselves, a capitalist logic expands deeper and deeper into our subjectivity. In his text *Genre is Obsolete*, Ray Brassier points out that the commodification of experience now takes place not only at the ideological level but at the neurophysiological level.

If we take the term literally, noise should not work 'smoothly' at the level of either aesthetics or experience. In fact its qualities radically challenge both of these notions. Rather than trying to reconcile knowing and feeling, noise can help us to dissociate the commensurability of experience and subjectivity in a sense that exceeds the logic of framing, by either being too much, too complex, too dense and difficult to decode, or too chaotic to be measured. One cannot have mastery over it. It is a kind of useless general intellect that suspends values of judgement such as good or bad, right or wrong. To think of it in moral or ethical terms seems ridiculous. Noise, with its epistemic violence, counters the division between activity and passivity. By making us aware of our inability to decipher it, noise alienates us. We all are no one in front of it. We cannot find reaffirmation of our accepted positions (either as audience or performer).

Unfortunately, in practice, noise has become just another musical genre and many people can predict what a noise concert might be. In noise concerts the performer/audience division is reproduced as it is elsewhere and players rarely deal with it. Rather than trying to perpetuate noise as musical genre, we would like to think through how noise, as it carries qualities such as chaos, density, saturation, precision, intelligibility, and so on, can be executed in order to dismantle the frameworks which so often shape the way we behave and how we relate to each other. Noise routes expression through the impersonal and indulges in a catastrophe of generic gestures. We will call 'anti-self' the nihilist process of exposing oneself to noise, as destroying one's own position by nullifying the attributes of accumulation that shapes our subjectivity today, such as confidence, contacts, recognition and attention (think here of Lou Reed's many years of ambivalent reaction to his *Metal Machine Music*; it is only now that this record has become accepted by its author and the establishment that it has ceased to be noise). The anti-self is being no one, being nowhere, being nobody, definitely not an artist, certainly not an audience, producing nothing that separates us from our objective conditions, having nothing to exchange because there is nothing to count that someone else can frame.

But how does a subject that *isn't* come to be at all? In the development of machinery in large-scale industry in the nineteenth century, Karl Marx apprehended a dynamic and contradiction which has become manifold in the twenty-first century, not only in the factory but across all work: 'the machine does not free the worker from work but rather deprives the work itself of all content' (Marx, 1990, 548).

As capital develops automation, labour power, the very source of value, is thrown out of the process. On a qualitative level capital simplifies and standardizes all tasks, making it possible for a machine to do them. On a quantitative level, by raising the productivity of labour, it requires ever fewer workers and ever more machines. Capital has a vested interest in reproducing human subjects as workers but also, over time, eroding the meaning and content of their work. Instead of employing ever larger numbers in growing factories the very opposite becomes true. In his own lifetime Marx experienced, with surprise, the way that this situation produced a massive expansion of a servant class as industrial production grew. We experience the later stages of the same contradiction as the production of surplus populations – a growing global population which cannot be absorbed into productive labour (both a flexible service class in the North and a landless, unemployed proletariat in the South). Other facets of questions of the content of work, understood in part as de-skilling, come increasingly to the fore. These may be characterized on the one hand by a growing dis-identification with work by workers, or even a disenchantment with work as the substantial content of human life. On the other hand, we see desperate attempts to identify with forms of work which have less and less substance. This desperate attempt to identify with work, or more precisely with value, becomes obvious when we measure all of our activities in terms of gains and losses. We build up an image of ourselves knowing what we can get from that image, as if we were embodying value itself. Increasingly our activities are directed towards either personal pleasure or self-valorization by representing ourselves through, for example, social networks. We work towards the production of our own subjectivity having internalized the values of contemporary capitalism which praises attention, reputation, confidence, innovation and creativity, as ways of producing value out of nothing.

Human companies: spectral objectivity

The openness of Noise allows me to explore my creativity in unimaginable ways. Noise is the ultimate act of freedom. Only while making Noise [do] I feel myself.
R. Holloway of The Bloody Unicorns, Detroit (personal conversation: GegenSichKollektiv and Holloway)

Notions of freedom, self-expression and creativity are the hallmarks of desperate attempts to produce value out of the unproductive forces in capitalism. Value seems now to have more to do with speculation, confidence and belief than with socially necessary labour time. An example of this is how artists and musicians 'work' without getting paid but, in their total identification with what they are doing, are ready to sell themselves for nothing but their own self-image. Within the experimental music scene this self-image is reinforced through the prising open of subjective experience, an anthropocentric perspective in which one sees oneself as the central and most significant entity in the universe:

> it would be naïve to think of the subject and the object as two separately subsisting entities whose relation is only subsequently addressed to them. On the contrary, the relation is in some sense primary: the world is only world insofar as it appears to me as world, and the self is only self insofar as it is face to face with the world, that for whom the world discloses itself.
> (Huneman and Kulich, 1997, 22)

The phenomenological approach described above fits perfectly well within an individualistic logic which avoids political implications: as if one is able to access reality through sound in an act of unmediated experience, in a moment of freedom from the determinations of the forces of production, just as it appears to us (as phenomena). It is not uncommon to then hear people making noise about or extemporizing on notions of form, structure, quality … basically aesthetic choices determined by subjective notions of taste. These personal choices feed into a notion of individual freedom, but this is a notion of freedom that is completely entwined with the development of capitalism. As Marx notes, it was not until we were equal before the eyes of the law that the logic of exchange could be developed universally. He explains that in order for workers to be able to sell their labour power as a commodity, two requirements must first be met: 'In order that its possessor may sell it [his or her own labour power] as a commodity; he must have it at his disposal, he must be the proprietor of his own labour-capacity, hence of his person' (Marx, 1990, 271). Second, he or she should also be free from any access to the means of production or substantive property. The worker is free to be, to have this equality as his or her content, but only as far as he or she is a worker and thus material for capital to exploit. Thus it is 'not only outside of the wage relation that we are nothing but outside of the *contradiction* of the wage relation, which changes everything, and by which everything can change' (Theorie Communiste, 2010; emphasis in original).

We can see how the conceptualization of experience emerges at the same time as the development of the bourgeoisie, at the same time as we are 'equal before the eyes of the law' (as opposed to the formal inequality of serfdom or feudalism). A constructed notion of the individual becomes naturalized through the notion of experience. One aspect of this process is the way in which aesthetic judgement affirms a universal society of equals – Kant's 'sensus communis'. Another aspect is that aesthetics reinforce this individuality by, for example, producing the concept of authorship and the division of labour under the audience/artist or performer distinction.

Today, artists and musicians outside the mainstream have insufficient means to produce any effectual change because their productivity is not directly involved in the production process. Therefore we consider ourselves both as property and as the means of production. In order to sell our property and potential (production of aesthetics) we have internalized a 'managerial logic' that is engraved in the latest developments of capitalism – one that sees human capital as its very currency. By managerial logic we simply mean how we frame our dubious creativity and innovation in such a way as to be able to market ourselves. Money may not be the primary currency in the noise scene. Instead, the key currency may be thought of as self-promotion. Young subcultures have learned this very quickly. In a YouTube video about the history of jerkin (street dance from Los Angeles) one of the teenage musicians explains how what they really wanted was to rack up hits on MySpace and YouTube.[2] This will give them credit and respect among their peers. This specific reputation is something one cannot buy with money. In this regard we can see how musicians and artists are paradigmatic subjects within contemporary capitalism: they give their all in the development and marketing of their 'own' individual skills so that the audience/consumers can have experiences that they cannot find elsewhere. This is yet another example of how commodification takes place at the level of experience, since musicians know there is a market for such experiences, and so they work towards it.

That this 'commodification' has nothing to do with a wage suggests two trajectories: that capital may now be drawing upon 'free inputs' of (gently) coerced labour power, as in so-called primitive (or primary) accumulation; and, perhaps more controversially, that capital itself has reached a point at which it is struggling to absorb labour, and this self-activity is either 'above' or 'beneath' capitalization. The struggle to capture this subterranean activity as intellectual property has comprehensively failed. Our anonymous hordes may seek recognition, but recognition does not equal value. Concrete human activity is therefore providing less and less of the substance which capital craves. Either the social relations of capitalism no longer necessarily pass through the labouring subject or the formerly labouring subject no longer recognizes the necessity of deforming themselves through work. Yet this 'going through the motions', this preening and constant work on the self, passes at least for work-readiness in the absence of any real materialization of the conditions for work to be done. The values of objectivity in noise production today are even more spectral than in the type of production typically based on wage labour:

> The 'substance of value' as a figure of speech has frequently been understood in a quasi-physical, 'substantialist' manner: the worker has expended a specific quantity of abstract labor and this quantity exists within the individual commodity and turns the isolated article into an object of value. That things are not so simple should already be made apparent by the fact that Marx describes the value-objectivity as a 'spectral objectivity' [in *Capital*, Vol. I (Marx, 1990, 128); corrected translation], [and] in the revised manuscript for the first edition he even speaks of a 'purely fantastic objectivity'.
>
> (Heinrich, n.d.)

What is this *spectral objectivity* if not the fetish character of the commodity? Marx understood fetishism as the inversion by which humans are dominated by the results of their own activity. When a thing becomes a commodity it is changed into something that transcends its sensuousness and ordinariness, becoming something 'mysterious' or, to be precise in its translation, a sensuous super-sensuous thing: 'sinnlich-übersinnlich' (see Bonefeld and Psychopedis, 2005). The production of ourselves as commodities cannot but produce schizophrenia as we are trying simultaneously to identify our subjectivity and to sell it as a thing. The production of experiences tries to emphasizes the sensuous aspect in order to supersede the ordinary, but still reproducing this mysterious thing called the self. Hence, for Marx, '[v]alue is a relation between persons – expressed as a relation between things' (quoted in Rubin, 2008, 267).

An experience-less subject – this person as a thing – is exactly what the value form produces as sociality: people regard each other merely as tools and commodities, as accretions of value. Experience today expands this spectral objectivity in our subjectivity, producing a sense of individuality that appears to transcend the logic of value and wage relations. In this process we become sensuous super-sensuous things, albeit with a human face. Yet, to take this creation and identify with it – to identify with non-identity – would put this abstract, purposeless purpose to work not in the augmentation of value but in the augmentation of human capacities, with sense-perception now expanded.

> Capitalism now produces subject positions; it has caused many variants of human beings to come into existence (via identity practices, and niche markets) which feel completely at home within the boundaries capitalism

has drawn onto them – from the perspective of its subject positions, capitalism has replaced nature. It has become, or it was always, almost impossible to consciously reject the values developed by capitalist organisation because consciousness itself is derived from the movement of its value – the refusal of capital is literally the refusal of reality.

(Dupont, 2007, 22)

This refusal of reality, as understood from the perspective of a subject position, would still mean today the reproduction of a subjectivity produced by capitalism. The question is whether there is a reality outside a subject position.

Critique of the self: objectivity independent of ourselves and capitalism

Ultimately, subjective experience is a biological data format, a highly specific mode of presenting information about the world by letting it appear as if it were an Ego's knowledge [...]. But no such things as selves exist in the world. A biological organism, as such, is not a self. An Ego is not a self, either, but merely a form of representational content – namely, the content of a transparent self/model activated in the organism's brain.

(Metzinger, 2009, 8)

Following recent scientific and philosophical developments, the notion of the self has become subject to serious questioning. In post-structuralist and postmodernist framings any notion of the self may have been very much called into question but this remained solely from the perspective of identity (or 'identity thinking' as Theodor Adorno put it). Because of the different backgrounds and influences of identities, and the different ways in which our subjectivities are produced, it has become impossible to talk of an objective or absolute truth, one that would transcend identity and the different struggles and power relations within which we are embedded. This led to forms of relativism and political victimhood – a situation in which the sovereign entity poses itself increasingly as a victim in order to assert power over others. However, neurophilosopher Thomas Metzinger suggests that the self is an illusion, a coping mechanism constructed by our brain, which has to reduce the complexity of the information it receives from the world in order to function. To facilitate our survival, our brain unknowingly constructs a reality tunnel. This is what Metzinger terms 'The Ego Tunnel' (Metzinger, 2009, 8). There is an objective reality, of course, but our senses would never be able to perceive it. We apply unconscious filter mechanisms, through our sensory systems and the workings of our brains. Our biological architecture is inherited which, together with beliefs and assumptions, builds an 'I' on this foundation. The notion of experience is not only a myth in the ideological sense *but also* an illusion that our brain creates in order to fashion a coherent understanding of the world and our relationship to it.

Taking into account different scientific discoveries, philosophers such as Quentin Meillassoux and Ray Brassier have pointed out that contemporary science is able to state facts about a reality existing independently of any subjective point of view. A fossil is that which indicates traces of life, but an arche-fossil is that which contains traces of matter before the emergence of life. Meillassoux argues that with the discovery of arche-fossils, science is able to talk about a time and a reality before the emergence of life and thought. This implies that there is a reality existing totally independently of thought. This calls into question what Meillassoux calls 'correlationism': the view that the very idea of an absolutely mind-independent reality is meaningless. Now, only that whose non-existence is unthinkable is necessary. But a fact is something whose non-existence is always thinkable: a fact is something that could have been otherwise. Science records the existence of facts: arche-fossils are facts. But if everything that exists is a fact, and facts are contingent, then everything that exists is contingent, and there is no necessity whatsoever underlying existence. The only thing that is necessary is that nothing exists necessarily. This constitutes what Meillassoux calls 'a new absolute': an absolute of un-reason. Everything is necessarily contingent or 'without-reason'. There is absolutely no reason for our existence or that of anything else. All existence is contingent and hence strictly meaningless. This absolute of unreason is what calls correlationism into question:

> By 'correlation' we mean the idea according to which we only ever have access to the correlation between thinking and being, and never to either term considered apart from each other. We will henceforth call *correlationism* any current thought which maintains the unsurpassable character of the correlation so defined. Consequently, it becomes possible to say that every philosophy which disavows naïve realism has become a variant of correlationism.
>
> (Meillassoux, 2009, 5)

A critical question emerges: how can we break out of the correlationist circle? Ray Brassier defends a radically anti-correlationist philosophy which claims that 'Thought' is conjoined not with 'Being', but with 'Non-Being'. For him, universality and our understanding of the absolute is inaccessible to experience in the way we understand it today as connected with subjectivity. It may be possible to break the relation between thought and being if, for example, we conceive of the subject as an organon or automaton. The objectification of experience would mean that we would be able to develop mind-independent concepts, to use Brassier's term. Could the objectification of experience in the cognitive sense transcend the socio-economic register? What would this require? Brassier:

> For once we have put science and philosophy on an equal footing before the real it becomes necessary to insist that there is no possible compromise between the claims of correlationism and the ancestral claims of science: if correlationism is true, science's ancestral claims are false; if the latter are true, correlationism is false.
>
> (Brassier, 2007, 63)

It is the development of science that gives us the knowledge that calls into question ourselves and correlationism. By taking into account its developments without positing ourselves at the centre of its discoveries we could achieve a better understanding of reality and perhaps, thanks to this, change it. The subject, as subject of scientific experimentation, might help us to develop a redefinition of politics beyond the 'free individual' that reproduces the logic of the commodity form.

Through the use of cybernetics we could also develop a radical conception of sex and gender relations, finishing with the tyranny of the biological family (following the propositions of radical feminist Shulamith Firestone in her seminal 1970 book *The Dialectics of Sex*; see Firestone, 1979, 12).

Spectral silence: generic gesture and impersonal expression

As people who work with noise we ask: What would be the most objective sound, the most independent of our subject position, the one that would counter the idea of self-expression that we have criticized before? What could be that sound which has no value at all? One could think that silence is the most generic and asubjective expression, the most uncreative and available. Because of this perhaps the very 'sound' of silence could critique or dismantle the logic of commodity as no value can be attributed to it. Silence proposes in its generic qualities the possibility of leaving behind notions of authorship. But here we will see how silence becomes reified in its different uses by being framed within the managerial logic we are trying to criticize here. Cage rightly pointed out that there was no such thing as silence. Is there silence after the critique of correlationism? When humanity ends, would there be silence? Silence only has conceptual importance within our mental reality, both in the hypothesis of the extermination of humanity, or in respect of a mind-independent reality, silence, as we conceived it, would make no sense.

That having been said, with Cage we can see how the problem of an author's authority can follow the form of value: the silence is no longer silence but somebody's property. Paul Hegarty, in his book *Noise/Music: A History* (Hegarty, 2007), singled out the first performance of *4'33"* as the first noise concert. Interestingly the noise is made by other people, not by Cage.

We can understand that silence is always specific and singular, that it works as a framework which allows things to happen. In recent years we can see that in noise, improvisation and contemporary composition, the use of silence is taken in some way as an aesthetic palette which is used as if it were a guarantee of a sound or event by which we obtain the desired responses from the public and the artist. This is the case of movements such as that which has been called reductionism (minimal improvisation) or the Wandelweiser group of composers. This music is largely based on long passages of silence accompanied by minimal notes, subtle tones, or field recordings with minimum interference or processing from its 'natural' recording.

These musicians found in silence a way of looking at situations and the infinite riches of the circumstances of reality, as subtracted from the action of the music, and evaluating critically the need to add something to that which already exists. While noise could emerge from Cage's *4'33"*, Waldenweiser and the reductionist improvisers tighten up their silences so that the revolting, unwanted, or alienating character of what could be noise becomes formalized, feeding a very specific aesthetic taste. Noise cannot emerge from their use of silence, a silence that gets subjectified in their personal desires and their authorities as composers.

These artists have taken care to make sure that supra-personal events (those which have to do with socio-political and economic structures) will be decisive in the analysis of their work, thereby ensuring, through their subjectivity, the value of their individual decisions. The phenomenological character of listening is accepting as real the subjectivity of the artist projected by our own consciousness. Therefore what may happen during a silence has a special meaning in relation to who has greater power in the situation. If it is a concert, then for the musician who has taken the decision *not* to play, this matter remains his or her decision while the public's collective decision not to move from their places is entirely expected.

We will call this silence a spectral silence – one which 'tames' the situation and sets limits on access to the reality that is. It is silence as an element bereft of any consideration other than aesthetics or the decision emerging from the artist's subjective process.

An object is created, ready to be experienced and tasted, as if it were itself a sublime event to be enjoyed, or savoured, and so on. It is a pleasure that can be derived from the hand of stillness, of quietness. It is a phenomenon of representation of that which we conceive of as silence, and not just an understanding of silence as an absence of sound, but also the conception of this set of sounds (a set that the performer or artist does not control) as unprescribed sound. Spectral silence neutralizes the insurgent nerve or noise that can emerge in any improvisation by reinforcing the notion of subjective experience.

The musician's intention to appropriate or 'generate' a silence does not waive the fact of our recognizing the enveloping conceptual framework as their own: a product of their own subjectivity. It is an aesthetic tool that subjugates the opportunity to reflect on the reality of each sound in this context. The musicians relate to the silence in such a way only through individual expression, the encouragement of his or her ego, and their aesthetic decisions. The obtained musical phenomena end up determining the cognitive processes which take place at that time.

We all know that the state of silence does not physically exist. Despite this, silence is likely to be objectified except when in its spectral form (i.e. commodified and valorized). Spectral silence arises to prevent (on the part of both the public and the interpreter) the objective analysis of this situation, to really know the reality of this situation or art object.

Once an artist decides to use silence, this silence becomes part of somebody's improvisation or composition. Therefore it is a silence that does not reflect on the objectivity of the situation but on the subjective authority of the improviser-composer, and his or her decision to use this silence.

Silences becomes subjectified in their productions of aesthetic experiences, which reinforces rather than questions the division of labour between the musicians and the audience. This limits the access to the reality of the sound in itself. *That* reality is dependent on the correlation we establish as cognizant subjects with the situation and what may be known of it. In this regard we can understand that spectral silence creates an effect similar to that created by correlationism – keeping an area of reality incognoscible. We are interested in both noise and silence, seeking their radical potentials as encoded objects which challenge the established concepts of knowledge, experimenting with the limits and liberties of a situation.

In a reductionist musical concert the artist and the spectators understand (just as Kant did) that the cognitive experience of the cognizant subject is active and that, in the act of knowing, the cognizant subject adjusts the known reality. This correlationism gives us access to what is 'in itself' a concert of noise (i.e. something independent of the subjective relationship we build with this). We can only know what the concert is 'for us', as it were. Thus what we perceive is conditioned by the conceptual decision of the artist and by, as it generates meaning for us, that set of ideas processed through our supra-personal level. We pay attention to something specific, to encourage the development of a meaning consistent with the authority of the artist, our own tastes, reinforcing our acceptance or dissent from the context created by the conceptual idea, and ignoring all other aspects that can remain censored. Nevertheless, these secondary issues might help us understand the reality of the situation. In addition, cognition may be distorted by the aesthetic experience. We recognize the significance of each environmental sound we perceive as a harmonious and artisan creation of nature and the subjectivity of the artist. We return to this in search of a shelter that guarantees the same sensory success as in our past experiences. This passive recreation and contemplation in listening drives us deeper and deeper into the idea of a positivist order in our relationship with nature – a nature typically perceived as peaceful, cosy and yet overwhelming (so that it is no surprise to see some of these composers, such as Michael Pisaro, using field recordings of nature as the inspiration for their compositions).

Towards anti-self: nihilism and truth

Nihilism is not, as Jacobi and so many other philosophers since have insisted, a pathological exacerbation of subjectivism, which annuls the world and reduces reality to a correlate of the absolute ego, but on the contrary is the unavoidable corollary of the realist conviction that there is a mind-independent reality, which, despite the presumptions of human narcissism, is indifferent to our existence and oblivious to the 'values' and 'meanings' which we would drape over it in order to make it more hospitable. Nature is not our or anyone's 'home', nor a particularly beneficent progenitor.

(Brassier, 2007, xi)

If we want to exploit these kinds of experimental practices (such as improvisation, composition or artistic interventions) as materials of emancipation, we must first destroy the naturalistic approach to listening to the silence, to stop looking at silence as a canvas full of pure, harmonious and subtle imperfections, and to release instead the full range of powers that reside in silence.

In distinction to the inertia that leads these musicians to build spectral silence, the idea of generating noise now appears. We usually think of the liberating power of noise – its inherent connection with chaos and disorder, noise's propensity not to fall into the trap of capitalism because noise itself seems to threaten the logic of generic classification as such. But noise, like any other sound, can be realized as an aesthetic category (note how noise has become a musical genre) – as happens when spectral silence loses its intensity as an abstract form, an intensity which it shares with silence.

Is it possible to implement silence or noise under the influence of the nihilistic conception proposed by Brassier?

We maintain that it would be interesting to think about how sometimes, in improvisations or compositions that work with silence, our relationship with 'nature' is somewhat confused. There is no clear relationship established by artists with this word 'nature'. We do not know if it is the 'natural world' or the structure of reality. This confusion, which leads artists to determine what is or is not natural for them, is very problematic.

We need to dismantle parameters such as 'sensitivity' or 'aesthetic values' in favour of processes of objectification (or non-subjectivity) in noise-making or improvising. How is this possible, keeping in mind that a Wandelweiser composer can object to the fact that the public is speaking during one of his or her concerts? They dare to think that perhaps the sound of the crowd is less 'natural' than the sound of birds or the traffic in the distance. Obviously it is no less natural – it is only less aesthetically desirable for their purposes.

If we assume that silence, as one of the more objective approaches to the reality of the situation (by silence's generality, which excludes the artist's hand), we have to analyse the problems of the cognition distorted by the aesthetic experience induced by the artist's decision – the decision that establishes the conceptual framework.

In Michael Pisaro's composition *A wave and waves* (2007) we can see how Pisaro and Greg Stuart work to re-create the natural dynamics of waves (after coastal observation) in a soundscape piece, to delight the listener with the grandeur of nature. What is the impetus for trying to mimic nature's processes? This interpretation, with its strong emphasis on phenomenological character, does nothing but deliver to us the idea of an overwhelming nature; a lapse back into nature is more like a naïve conformity to nature and, in a way, is reason's own fatal submission to the dictates of nature. We can see through the reception of the work how music composers encourage escapism and the unconditional acceptance of the phenomenological immersion of the work. This process of identification with nature according to the transcendental perspective, engenders a subjective identity, belonging to various positions, while forgetting that nature is completely indifferent to us.

In the praxis of an objectified silence/noise, the artist's decision, which activates certain conceptual processes, must be overturned. We should work in a constant stage of sabotage of the self. We will not take conceptual decisions, invested in our own individuality. Rather our praxis should be the result of generic gestures or impersonal expressions. Otherwise we are doomed to access only the meanings of a 'reality' created through the filter of the artist's subjectivity (as with Pisaro), and thereby we continue to ignore and censor sounds and acts depending on how they comply or not to the dictates of our subjectivity and how we wish that this should be projected (for example, the Milan performance in 1977 of Cage's *Empty Words*, which prompted a strong protest from communist students).

A praxis is not based on individuality but questions individualism and the self, both in respect of its ideological position (and what interests this position serves) and its neurophysiological position (what are the limitations of our senses and how can we change them through the use of technology?). As Brassier suggests: 'The failure to change the world may not be unrelated to the failure to understand it' (Brassier, 2011, 54).

14

Music for cyborgs:
the affect and ethics of noise music

Marie Thompson

Example 1a. The car alarm. A sound designed to provoke alertness, awareness, a response. Never is this sound more effective as in the (relative) dead of night. It cuts through the cityscape, flowing through walls, seeping in through the gaps of the brickwork. It holds me hostage, grabs me by the shoulders and shakes me from my sleep. A faceless cause of disturbance. My heart pounds. I am disorientated by this invisible invader, their intrusion into my most personal space, my home, my bedroom.

Example 1b. Melt-Banana's opening at the Star and Shadow, Newcastle upon Tyne, 18 October 2010. A darkened room is filled with noise. It bounces off the walls, invades my body, sweeping me up with its pulsating waves. The extremes of frequencies push my hearing to its limits but I am excited, my heart racing with anticipation, or is it fear? Where will the noise take me? When will it break? What comes next?

I have described here two very different experiences with sound; one of fear, intrusion and disruption, the other of an overwhelming of the corporeal, an adrenaline-fuelled mixture of excitement and anticipation. Both sonic experiences could be described as an affective encounter with noise. Affect, it would seem, remains necessarily vague and elusive; as a concept it resists being pinned down to a single, clear definition. Affective thinking has afforded a new perspective, *contra* the Cartesian philosophical tradition, on the synthesis or resonance between body and mind, the corporeal and the intellectual. In the work of Spinoza, the body and mind are treated as autonomous entities; however, their developments are parallel: a mind's power to think corresponds to the body's power to act, or, in other words, to affect and be affected. Fast-forward to Deleuze, and affect becomes trans-corporeal swarms of intensities and pre-subjective. For Massumi, following on from Deleuze, affect, when pinned down and qualified, becomes emotion. Whereas emotion is meaningful, conscious and categorized, affect, by contrast, is unqualified, intensive, synaesthetic, insomuch that affect involves the participation of the senses in each other. Moreover, affect is synonymous with noise in that it may be thought of as excess; it is that which is prior to, or the residue after intensity's qualification as emotion.[1] To put it another way, and to perhaps draw the analogy with noise closer still, Steve Shaviro contrasts affect and emotion by arguing that: 'subjects are overwhelmed and traversed by affect, but they *have or possess* their own emotions' (Shaviro, 2010, 3). Affects do not 'belong' to an individual but rather pass through them. Subsequently, in thinking of noise in relation to affect, the question stands not as 'what is noise?' but rather, 'what does noise do?'

In the first exemplar, of 'everyday noise' as it were, noise is an unwanted intrusion into space; it functions as an interruption. Noise, in this instance, threatens 'my' boundaries; when the neighbour's music passes through the walls, it is a vibrational attack upon what I understand to be 'my' sonic space, the space in which I am the guardian and legislator of sound. Similarly, when someone's music spills out from their headphones, leaking into a public sphere, the train or the bus, 'I' am irritated by this violation of an unspoken social contract, the other's breach of the peace. Noise is a force that dominates; it is beyond the grasp of my control.

This is all well and good but what about noise in its alternative guises; does noise still function structurally, that is, as a threat to structures? If we take noise in its communicative definition as interference within or between informational channels, for example, then noise becomes unwanted or extraneous sound that threatens to corrupt signification. This is not to suggest that noise as extraneous sound is meaningless; to be sure, as Attali's thesis in *Noise: the Political Economy of Music* has shown us, noise can be full of information, the base material from which meaning emerges. He states:

> For despite the death it contains, noise carries order within itself; it carries new information. This may seem strange. But noise does in fact create a meaning, first, because the interruption of a message signifies the

interdiction of the transmitted meaning, signifies censorship and rarity; and second, because the very absence of meaning in pure noise or in the meaningless repetition of a message, by unchanneling auditory sensations frees the listener's imagination. The absence of meaning is in this case the presence of all meanings.

(Attali, 1985, 33)

Thus the fault line of noise cannot simply be drawn between the meaningful and the meaningless; nor is it enough to render this ambiguity of meaning as simply a matter of perception. Noise, in its metaphysical guises, is often posted as the not-yet-meaningful or as that which lies beyond or below meaning; a whirlpool of chaos from which sense emerges. Nor can noise be distinguished as unwanted sound, since this posits it as a purely auditory phenomenon. However, noise can remain hidden even within the quiet Cagean concert hall. Noise can reside within unclear handwriting; it can be the granulation or 'snow' on a television image, or unwanted pixilation on a photograph. Similarly, noise may be silence itself; imagine, for example, the silence of an electronic performance due to technical failure, the desperation for repair it can induce. In these instances noise may be thought of once again as the invasion of excess flow of material, a force that disrupts and intrudes. To refer to noise as excess does not require it to come 'from the outside', a radical exteriority, nor does it come from a binarism between inside/outside. Rather, noise exists structurally or relationally; its presence relies on an assemblage of perceivers, generators, borders, vibrations, ideas, geographies, spaces and materials.

Generally speaking then, in its everyday, empirical contexts, noise tends to be understood as negative affect; an unwanted or excess flow of vibrations that invade 'my' world, drowning out other sounds in the auditory or informational plane. It is an attention-seeking nuisance. However, how does noise function in its aesthetic contexts, when noise is used as music, or noise is used in music? The exemplars above exhibit two affectively and, indeed, materially distinct sonic experiences. Yet there has been a tendency to conflate noise 'proper', as it were, and aestheticized versions of noise. Salomé Voegelin, for example, in *Listening to Noise and Silence*, does not seem to draw a clear distinction between noise and noise music. Her claim that 'it is as if noise music lives out the trauma of the beginning of the twentieth century: sounding out its consequences for community and tolerance' (2010, 43) would seem to render noise as negativity and thus, arguably, fails to account for the possible positivity of noise in its performative and aesthetic contexts. Subsequently, she jumps between talking about the 'noise' of my neighbour's music, to the experience of a rave, to a performance

of Otomo Yoshihide, with little explicit consideration of the affective specificity or difference of noise in these three distinct encounters with sound.
Likewise, Douglas Kahn seemingly does not draw an explicit distinction
between noise and noise in music, although he does (correctly) acknowledge
that the 'framing' of sounds changes their impact. Apropos the modernist
scream, he argues that, in its 'natural habitat', the scream 'is thought to be
an irrepressible expression, instantaneously understood through unmediated
communication' (Kahn, 2001, 4). However, the scream in its literary, theatrical
or musical habitats takes on alternative significance, affects and rhetoric:
'does anybody rush to the stage to lend assistance?' (Kahn, 2001, 4). In
Attali's thesis, the negativity of noise becomes integral to its ontology; noise
exists as that which remains outside of music, the violently new. Over time,
noise is gradually assimilated into the musical and is disarmed. However,
Attali's primary thesis of noise as negativity or the negative arguably fails to
account for the positivity of noise, or at least its affective complexity, within
its aesthetic contexts.

Thus a clearer distinction is required between noise and noise music. This
is not to suggest that there is no correspondence between noise 'proper' in
its social and metaphysical conceptions and noise music's aestheticizations of
noise; to be sure, there is a resonance between these noise spheres, with noise
music often harnessing rhetoric regarding invasion, submission, transgression
and so on.[2] However, there are significant affective differences between them;
while noise 'proper' tends to be conceived of in terms of negative affect,
as excess, the sonically abject or as impossible, incomprehensible chaos,
noise music embraces this negativity as positive, productive and desirable;
as a means of gaining new or alternative sensuous experiences. In order to
portray this difference, or rather the specificity of noise within its performative
contexts, noise music may be conceived of as a 'theatre of affect'.

Antonin Artaud's notion of the 'theatre of cruelty' marks a desire to
return, or move beyond, the language of representation to a plane of physical
expression, directed by and towards the corporeal. He states: 'one cannot
separate body and mind, the senses and intellect, and above all, in a domain
where the repeated fatigue of organs, needs sudden shocks to revive our
comprehension' (Artaud and Morgan, 1958, 76). When Artaud speaks of
cruelty, he is not referring to 'martyred flesh, crucified enemies' or 'tortured
victims', nor is this cruelty 'a matter of sadism nor bloodshed, at least not in
any exclusive way' (Artaud, 1958, 101). Rather, he is referring to an 'implacable
intention' and violent physical determinism, capable of rendering perceptible
the lost 'truth' of reality; the inhumanity of humanity, the spectator's hidden
dreams for cannibalism, eroticism, violence.

In short, Artaud wishes to move away from the plane of representation and into the realm of sensation. Similarly, noise music, as a theatre of affect, foregrounds the plane of sensation. Rather than simply representing noise as an auditory phenomenon, that is, merely appropriating those sounds typically considered 'noise' in the everyday, noise music seeks to emulate noise as force; noise music does not borrow from, or not just borrow from, the everyday soundworld of (that which is typically understood as) noise but rather finds ways and means of staging the *feeling and intensity* of noise.

Flesh

What does it mean to be flesh? For we know not what the flesh can do.

Another anecdote: a few months after I moved to Newcastle to begin my Ph.D., a friend and I went to see the noise band Sunn O))) at the Sage Gateshead. As we approached the hall, we were handed earplugs and were advised (via warning signs) to wear them during the gig. When the band began to play, the sound expanded, filling the spectrum, creating a wall of noise. My whole body began to vibrate; my attention was turned inside, to my lungs, my stomach. The sound was, quite literally, force; many people not wearing the earplugs covered their ears as the sound invaded, seizing the bodies of the room, bringing to the fore my existence as vibrating, affective matter. This was not music for hearing, for the sound, without earplugs, was painful. This was music for feeling.

At its most intense, noise music disorganizes the body; it disrupts the organization of the organs. It transforms the organs into a thousand ears, the ears into a vibrating, fluttering drum skin. Noise music addresses me as matter, rendering the body porous. I can feel it in my lungs, my stomach, my throat; it can turn me inside out.

I become flesh. Michael Hardt posits incarnation as an abandonment – an abandonment to the flesh. Christ emptied himself from his transcendental form by becoming-flesh, by taking on a limited materiality, transferring divinity to the immanent. Thus incarnation refuses the dualism of the transcendent and the immanent:

Transcendence, the condition of possibility of being, should not be imagined as above or below the material – it dwells, rather precisely at its very surface. Incarnation is the claim that there is no opposition and no mediation necessary between the transcendent and the immanent, but an intimate complementarily. This immanent transcendence is the most innermost exteriority of being, the potentiality of flesh.

(Hardt, 2002, 79)

The flesh is not simply the body, since the body is discontinuous and hierarchical, bound up in its historical, dialectical opposition to the Cartesian mind. Rather, the flesh is 'the vital materiality of existence'. It contains both corporeality and consciousness; 'the paths of thought and existence are all traced on the flesh' (ibid., 82). To abandon oneself to the flesh is to take on an intensive, continuous existence, to lose oneself, my separations and discontinuities. It is to become immanent, immersed in an impure world. This is the lesson Christ teaches us; through incarnation, his existence as material, matter, slave, Christ 'renounces any divine separation not as a demonstration of ascetic denial, but rather in search for the continuity of life and community (ibid., 81).

There is an ethical content to becoming-flesh; it is an option of joy and love, a belief in this world, this imperfect world. Torture often demands that we separate ourselves from the flesh, distancing ourselves from the corporeal, even in situations of close proximity and intimacy: 'it's not me they are hurting, for they can only touch my body'. In torture, I hide outside my body. Torture is a form of exile; an exile from life. Thus Hardt argues that we should take back the flesh, live in it to its full, affirmative, intensive existence. Through flesh we find freedom. Hardt states:

> The miracle of Christ is to take back the flesh from the soldiers of empire who nailed him to the cross. Even in his torment Christ lived the flesh in all its intensity. The critique of Torture does not require that we should live in such a way as to avoid all violence and all pain – that would be a life without intensity, always already separated from the violence of experience. Rather, we should refuse the separation from the flesh that torture entails: live the violence of experience in the flesh, make our pain a mode of intensity and joy.
>
> (ibid., 81)

Refuse the separation, find the immanent, erotic, common language of intensity; this is how we can overthrow the alienation and isolation that torture demands.

Noise and noise music may be seen to play out this tension between torture and an intensive, joyous existence; noise 'proper', as it were, is often used to control our bodies, separate us out, break us down; I am thinking here specifically of 'everyday' sonic warfare devices such as the Mosquito, used for dispersing groups of 'undesirables'; from rats, to teenagers, to the homeless. Noise music takes this negative force and revels in it, taking us to existence in all our materiality. Noise music is a shared intensity, a shared, sensuous language of the flesh. What do I even mean by me any more? For my boundaries are no longer stable. My body becomes a component within the body of noise; a maelstrom of forces, affects, materials, spaces, technologies and organs.[3] A vibrational mass. It is a dangerous eroticism; it can take (or at least, is imagined to take) 'my' body, the bordered body, to its outer thresholds, its margins. I exist on my skin, at my innermost exteriority. The negativity of the sonic invasion that noise can encompass during its everyday existence thus becomes a positive dimension of noise music: take the force of torture and find a joyous, intensive existence in it.

However, to talk about noise music as a vibrational continuity is by no means to simply align noise music with extremes of amplitude. Noise music is not merely that which is loud; quite the contrary, quiet materials can also generate an intensive noise force. Ryoji Ikeda's album +/−, for example, exploits frequencies on the edges of human hearing, with the album concluding with a tone that only becomes present in its absence; the listener only becomes aware of the tone on its disappearance. Ikeda's music thus makes perceivable the process of hearing itself, toying with its limitations and questioning hearing's purported (ideological) immanence.[4] The barely audible, high-pitched frequencies are often analogous to the sound of the Mosquito device; the sound used for dispersal, separation. Ikeda's music thus takes the negative force of noise and renders it positive; a means of finding new, intensive pleasures; again, take the force of torture and find a joyous, intensive existence in it.

Becoming

What does it mean to be a voice? For we know not yet what the voice can do.

Contra the notion of being, becoming infers non-linear, dynamic processes of change that destabilize the fixity and separations of an entity in revealing not what it is, but what it might be, what it might become. What am I, for example – when do I become a being, since I am always changing, always learning and experiencing new things? Becoming can have an ethico-political agenda. Deleuze's becomings; becoming-animal, becoming-child, becoming-woman are instances of a molecular politics that run against the normative categorizations of the asymmetric binarisms of Western societies; male over female, adult over child, rational over animal, white over non-white. The challenge of becoming does not simply require us to become the opposition, the other side of the binary; it is not enough to imitate child or woman or animal, for this would only repeat and reinforce the cleavages of normative dualisms. Rather, becoming is a disruption, an exposure of the grey area, the 'noise', as it were, of purportedly fixed identities.

For Deleuze, the grey area of becoming is expressed visually in the paintings of Francis Bacon. *Contra* abstraction, which steps outside of the realm of representation and figuration, Bacon's painting instead takes apart the figurative from the inside, 'noisifying' its signification, stripping it of its narrational or representational contexts:

> The abandonment of simple figuration is the general fact of Modern painting [...] but what is interesting is the way in which Bacon, for his part, breaks with figuration: it is not impressionism, not expressionism, not symbolism, not cubism, not abstraction. Never (except maybe in the case of Michelangelo) has anyone broken with figuration by elevating the Figure to such prominence.
>
> (Deleuze, 2004, xiv)

In Bacon's landscapes, the dismantling of representation is achieved primarily through two techniques: 'local scrubbing' and 'asignifying traits', which are devoid of any illustrative function and belong to a precise system of blurriness; they destroy clarity through clarity. Likewise, in his portraits Bacon dismantles the faciality of the figure in order to reveal what lies beneath, which Deleuze identifies as the head. The face is 'a structured, spatial organization that conceals the head' which belongs to the realm of signification, of language, of identity, produced by the abstract machine of faciality. The face is autonomous: 'the inhuman in human beings: that is what the face is from the start' (Deleuze, 2010, 189). The head, by contrast, is integral to the body and dependent on the corporeal. In distorting the face, Deleuze argues that Bacon reveals the becoming-animal of the head. This is not to simply suggest that Bacon paints animal heads as opposed to the human, or paints human faces with animal features, but rather that there is 'a zone of indiscernibility or undecidability between man and animal [...] it is never a combination of forms, but rather the common fact: the common fact of man and animal' (Deleuze, 2004, 21). This common fact is the 'meat' of the head, the human body as flesh and bone, or rather the confrontation of flesh and bone:

> Pity the meat! [...] Meat is not dead flesh for it retains all the sufferings and assumes all the colors of the living flesh [...] Bacon does not say 'pity

the beasts' but rather that every man who suffers is a piece of meat. Meat is the common zone of man and beast.

(Deleuze, 2004, 23)

Destroy the face; reveal the head, the becoming-animal of the human. This is not to return to a better, 'primitive' past, but rather to take up new lines of flight, new lines of intensity, to get outside of what Deleuze refers to as the 'black holes and white walls' of signification and subjectivity. He states:

If human beings have a destiny, it is rather to escape the face, to dismantle the face and facializations [...] not by returning to animality, nor even by returning to the head, but quite spiritual and special becomings-animal, by strange true becomings that get past the wall and get out of black holes, that make faciality traits themselves finally elude the organization of the face – freckles dashing towards the horizon, hair carried off by the wind.

(Deleuze, 2010, 189)

Noise music in general may be understood to be, quite literally, the musicalization of indiscernibility. Noise music relies on an exploitation of the grey area of contradiction; it lies on the fault line between music and non-music, wanted and unwanted, the pleasurable and grotesque, and so on, pulling in various, conflicting directions. Too far towards noise, and noise music gets lost at sea; it becomes nothing but noise. Too far towards music, and it becomes too grounded on the shore; it becomes fully assimilated into the realm of the musical and becomes something else. Moreover, as Hegarty argues with reference to Merzbow, it is not enough to reach the 'extreme' of noise, the end-point, as it were, of a full noise, the 'ultimate noise' within noise music, since this point is always already an impossibility. Thus, for Hegarty:

Merzbow's noise music brings a terminal condition that turns out to have always been the case – music, language, meaning, culture, always haunted by that which it is not, that which surrounds it, threatens it and structures it by providing a frame that dissolves itself. Over and over. Merzbow is the playing out of the fundamentals of music, to the point that there is little left.

(Hegarty, 2007, 157)

Like Bacon's destruction of face, noise music may be understood to take up new lines of flight from music, from *within* music; it takes apart the musical from the inside, in order to make audible the force of noise. This destruction from within is perhaps most explicit with noise music as 'noise rock'; bands such as Boredoms, Ex Models, Sonic Youth and Monotonix may be heard to blur what a 'rock band' sounds like, from within that convention, in their use of unusual forms, sonorities and instrumentations. Similarly, Lou Reed's *Metal Machine Music* (1975) and other guitar-based noisescapes push the question of what the guitar might be, what it can do, exploring its sonic potentialities beyond its conventional modes of existence.

The Norwegian vocalist, Maja Ratkje, provides an interesting parallel to Bacon's 'noisification' of the face, in her 'noisification' of the voice from within itself. In the auditory realm, the voice occupies a similar position to the face; it typically relates to notions of identity, language and subjectivity.[5] However, Ratkje, through her use of technologies and extended vocal techniques, allows the voice to take on new becomings, beyond its traditional functions and expressions. In the track 'Vox',[6] for example, beautiful, melancholic voice tones are juxtaposed and interrupted with various noise sounds: high frequencies, granulated tones and what sound like the screeches of tape-recorders. The (technological) voice is pushed higher and higher, until it is eventually swallowed up by the other textural noise sounds. Suddenly, the building chaos stops and glitches, clicks and fragmented manipulations of the voice may be heard. Out of this emerge more and more layers of granulated sounds, this time accompanied by a melodic yet distorted voice, until it is again swallowed up by the sound of static and other noise sounds. What seems to be Ratkje's voice, or perhaps recordings of her voice, takes on a high-pitched, gibberish, mewing quality. The volume is altered so that there is a sweeping motion in the static, similar to that to a radio being tuned. The track ends with twittering, birdlike sounds that also open the track, accompanied by little but static.

What is interesting about 'Vox' is that Ratkje does not simply abandon the conventional musicality of the voice. Just as Bacon maintains the figure beyond figuration, Ratkje maintains up to a point the 'musical' voice. However, like Bacon's figures, it is radically deconstructed, distorted. The growing indiscernibility for the listener of the voice and the non-voice, the organic and the inorganic, the 'original' (whatever that may be) and the recorded, in 'Vox' may be read as a destruction from the inside; Ratkje cracks open the voice to find a mouth full of wires. In doing so, Ratkje does not assert what the voice is, or rather what her voice is, but instead pushes the question of what it might be; its potential to take on new forms, new modes of existence. With the assistance of inorganic intervention, the voice is loosened from its identity; it no longer faces the organic limitation of the human voice box. Nor is it limited to representation, meaning, logocentrism: it flees Deleuze's 'black holes and white walls' of signification and subjectivity. The voice is cut loose from its organization and function, and is instead free to run within, as part of, the plane of noise sounds, as a voice for itself.

Cyborg

What does it mean to be music? For we know not yet what music can do.

As a means of moving towards a conclusion, I would like to open up this ethico-political project of becoming that Deleuze presents to the notion of noise music as a space with a radical potential that exists within the structures of capitalism. It would be problematic to suggest that noise music, as many have previously claimed in the name of the avant-garde, is simply subversive towards musical, and by extension, socio-political codes due to its oppositional status. Noise music as commercial object can be subject to a vulgar Marxist critique of commodity fetishism; Nick Smith has identified the 'blatant contradiction' of the commodification of noise.

Apropos Merzbow's *Merzbox*, he states:

> Marketed as a limited edition collector's item, it has sold for upwards of two thousand US dollars. While such a quantity would be a monumental purchase for any musical collection, the fact that this buys a case-full of noise adds to its conspicuousness. ... Rather than entering the market kicking and screaming, noise plays along as well as Pokémon cards and Beanie Babies
>
> (Smith, 2005, 54)

Similarly, *contra* to the rhetoric pertaining to noise music's power of subversion, Simon Reynolds points to the 'subversive fallacy' of the use of noise in music. The subversive nature of noise is, in fact, when one considers its audience, self-subversion; such rhetoric creates a fictive enemy, be they grown-ups, or 'straights' or those complicit with the values of pop music. However, the only power structures overthrown by noise are those that exist in the (complicit) listener's head.[7] Just as Deleuze insists that Becoming cannot simply involve becoming the other side of the binary, since this merely reasserts the normative cleavages that govern us, noise music's purported disavowal of the musical and its broader socio-political structures relies upon an investment *in* these structures.

Thus the aim of the game is not transgression, since transgressions reassert that which they seek to oppose, escape or overturn. What is needed, rather, is an exposure of the anomaly, the blurring of the binary, an entangling of the wires. Dealing with that which is at hand rather than seeking to step outside altogether. With this in mind, noise music may be seen to have an ethico-political potential in spite of itself; from within the walls of the capitalist fortress, of performative spaces, of music, from which it can pose questions regarding what it means to be included within these spaces. What does it mean to be musical? What does it mean to be virtuosic? What does it mean to perform? What does it mean to hear? What does it mean to fail?

Regeneration, not rebirth: this is the repositioning that Donna Haraway's cyborg seeks. The cyborg finds a sister in Maja Ratkje's noise voice; in the same way that Ratkje's indiscernibility undermines normative 'molar' categorizations that govern the identity of the voice, the cyborg, likewise, poses a problem to dualisms between man and machine, organic and inorganic, corporeal and incorporeal. The figure of the cyborg is not innocent; it was not born 'outside', nor does it stand in a 'pure' position, but rather is the offspring of war, of imperialism and capitalism. But it is only from this position, from the inside, that the cyborg can begin to decouple normative binaristic codes and, moreover, offer new lines of flight, to move beyond. Haraway states:

> We do not need a totality in order to work well. The feminist dream of a common language, like all dreams for a perfectly true language, of perfectly faithful naming of experience, is a totalizing and imperialist one. In that sense, dialectics too is a dream language, longing to resolve contradiction. Perhaps ironically, we can learn from our fusions with animals and machines how not to be man, the embodiment of Western logos.
>
> (Haraway, 1991, 173)

Imperfect, partial, of questionable origins but potentially disruptive; the cyborg figure may find its voice and its stage in noise music, as that which exists as, or at least, has the potential to exist as, a problem, as contradiction. To be sure, cyborg politics is a politics of noise:

> Cyborg politics is the struggle for language and the struggle against perfect communication, against the one code that translates all meaning perfectly, the central dogma of phallogocentrism. That is why cyborg politics insist on noise and advocate pollution, rejoicing in the illegitimate fusions of animal and machine.
>
> (ibid., 176)

I finish, then, not with grand or profound insights or conclusions but rather gesturing towards a potentiality for exploring noise music's political potential; noise music as cyborg music.

15

What is noise?
An inquiry into its formal properties
Saeed Hydaralli

Introduction

Today, due to a number of recent developments, the phenomenon of noise as sound requires some clarification. For instance, while loud sounds have always been a source of disquiet and worry,[1] the increase in the cacophony of cities as a function of the technologies of industrialization has raised concerns around the unhealthy consequences of those loud sounds which have been named noise pollution:

> In European countries about 40% of the population are exposed to road traffic noise with an equivalent sound pressure level exceeding 55 dB(A) daytime and 20% are exposed to levels exceeding 65 dB(A). Taking all exposure to transportation noise together about half of the European Union citizens are estimated to live in zones which do not ensure acoustical comfort to residents.
>
> (WHO, 1999, iii)

What is interesting to notice in that characterization is the way in which noise is understood as a quantitative measure – dB(A) – that complies with some minimum sound pressure level measured in decibels.[2] Sounds which register below that level are not considered noise and are therefore not perceived as a source of worry (a danger to health and well-being). A differing view holds that policy inspired by a perspective where the sonic environment is conceived as suffering from noise pollution and therefore in need of amelioration fails to distinguish between noise which is wanted ('positive sounds') versus that which is unwanted ('negative sounds') as if there are two distinct (differently charged) and irreconcilable types of sounds that pervade the urban soundscape.

> One problem with the European process of noise policy [exemplified by the WHO] ... is that it is ... based on metrics and treats noise as something unwanted that is to be controlled, whereas in the area of sound management a different approach is necessary due to the localized nature of sound production. [...] So, how can the positive sounds that people value in an area be mapped or included in the process?
>
> (Adams *et al.*, 2006, 2396)

Instead of the WHO and European public health policy that conceives of the typical physical environment of the city as saturated with noise pollution, this view proposes that the urban soundscape comprises good and bad sounds, what it calls 'positive and negative soundmarks' (Adams *et al.*, 2006, 2396). According to this view, a sound could meet the WHO's criteria for noise (a specific decibel level, depending on whether it is daytime or night-time) but yet be acceptable if it is a 'positive' sound.

While these seemingly contrasting positions disagree over which loud sounds of a certain prescribed decibel measure comprise noise (all loud sounds versus only some loud sounds), they are none the less united by the view that noise is ultimately a metric. Yet it has long been noted that noise exceeds a strictly quantitative consideration: 'Noise that may be highly vexatious may register little in decibels, as in the insistent cough or sniff in a library' (Bailey, 1996, 50). Consequently, if different sounds that register on the higher and lower ends of the decibel scale can both be named noise, then a clarification of that phenomenon (noise) is necessary. Can noise take the form of sounds that do not meet the prescribed public health policy criteria? And can there be loud sounds that meet or exceed that quantitative criterion that are none the less not received as noise? In order to pursue these questions we begin with an empirical example where noise is being claimed as being present, even though the corresponding sound levels which inform that claim often do not meet the criteria set out by public health policy. We find such an example in the widespread occurrence of complaints in relation to neighbour noise in the city. Neighbour complaints launched against sounds that are received as noise are often not grounded in decibel measures. For instance, in trying to tackle the problem of noisy neighbours in a Dutch city, the following was noted: 'the minister Irene Vorrink ... claimed that such ordinances [in relation to noisy neighbours] were not effective anyhow because [...] people's standards differed; what some considered normal, others saw as nuisance' (Bijsterveld, 2003, 191). The minister proposes that neighbour noises are difficult to regulate owing to the seemingly differing criteria used by city-dwellers to identify noise. Similarly, the WHO shares the belief that neighbour noises are difficult to regulate due to what it calls 'lack of methods to define and measure it'.

> Although many countries have regulations on community noise from road, rail and air traffic, and from construction and industrial plants, few have regulations on neighbourhood noise. This is probably due to the lack of methods to define and measure it, and to the difficulty of controlling it.
>
> (WHO, 1999, 1)

The point not to be missed is that neighbour noises are inconsistent with the quantification of noise; that is, noise as an objective measure.[3] That something as prominent as neighbour noises defies the official view of noise raises questions about noise as officially formulated. It also suggests that an understanding of how sounds are construed as noise by neighbours might provide necessary insight that clarifies the phenomenon of noise. Perhaps neighbour noises represent the site where the complexity of noise best comes to view (and may best be heard). After all, it is here that sounds of various measures are often construed as noise, many of which do not meet the objective criteria as formulated by regulatory policy: 'even though the decibel became a major factor in measuring and controlling urban traffic noise, decibel- and noise level-based legislation aimed at regulating distur-bance from neighbors has not been realized in any comprehensive manner' (Bijsterveld, 2003, 174). As a consequence,

> in the mid-1980s, local police needed to intervene about 70,000 times in neighborly noise disputes .... In the Netherlands today, nearly one out of three citizens complains of noise produced by neighbors. The country's Noise Abatement Act, however, does not encompass noisy behavior of neighbors.
>
> (Bijsterveld, 2003, 174)

All of this confirms the limitation of a quantitative orientation to noise. Thus, we set ourselves the task of recovering the elementary form of noise, those characteristics that are essential to the phenomenon. In other words, what makes a sound noise? Does the commitment to quantification ('trust in numbers'; reliance on objective scientific standards) undermine the ability to grasp noise in its most elementary form? It would appear that the very thing that needs clarification – the concept of noise – is taken for granted by public health policy in order to formulate it as noise pollution.

The phenomenology of noise

If loudness that satisfies a certain decibel measure, in the way that regulatory policy proposes (cf. the WHO), is not sufficient for a sound to be classified as noise – after all, loud sounds can also be engaged as stimulating, exciting, and the like (cf. Adams *et al.*, (2006) on 'positive soundmarks'), and at the same time, many soft sounds are often received as noise (cf. Bailey, 1996, 50) – then what criteria exactly would provide for the presence of noise? Our inquiry into the form (phenomenon) of noise might be assisted by bringing to bear some reflection on the following:

> what Thomas [Carlyle] insisted on attacking as noise, his wife came to perceive as the necessary and innocuous bustle of constructing and managing a home, the working sounds, so to speak, of one facet of her profession ... their contrary perceptions do indicate the difference between the socially-defined labor of the homemaker, who oversaw the often noisy inhabitants and affairs of her house, and the hushed sound of the isolated author at work under her roof.
>
> (Picker, 2000, 436–7)

We are confident that neither Carlyle nor his wife had relied on some quantitative standard to determine whether those sounds were in fact noise. We say this knowing full well that the concept of the decibel (and the complementary decibel meter) had yet to be invented. At the same time, we know that an absolute measure has never been at the everyday basis of what is construed as noise. This we know from observations such as the following: 'contrary to the common usage of the word, noise is not necessarily loud. There are soft noises: the turning of a page, distant footsteps, normal breathing' (Levarie, 1977, 21–2). It should also be noted that the noise which Thomas Carlyle complains of would likely hardly qualify as 'noise' according to regulatory criteria whereby 'noise' are loud sounds of a certain decibel measure. After all, the sounds in the Carlyle household are produced as a by-product of the 'bustle of constructing and managing a home'. Noise as a decibel measure, in the way that policy proposes, would suggest something like a mechanical relationship to sound. According to that view, either Carlyle or his wife would have to be wrong. That is, noise is either present or absent, but cannot be both absent and present. Such a view, with the assistance of an external standard, believes that the 'dispute' can be unambiguously resolved. In other words, noise is empirical and quantitative. However, we resist (defer) such judgement and direct our interest at trying to understand why the same sounds were differentially perceived by Carlyle (as noise) and his wife (as not-noise). Such a deferral is designed to allow for the phenomena of noise to come to view (to be heard) in the ways that it makes its appearance in everyday life. Let us listen to Michel Serres, when he writes: 'following scientific tradition, let us call *noise* the set of these phenomena of interference that become obstacles to communication' (Serres, 1982, 66). Serres reminds us that noise, whether sound or otherwise, is that which interferes with communication.[4] Communication is that process which joins sender and receiver, the uniting of an objective with its realization. Thus it may seem as if noise only interferes with communication when it undermines the signal between an actor and her interlocutor, which might include that actor's work or some other interlocutor that is separate from the actor herself. Yet, as Arendt (2000, 408–16) tells us, the thinking actor is dual, and thus noise also interferes with activity, the communication represented by the dialogue between ego and alter, involved in thinking. Noise, it appears, are sounds that prove to be obstacles to the achievement of everyday objectives. Put differently, noise, it seems, works to undermine the ability to concentrate one's focus on a desired outcome. An absence of such interference would then mean an absence of noise. We might say that for Mrs Carlyle the sounds are indeed 'working sounds', coextensive with her commitment, and therefore comprise part of her focus. They serve to confirm that the necessary tasks are being tackled, and as such assist in the discharging of her mandate of household management. Indeed, she finds the sounds to be stimulating rather than any kind of interference or obstacle (noise). On the other hand, for her husband (Thomas Carlyle), those very sounds conflict with his writerly interest. That is, they amount to interference in relation to his writerly projects, and it is on that basis that he perceives those household sounds to be noise.[5]

To better understand how noise functions, that is, how it manages to do its work of interference, we might consider the following observation: '[For Serres] "Noise" is … where it becomes impossible to clearly differentiate one thing from another. There is only a continual movement which seems to overrun place, take up and confuse space' (Brown, 2002, 13). In effect, noise erases borders (distinctions), making previously delimited spaces into one indistinct space. There is no longer a foreground and a background. Indeed, the background supplants the foreground providing for what Serres (1982) called an interference with communication. For example, in the case of the Carlyle household, the sounds proved to be noise for Thomas Carlyle because they erased the border between his study and the rest of the house. The entire house assumed a similar sonic ambience, as if the distinction between Carlyle's study and the rest of the house was contrived, without any real difference. Such a sonic continuity proved inhospitable to Carlyle and his work because it deprived him of that sonic distinction between foreground and background that he found suitable, and necessary, for such work. In other words, the border between the study and the rest of the house was of the utmost significance as far as sounds were concerned. Whereas for Mrs Carlyle, no such breach of a boundary transpired because the sounds that resonated in the house confirmed her understanding of it as one continuous (uninterrupted) sonic space versus her husband's different understanding of that space as distinctly divided along sonic parameters. For Mrs Carlyle, the sonic border was between the inside of the house and that which transpired outside of the house.

To elaborate further, the sonic character of any space or place takes its shape, in part, from the surrounding soundscape in which it is immersed. Such a surrounding soundscape we might call the background. The typical and predominant sonic character of any space or place may be thought of as its foreground. For Mrs Carlyle, the 'working sounds' heard in her home represent the typical and predominant sonic character of that space and therefore comprise her sonic foreground. Her background (of sounds) would be those that are part of the larger ambient soundscape in which her household is situated, say, the sounds of the neighbourhood. Noise for Mrs. Carlyle would be sounds that interfere with her ability to, in this case, do the work of 'constructing and managing a home'. Similarly, for Thomas Carlyle, his foreground is represented by the ambient space in which he pursues his work, a foreground that is typically absent of insistent sounds such as those associated with 'the bustle of constructing and managing a home'. In other words, the foreground (including sounds) is constitutive of that which makes it possible to realize the objective at hand. His background (of sounds) would also be the larger ambient soundscape in which his household is situated, and includes the activities conducted in the areas of his house outside of his study. Noise for Carlyle would also be sounds that interfere with the task at hand, in this case writing. The point not to be missed is that though noise would be made up of different kinds of sounds for each of Carlyle and his wife, the constitution of noise remains the same. That is, noise is experienced when background sounds (the larger ambient soundscape in which one is located, for example, the sounds emanating from areas of Carlyle's house outside of his study) become discernible to the foreground in ways that interfere with foreground activities. In other words, we might say that noise is experienced when background sounds supplant the ambience of the foreground. Noise is sound which inverts or undermines the foreground–background relation. Here we also begin to see that a sonic background is inextricable with every social environment. It is when that background supplants the foreground that noise results. Noise is not a matter of decibels. A sound is construed as noise when it interferes with (makes impossible) one's ability to perform the task at hand. It is this phenomenological understanding of noise that permits the range of sounds, from the very loud to the very quiet, in the social landscape to be differently interpreted, spatially and temporally, as noise, as ambient sound, or as stimulating.

Let us look at another example which in some ways is similar to the Carlyle household, but more directly addresses the conflict between policy and social theory vis-à-vis noise, to see if it corroborates the understanding of the phenomenon of noise that we have been developing.

With the exception of damage to the hearing organ, the exposed organism's reaction to the perception of sound is strongly dependent on the context of exposure. The effects of noise exposure cannot be understood only by taking mechanisms of toxic action into account. For example, the sounds in a discotheque are music to the dancers but noise to the neighbors. In the first case, the exposure would not be annoying but is expected to contribute to hearing loss; for the neighbors, hearing loss would be improbable, but annoyance would certainly occur.

(Passchier-Vermeer and Passchier, 2000, 123)

The speech here expresses the desire to transcend the public health understanding of noise which is exclusively in terms of decibel levels that have negative physiological consequences ('damage to the hearing organ'; 'mechanisms of toxic action'). The example of the neighbour who is annoyed by sounds (in this case music) that pose almost no threat of damage to their ears is meant to signal a more complex understanding of noise than that proposed by the WHO (public health). What such a representation is unable to (or does not) do however is tell us what none the less makes those sounds noise to the neighbours; that is, what makes them annoying, which we understand to mean interference as a consequence of erasing the sonic border between the discotheque and residential quarters (even though 'hearing loss would be improbable'). What is it about the sound of the music that permits us to call it noise if in this case it has little to do with approaching or exceeding the scientific measure of noise (that is, sound that is a threat to hearing impairment)? What makes a sound music to one person and noise to another? To say that it is noise because it is annoying is not a clarification of a problem but only a tautology, since noise, in its etymology, is related to nausea (Porteous, 1990, 63; Serres, 1995, 20) which has as one of its lesser characteristics the quality of being bothersome or irritating (both synonymous with annoyance).

Although Passchier-Vermeer and Passchier are not able to adequately develop the relationship of annoyance to noise in ways that provide a clarification of the phenomenon of noise, they none the less supply the material from which we might be able to do some of that work. For instance, they tell us that 'noise annoyance is a feeling of resentment, displeasure, discomfort, dissatisfaction, or offense when noise interferes with someone's thoughts, feelings, or actual activities' (Passchier-Vermeer and Passchier, 2000, 126). We can begin to discern the character of noise in statements such as 'noise interferes with someone's thoughts, feelings, or actual activities'. Noise, it becomes evident, is sound that reorients our attention away from that with which we are or wish to be engaged.[6] It is in that sense that sound from a discotheque may be annoying in the way suggested by the authors. If, however, those sounds are not received by the neighbours as that which reorients their focus (remains in the background; or they choose to orient to it as their foreground), then it is not understood by those subjects as noise. Additional data are provided by these authors that permit us to further clarify the problem of noise. They cite a 1991 study which showed that the 'psychosocial well-being of subjects exposed to high levels of road traffic noise was not related to daytime noise exposure but to night-time equivalent sound level in the bedroom and to subjectively experienced sleep quality' (Passchier-Vermeer and Passchier, 2000, 128). We are told that whereas high levels of daytime road traffic noise did not impact upon the psychosocial well-being of subjects, equivalent night-time sound levels did indeed negatively impact upon psychosocial well-being. The authors however did not account for that difference, an accounting that would be necessary if we are to understand why those equivalent sounds are differently experienced, one as benign, not noise (daytime road traffic noise), and the other as noise, harmful to psychosocial well-being (night-time road traffic noise). Of course, the obvious difference is that background noise levels are lower at night, thus amplifying the night-time resonance of equivalent daytime sound levels. Yet, even that insight does not account for why the same sound levels are differently received, one as noise, the other as benign. It is crucial that we understand that during the day, those high levels of road traffic noise are part of, and indeed significantly contribute to, an already amplified soundscape which serves as a sonic background such that they do not typically interfere with whatever it is that one is absorbed by, since one's foreground is already calibrated to account for that higher everyday sonic background. Whereas those same sound levels at night, since they are intermittent rather than typical, would represent a sufficient contrast with the foreground to the extent that they become the foreground, such that they would prove disruptive to one's immediate preoccupation, particularly pursuits having to do with sleep, rest and the like. Put differently, at night, because of the typically lower level of background sounds, road traffic (or other sounds) comparable with those occurring during the day would have the capacity to sufficiently interfere with one's preoccupation, and as such constitute noise. Noise is essentially the condition where the background becomes the foreground to the extent that it impairs one's attention to the undertaking at hand (the foreground). We typically experience the sounds of traffic in the city as ambient sounds and therefore unnoticed. What is really interesting here is the implicit concession that the background 'noise' of the city, however loud that may be, is not typically considered noise because it is experienced as inextricable with city life and therefore more or less unnoticed (or at least, not sufficiently noticed to interfere with the foreground). Of course, there is a limit to how much background 'noise' is permissible before it damages the human ear (cf. sound barriers vis-à-vis highways, even though traffic noise is typically considered background noise).[7]

What is noise cannot be substantively predefined or known in advance in the way that public health policy proposes. It is however conceptually known in advance as a certain kind of relation, one in which the foreground is supplanted by the sonic background. It is the collapsing of the foreground and the background that is appealed to by social actors in their understanding of noise. Noise, we might say, is always reflexively determined. Even the most violent and deafening sounds are not received as noise if they are the foreground to social action. For example, the sounds at a Formula One race are not noise to the spectators, since that is their object of engagement. Here again we are reminded that noise is a social relationship, always socially grounded, rather than a natural fact.

Can such a formulation hold up to scrutiny? Can this be what social actors mean when they complain about noise? Moreover, can it be that it is precisely the understanding of noise we have developed that accounts for why the public health understanding of noise as a metric (articulated by WHO and the variety of noise policy initiatives it has inspired in the form of noise by-laws) does not resonate with city dwellers and is unable to mediate the innumerable noise complaints that cities relentlessly generate? In order to answer these questions adequately, it is necessary to examine a case where the question of noise is subject to legal argument.

The case of The Docks versus Toronto Islands Residents Association (TICA)

On 17 February 2005 the Alcohol and Gaming Commission of Ontario (AGCO) commenced a hearing, which ultimately lasted 26 days, to determine whether The Docks nightclub was guilty of consistently violating the city of Toronto's noise by-law. That hearing was convened after almost 10 years of persistent, and unresolved,[8] noise complaints against The Docks by the residents of the Toronto Islands. We propose that such a long-standing dispute is only possible because of an insufficiently developed formulation by the city and its representatives of both the problem of noise *and* the relationship of the soundscape to the health and well-being of the city (as evidenced in their interpretation of the existing noise by-law). That such is indeed the situation is revealed to us by attending to the transcript of the conflict between The Docks and Toronto Islands Community Association (TICA) as adjudicated by the AGCO. What is more, it is precisely in the transcript of that conflict that we will be able to locate the evidence which confirms the understanding of noise we have been developing.

We will begin by recovering the official understanding (consistent with the public health view) around which sounds are heard as constituting noise. Such an understanding is articulated within the transcript of the conflict between The Docks and TICA as adjudicated by the AGCO. Here is Detective Sergeant Brian O'Halloran of the Ontario Provincial Police discussing how the police go about determining whether a noise complaint is legitimate; that is, whether such a complaint points to the presence of noise.

> Well, the only noise that we would look after is patio noise. I know, I'm familiar with the Coulter report and encouraged to enforcing that, our inspectors don't have the capability or equipment to do that. In the Coulter Report because they started talking about decimals[9] [*sic*] and other noise, it's measurements, that really our department can't or don't have the equipment to enforce.
>
> (Alcohol and Gaming Commission of Ontario, 2005, 840, 843)

Notice here the quantitative understanding that the police have vis-à-vis noise. The police based their understanding of the city of Toronto noise by-law as refracted through the Coulter report which had been commissioned by the city of Toronto in 1996 to prescribe the sound levels to which The Docks needed to adhere in order to abide by the city's noise by-laws (Alcohol and Gaming Commission of Ontario, 2005, 102–4). They are therefore using the working assumption that noise can only be determined through measurement. In other words, for a sound to be noise, it must conform to a prescribed decibel measure. And since the police do not have the appropriate equipment to conduct those measurements, they have taken the position that they are ill-equipped to intervene in the dispute between The Docks and TICA around noise. Thus it appears that the noise by-law, whatever it might actually say in its 'fine print',[10] suggests to those charged with its enforcement that noise is a function of measurement, and tends to correlate with the loudness of the sound. Indeed, if counsel, Mr Macos, for the defendant (The Docks) is correct, it appears that the Medical Officer for the province of Ontario also shares that quantified understanding of noise: 'and I also notice from Dr Basser's[11] [sic] report, for example, that 70 [decibels] seems to be a level which raises some concern for her' (Alcohol and Gaming Commission of Ontario, 2005, 1205). Such a stance by Dr. Basrur would conform to the public health view of noise which we have previously articulated above. That the official view of noise seems to be one grounded in an abstract relation to quantification makes it unsurprising that The Docks would attempt to defend itself against the charge of noise pollution by resorting to an argument grounded in such logic. Thus counsel for The Docks asks:

> why is the City then approving residential development along these arterial roads, where you've just discussed; we've got Queen's Quay; we've got Front Street in the Donlands; yet you're proposing that five thousand people live in each of these areas, in an ambient that's already 70 decibels?
> (Alcohol and Gaming Commission of Ontario, 2005, 1205)

Mr Macos means to say that if the city does not consider 70 decibels noise (and how can it if it proposes to build housing in such an ambient space?) then it is entirely likely that his client is not guilty of noise pollution if it can be shown that the sound level The Docks produces is lower than 70 dB(A). Counsel's question clearly suggests, even though he is seemingly unaware of the implications of that question, that noise exceeds a concern with the level of sound, something which the city implicitly concedes by promoting residential development in areas where sound levels meet and exceed its implied criteria for noise. Let us listen to Island residents speaking about noise, which they attribute to The Docks:

> I can often perceive the music coming from the venue above and beyond Peter Mansbridge's [a television newscaster] delivery. (Gaskin in Alcohol and Gaming Commission of Ontario, 2005, 81)

We went inside. We closed the windows, closed the doors, and it was still impossible for us to talk, so she just left. (Jackson in Alcohol and Gaming Commission of Ontario, 2005, 91)

I must admit it causes me to be quite agitated and restless. And, if I'm studying or doing work or trying to do work at home, I can't. (Jackson in Alcohol and Gaming Commission of Ontario, 2005, 91)

Okay, to have constant bass go all night is like torture. It does not have to be loud. It goes through my pillow and into my heart. (Pitcher in Alcohol and Gaming Commission of Ontario, 2005, 445)

We note that in all instances, Island residents, without necessarily understanding it explicitly, formulate noise as sounds that interfere with their ability to fully engage with whatever it is that they wish to at that moment, whether it is watching television, having a conversation, studying or working. Noise, it would appear, comprises sounds which distract from that which one is immersed. Could that be the characteristic which unites disparate sounds as noise? If that were indeed the case then it would not necessarily matter how loud the sound is, as long as it manages to insinuate itself into one's psychic space such that it meaningfully distracts from the project at hand. And is this not precisely what is being suggested by the following?

[A]nd even a low bass constantly pounding for hours is distressing, and I don't mean that low frequency bass at this point. I mean just a quiet – as you referred to, 'a whisper', Mr. Macos. That can be annoying after hours, just a very light bass, when you're trying to sleep.
(Pitcher in Alcohol and Gaming Commission of Ontario, 2005, 452)

In other words, sounds that distract (noise) can be as soft as a whisper or as loud as a jackhammer.

We can understand the background–foreground relationship as one where the foreground is where one's interest is directed. Noise is that which distracts from (interferes with) that interest, whether in intermittent or sustained ways. For example, if conversation is the primary interest that collects a group, then sounds which undermine that conversational interest would be classified as noise. In this case it is typically loud sounds that are more readily able to prove disruptive. However, if a group collects for the purposes of being among others in public, then conversation, while likely a feature of such a setting, is not necessarily central to the definition of the situation. As such, sounds that would have been considered noise in the prior scenario (the background intruding on the foreground) are considered legitimate to the situation (those sounds are part of the foreground in the first place) and are handled as ambient sounds. Noise in such a scenario would represent sounds that subvert the typical foreground experience of such a setting. City residents, and others, identify noise by acting on the 'seen, but unnoticed' assumption (Garfinkel, 1967) that city life, in its various domains or appearances, is inextricable from a background quantum of sound that is inescapable and particular to that domain. To the extent that they are the background sounds, they are taken for granted and are typically unnoticed. Indeed, such sounds are often unnoticed to the degree that many can no longer hear them, so accommodated are social actors to them. That a consideration of the ambient soundscape (background sounds) is indispensable to the determination of the presence or absence of noise is fleetingly alluded to by in the Appendix to the City of Toronto's Noise By-Law No. 111–2003 (see endnote 10); yet the by-law does not at all develop that recognition in ways that would provide for a robust understanding of the phenomenon of noise.

It is only when we come to understand noise as a situation where background sounds intrude on the foreground to the extent that foreground activities are undermined that we can shed some light on the conflict between The Docks and the TICA. Because The Docks was located on the mainland, which has a higher level of background sounds, it did not pose a significant noise problem for its neighbours on the mainland. This may be why The Docks insisted on defending itself by arguing that if its sound levels were not a problem for its mainland neighbours, then how could it be one for the Islanders? The defendant found itself in a situation where it was proximate to a residential area (the Toronto Islands) whose background sound levels were not typically urban (what the City of Toronto Noise By-Law refers to as a 'Class 2 Area'). Yet it had been given a liquor licence for activities that necessarily produce a certain quantum of sound which might be largely consistent with the background sound of a large city ('Class 1 Area'). Thus counsel for the defence articulates this incompatible situation in the following: 'what the licensee is really seeking is some clear rules of operation' (Macos, Docks Transcript, 2005, 20).

Noise is sound which erases the border between spaces in ways that undermine a previously established foreground–background sonic relationship. In this way it interferes with the discharging of the preoccupations of that foreground. It is here that noise itself is revealed to be ambiguous, comprising of the full spectrum of sounds. The noise that is a problem for most city residents is the kind which interferes with intended activities, but defies quantification (a metric). It is this ambiguous aspect of everyday noise that public health policy finds impossible to master. Now that we have formulated the essential character of noise, we are in a position to clarify the public health representation of the urban sonic environment as one that is buffeted by a relentless torrent of noise pollution. Our analysis has essentially shown, among other things, that noise is an inescapable feature of urban (and indeed, collective) life. The inevitability of noise is a function of that essential character of noise whereby, as we have shown, it (noise) amounts to a situation where the distinction between the background and foreground, as they pertain to sounds, collapses (is erased) resulting in a disturbance. In other words, noise tends to present itself in the most innocuous of situations because, rather than being a statistic (a metric), it is a relationship or ratio. Yet, because noise is an abiding source of tension in urban life (ranging from neighbour noises to traffic), and because it can cause real physiological and perhaps other kinds of harm to members, and because of its elusive quality (what is and what is not noise cannot be known in advance, but can only be determined at the moment of its happening), noise represents a seemingly impossible dilemma for city dwellers and authorities alike.

Conclusion

The recent global concern with urban noise pollution has provided us with the incentive to seek to clarify the phenomenon of noise since, in its everyday understanding, it seems to exceed the quantitative characterization it has been given by public health policy. Yet that everyday understanding, which informs the distinction, for social actors, between the presence and absence of noise, has largely remained implicit and therefore in need of unconcealment.

By engaging in an analysis of noise as an everyday phenomenon, exemplified by complaints in relation to what is called neighbour noise, we have shown that noise cannot be substantively predefined or known in advance in the way that public health policy proposes. It is however conceptually known in advance as a certain kind of relation, one in which the foreground is supplanted by the sonic background. It is the collapsing of the foreground and the background that is appealed to by members in their understanding of noise. Noise is always reflexively determined.

16

Considering Sound:
reflecting on the language, meaning and entailments of noise

Khadijah White

The aural landscape is an ever-present site – keys fall, doors open, dogs bark, children laugh, sirens wail, phones ring and spouses snore. Each movement, each motion produces vibrations that move through the air and connect to the human ear. This connection, the moment in which the human ear can perceive vibrations and waves across space and access events that the eye has yet to see and the mind to grasp – this is the phenomenon that both scientists and laypeople alike call sound. Sound orients people to the visual landscape through a process that includes perception, recall, identification, evaluation and response.[1] These final two stages, evaluation and response, mark the point in which a sound's 'signal' can become a social problem – otherwise known as 'noise'.

According to one scholar, noise in the United States is considered as 'the scourge of the 20th century' (Baron, 1970, 27). Generally speaking, the label *noise* is used to designate a sound at an extremely loud volume and is considered to be a physical reality, measurable and quantifiable, much like water, air or heat. Instead, I offer up scholars George Lakoff and Mark Johnson's notion that 'what is real for an individual as a member of a culture is a product both of his social reality and of the way in which that [social reality] shapes his experience of the physical world' (Lakoff and Johnson, 2003, 146). Through everyday movement within the physical world, sounds interact with the norms, customs, memories and space of every person and, in perceiving them as unwanted, these sounds become noise. As such, one person's loud noise may very well be another person's pleasant sound.

Scholars have used the term 'soundscape' to examine people's negotiation of sound and noise within a space and, in doing so, displace the primacy of visual symbols within the physical landscape and emphasize the significance of aural markers within shared environments (Smith, 1994; Arkette, 2004). As Sophie Arkette observes, 'there is a growing schism between the space that physical objects occupy, and the acoustic space that is taken up with a sounding object' (2004, 166). In this environment the sound of objects becomes noise through the influence of cultural norms, existing power and authority structures, regular uses of place, and temporal practices in various communities. Thus, noise is always socially constituted and in need of determination, debate and agreement about its existence or to permit its presence. Noise is a regularly contested social object, a territorial claim, and a violation of the social and legal contract, triggering conflicts that often demand outside intervention and require resolutions governed by language. This chapter is an examination of the language that constructs noise as a social problem. Lakoff and Johnson (2003, 125) note that:

Individual concepts are not defined in an isolated fashion, but rather in terms of their roles in natural kinds of experiences. ... Rather than being rigidly defined, concepts arising from our experiences are open-ended. Metaphors and hedges are systematic devices for further defining a concept and for changing its range of applicability.

I will begin with a broad discussion of how noise has been socially constructed as both a physical and intangible reality within a communal sphere. I will then examine the related metaphors of noise and their significance in impacting upon the use, abuse and treatment of noise in the everyday world.

Hearing noise: the (physical) reception of sound

The scholarly study of sound has defined itself primarily around the human act of hearing, which involves numerous physical phenomena and processes. First, two materials interact and cause some proportion of an object's energy to produce mechanical vibrations that consist of high- and low-frequency waves (Gaver, 1993, 286). Frequency waves that are audible to the human ear are 'sound'. Sound moves through the air and travels to listening ears. It may be conducted through the skull bone or its vibrations may be felt through tactile receptors, such as the fingers or the hairs at the nape of the neck (Blauert, 1997, 200). Thus, a simple move of one's head can change the perceptual quality of a sound. Upon receiving the sound signal, people use memory recall to identify the source, distance and characteristics of the sound. These recollections are usually based on the sound's social context and location, and past experiences with similar sounds and locales (Schulte-Fortkamp and Nitsch, 1999). After identifying the sound, the hearing person makes an evaluation of the sound and decides how to respond. These final two stages, evaluation and response, mark the point at which a sound's 'signal' can transition into the phenomenon known as 'noise'.

Sound is measured in decibels, a system based on the auditory threshold of healthy and young human ears; thus, zero on this scale does not mean silence but, rather, sound a person cannot hear (Baron, 1970, 83). Decibels, as opposed to some linear measurements, such as feet or metres, progress logarithmically instead of arithmetically. This means that 'each change of decibel level represents a sizeable change in acoustic energy' (Baron, 1970, 40). According to physicist Amando García (García, 2001) regular exposure to sound of 100 decibels can impair hearing and 120 decibels is the officially agreed pain threshold of sound for human beings (Sim, 2007, 31). At high decibels, sound can bend or break the hairs that carry its waves within the inner ear, causing deafness in the affected (Baron, 1970, 78). In the United States, about 10 million people suffer from permanent hearing loss due to sound exposure (Kosko, 2006, 52). 'Sound' in this context is harmful and is consequently labelled as 'noise'; indeed, 'Noise Induced Hearing Loss' is a recognized occupational illness (Kosko, 2006, 48). However, the many sounds that people call 'noise' and encounter in everyday life are rarely physically deleterious.[2] Traffic sounds are generally no more than 80 decibels and quiet urban areas measure 50 decibels in background noise (Kosko, 2006, 50). It is rare to find any place on earth where the sound level is as low as 20 decibels – and, if you recall, the range of human hearing begins at 0 decibels. The world for human beings is never really silent and yet people complain about noise every day.

So, if physical harm does not mark the distinction between sound and noise, and if it is virtually impossible to locate a space free of sound, how do people identify noise? In the United States, studies of people's responses to sound have provided some clarity in answering this question. One study

(Blechman and Dannemiller, 1976) showed that participants who believe they can control a noise perform better on a physical task than those who do not. In this case, a person's perception of control and their physical response to noise are mutually dependent. Similarly, another study found that:

> Noise, per se, does not impair simple task performance probably because of the adaptation of stress responses. However, the introduction of cognitive factors, for example, aperiodicity or uncontrollability of the noise schedule results in appreciable failures on complex tasks.
>
> (Glass and Singer, 1972, 4)

Thus, a sonic event becomes noise when it is unpredictable, or when people are not accustomed to it and/or feel they cannot control it, regardless of its physical loudness (i.e. decibels at non-deaf-causing levels). Noise returns to being 'sound' once people adapt to its presence.[3]

In the United States, noise has come to be defined as unwanted, obtrusive and anxiety-causing sound, often predicated and identified through culturally informed behaviour codes. For instance, the noise regulations in Philadelphia describe noise as: 'The presence of a sound or sounds of such intensity, duration, frequency, or character which annoy, disturb, or cause or tend to cause adverse psychological and physiological effects on persons' (Phila. gov, 2008). This example of noise in American law is historically rooted in the rapid rise of technology, particularly supersonic and jet engine aviation, in the United States. While studies suggest that noise annoyance is a process that actually wreaks mental (and consequently physiological) havoc on the 'victim' of 'noise assault', Americans live in a culture with certain ideological commitments about private versus public space, property and silence which also make it difficult to accept unwanted environmental sound.

The power/territory of noise

The temporal, spatial, situational and authoritative characteristics of a sound are critical to its social construction as noise. Consider the following selection from a news report about a conflict over drumming in Harlem, New York:

> NEW YORK – On Saturday nights in summer, hundreds of fingers pound out mesmerizing rhythms on African drums – a ritual repeated for decades in Harlem's Marcus Garvey Park.
>
> This year, the drums have a counterpoint: the complaints of 'new Harlemites'. 'African drumming is wonderful for the first four hours,

but after that, it's pure, unadulterated noise. We couldn't see straight anymore', says Beth Ross, who lives in a luxury apartment building near the park. 'It was like a huge boom box in the living room, the bedroom, the kitchen. You had no way to escape except to leave the apartment.'

(Dobnik, 2007)

This passage highlights the importance of space and time in conflicts over noise, particularly in identifying what defines noise. A period of four hours becomes the residents' established boundary for the drumming before it becomes noise. Thus, the woman identifies neither the presence of the drummers nor the noise of the drums as the primary reason for her complaint – it is the *time*. Temporal boundaries are integral to the contestation over the noise in this incident, especially because time in urban space is fashioned to facilitate movement and labour. According to Westwood and Williams (1997, 6):

Urban time appears to be transparent, organized for business and the transportation of people across the spaces of the city and routinely expressed in the preoccupation with timetables, starting and finishing times, opening and closing times.

Thus sound corresponds to time, creating a noise wherever and whenever sound appears out of 'appropriate' context. Temporal restrictions regarding noise also reveal how, through assigning sound versus noise designations, one also designates what is allowed in a space and identifies those who retain the power to set and enforce codified norms. Time and sound are thus mutually dependent in constructing boundaries of an aural landscape – since, while time is important because it allows for the presence of a certain public within a space, noise is integral because it establishes an aural public who is being addressed. Thus, the establishment of temporal and aural boundaries alludes to the 'noise' of the deviant 'other' and functions to exclude those 'others' from a space, while embracing the sounds of more valued individuals or groups. Consequently, the regulation of noise in urban space also facilitates the exclusion of unwanted others and the inclusion of those desirable within existing societal relations.

Moreover, people use the *language* of noise to marginalize sounds (and sound-makers) that violate social mores while expanding the sphere for other dominant conceptions of appropriate sound. In a world where people establish themselves as aural beings in culturally specific ways, the potential for a tyranny of the sound majority is clear. On the other hand, noise can be equally useful in redefining a space for a marginalized group. For example, scholar Clare Corbould writes about how sound and noise in Harlem was a point of ethnic and racial exclusion, division and identification in Harlem (Corbould, 2007, 860). She describes the ways in which black residents used noise to create a counter-public sphere in response to the presence of white landlords, shopkeepers, policemen and visitors.

> What white visitors found 'noisy' – whether they were excited or repelled by it – marked out the territory, as it were. ... This use of public space had as its analogue the formation of a black public sphere. Members of this counter-public sphere, including those associated with the Harlem Renaissance, defined themselves as aural beings, rather than as individuals oriented by sight. Debate erupted frequently within this sphere as to what was appropriate sound or noise, on the streets and especially in political and social agitation. The multiplicity of voices was ultimately the defining characteristic of the black public sphere, and of black modernity itself.
>
> (Corbould, 2007, abstract)

By offending white listeners, black Harlem residents created an aural community through which they could assert black self-expression as a political act (Courbould, 2007, 862). Similarly, in Europe, bells in the colonial period proclaimed the political and religious power of the Church and established sonic boundaries that separated the civilized territory from heathen areas where the ringing tolls could not be heard (Arkette, 2004). In this way, sound articulates a cultural and territorial claim to a space, as does its characterization as noise. According to Arkette, the term 'community' has 'traditionally been associated with a close-knit group of people all within audible reach, and further connected by a group of sounds which make that community distinctive' (2004, 164). 'Being heard' literally produces belonging and unity within a community, and sounds that clash with or disrupt these distinctive community sounds are seen as noise. These 'noises' agitate homogeneous acoustic spaces and demonstrate the potential for noise to function both as a tool of political and social activism, as well as disruption and brutality.

The language of noise

Scholars Nelson Philips and Cynthia Hardy tell us that 'epistemological and ontological assumptions maintain that there is no "real" world other than one constructed through discourse' (Phillips and Hardy, 2002, 79–80). Communication theorist Klaus Krippendorff also contends that language is essential to processes of social construction. Specifically, they argue that we use metaphors in language to create conceptual systems that structure our everyday reality. A metaphor, according to Krippendorff (1991, 181), is

A pattern, an explanatory structure, tied to a word or expression and carried from a familiar domain of experiences into another domain whose experiences and actions it thereby organizes and coordinates in its own and usually novel ways.

In this language paradigm, a metaphor links an object to an experience with which one is familiar and, in this way, imparts that experience's characteristics to the object. While metaphors draw on experiences to define and explain a concept, metaphors also construct and expand those experiences: 'Thus, they can give new meaning to our pasts, to our daily activity, and to what we know and believe' (Lakoff and Johnson, 2003, 139). Lakoff and Johnson refer to the related connotations that experiences produce as 'metaphorical entailments', which 'arise from our beliefs about, and experiences of, what it means for something to be' (Lakoff and Johnson, 2003, 139).

Entailments are useful in considering the way in which we understand the meaning of an idea or object through the associations we give its metaphors. For instance, if we use language to suggest that love is magic: 'She *cast her spell* over me. The *magic* is gone. I was *spellbound*. She had me *hypnotized*' (Lakoff and Johnson, 2003, 49; italics in original), then we understand love in the ways we may understand magic – magic is fake, magic is mysterious, magic is dark, magic is evil, magic is dangerous, magic is power. The metaphorical entailments would be that love is fake, evil, dark and mysterious. We may avoid love, mistrust love, or dismiss love as a result of these entailments. The importance of understanding the significance of entailments is that the language we use to describe a concept draws on metaphors that also affect our beliefs, understanding, and, even, actions.

For a noise-related example, the woman cited above in the article about the Harlem drummers claims that she had 'no escape' from the noise of the drums – it had trapped her and become something from which she had to seek refuge. Noise, according to her, is a prison. Thus, through her statement, we identify one metaphor for noise: *noise is a prison*. In complaints about noise, such metaphors are frequently used to make appealing arguments about eliminating undesirable sound. In the metaphor 'noise is a prison' some possible entailments are:

Noise is a physically confining space.

Noise holds someone against his or her will.

Noise is a punishment.

Noise is isolation from others.

Noise takes away someone's freedom.

Noise is involuntary restraint.

These entailments surrounding noise are extremely important, as we will see, because such entailments have been useful in arguments that aim to convert various sounds into noise through the use of metaphor. Metaphor, as Lakoff and Johnson point out, also provides a reality with meaning through which people can determine and justify a course of action. Or, as Stuart Hall argues about crime, 'the use of the label is likely to mobilize *this whole referential context*, with all its associated meaning and connotations' (Hall *et al.*, 1978, 19; emphasis in original). For example, throughout the twentieth century, arguments about noise have relied upon the language of war, describing *noise as a weapon*, which one community member can employ in dealings with an unwilling 'other' (Kosko, 2006). Again, this connotation relied not so much on the actual physical harm that noise could cause another person, as its emotional impact based on expectations regarding residential space. In recent years this particular metaphor has become reality. For the past decade, Israel has been using sound bomb technology in military campaigns and strikes against its rival neighbours (Sim, 2007). The US Army has also been accused of using music to torture and interrogate Iraqi captives (Goodman, 2010, 21).

In one passage, Kosko describes his feelings regarding sounds that become noise, which depict the related metaphors that underlie his perspective on that transition:

I hate noise. I hate the roar of car traffic and leaf blowers and airplane over flights. I hate the screech of car alarms and police sirens and the public speeches that too many of my fellow citizens make into their private cell phones. I dislike any unwanted signal that impinges on my humble sense organs. The same holds for the cyber-equivalent noise that arrives as spam in an e-mail mailbox or that flashes on the side of the computer screen as the latest product advertisement.

(Kosko, 2006, xv)

In the above quote, Kosko expands upon the metaphors *noise is a nuisance* and *noise is interference,* thereby, converting noise into a metaphor itself for email spam and unwanted advertisements. One philosopher even argued that noise interferes with communication to and from God, thereby becoming an obstacle to spirituality (Sim, 2007, 41). Author David Brock also employs this entailment of noise as interference in his book *The Republican Noise Machine* (Brock, 2004). For Brock, noise represents the voices of conservative Republicans that 'drow[n] out competing voices across all media channels' (Brock, 2004, 3).

Scientists, such as engineers and mathematicians, have developed an entire science around these noise-related metaphors. For them, noise is any type of harmful energy, something that interferes with the successful communication of a message (Kosko, 2006, 3). In this paradigm, heat is a form of noise (Kosko, 2006, 21). Cancer, too, has been described as noise (Sim, 2007, 47). Furthermore, noise can also infect other people and adversely affect their health. Thus *noise is a disease,* with the following associated entailments: *noise is an invading substance, noise is unhealthy, and noise is a contaminant.*

In the US noise as a contaminant became such an active entailment that the government assigned the Environmental Protection Agency (EPA) to regulate noise alongside other ecological hazards such as toxic waste and noxious fumes (Bragdon, 1979, 13). In this scenario, noise contaminates and taints the purity of silence. For instance, some people complained that aircraft noise 'soiled their home and property' (Bragdon, 1979, 44). Thus *noise is a pollutant.* Noise as a pollutant is perhaps the most fascinating metaphor, since it requires one to distinguish between the pure, non-contaminated sounds and noise, while invoking the entailment that noise is a harmful physical substance. One newspaper editorial on noise pollution reads:

> NEW HAMPSHIRE – Noise pollution is what we suffer from when we sit on the rocks looking out to sea enjoying the sense of the wind and the waves, but not enjoying at all the blast of soul music from the transistor radio on nearby table.
>
> What is interesting from this selection is the distinction between appropriate Sound – the waves and wind on the sea – from unwanted Noise – 'the blast of soul music.'
>
> (Baron, 1970, 20)

The 'soul music' (and not missing the racial implications of this phrase) for this complainant was the 'noise' here – unwanted, invasive, violating. As psychologist Susan L. Staples writes, 'noise impacts that penetrate the interior of the home represent an inescapable violation of the safety presumed of a primary setting' (Staples, 1996, 147). Another researcher noted similarly that '[n]oise is noise regardless of the source, and communities should protect themselves against all intruders' (Bragdon, 1979, 49). The metaphor here is clear:

Noise is a trespasser.

In the US, the metaphor of noise as trespasser is particularly important in the history of noise ordinances, and legislation and trespass law marked the initial foundation of the regulation of noise. The history of noise as a social problem, however, would show the metaphors of noise as a disease and pollutant to be much more useful in the political rhetoric and policy mobilized upon entailments.

In agreement with Glass and Singer, I do not want to minimize the importance of noise as a source of annoyance for human beings. However, it is also important to note that factors like habit, normativity and expectations are extremely important to the construction of noise as a social problem. García says it best when he sums up a number of studies about noise and writes:

> The subjective evaluation of a given sound landscape not only depends on the corresponding sound intensity but also, and perhaps even in greater proportion, on the contained information, on the context in which it is perceived and on the social and cultural meanings attributed to it by different individuals.
>
> (García, 2001, 5)

Summary

There is, perhaps, no happy ending to the problem of noise that an interrogation of its linguistic transition from sound can resolve. Linguistic meanings and evaluations connect sound to experiences that underpin contemporary arguments about noise. The frequent emergence of noise as a social problem reveals a complex system of contributing factors and interest groups. While the language of noise may be used to build community, it also finds troubling ways to exclude unwanted others. In contemporary rhetoric, noise continues to be considered a pollutant, a trespasser, an invader, interference and a weapon (Kosko, 2006; Sim, 2007). Moreover, advances in technology have altered the context of the twenty-first century soundscape, redefining communities and leaving ill-prepared citizens to fight against unfamiliar and unwanted sound – better known as noise.

These connotations promote an ideology of warfare around noise. In fact, as mentioned earlier, it is actually used as a weapon today. If noise is a *trespasser and invader*, then, in the language of war, the invasion can be stopped and, perhaps, peace can be restored. Since the locations for noise conflicts occur most frequently in our own deeply embedded senses of entitlement, time, volume and propriety, the place to reimagine sound and refit it with a different identity lies in our minds and words. Lakoff and Johnson (2003, 104) suggest that one should:

> Imagine a culture where an argument is viewed as a dance, the participants are seen as performers, and the goal is to perform in a balanced and aesthetically pleasing way. In such a culture, people would view arguments differently, experience them differently, carry them out differently, and talk about them differently. ... Perhaps the most neutral way of describing this difference between their culture and ours would be to say that we have a discourse form structured in terms of battle and they have one structured in terms of dance.

Klaus Krippendorff also argues that discourse can 'us[e] new metaphors for reorganizing experiences heretofore taken for granted, enabling multiple perspectives to be taken' (Krippendorff, 1991, 192). Rather than reduce the unpredictability and unexpectedness of noise in our environment and, thus, emphasize the importance of controlling a non-compliant environment, we can embrace the notion that sound is unpredictable and unexpected. We can welcome the possibility and surprise of discovering the 'other' in unplanned and serendipitous ways. This investigation shows that noise is a problem largely because people construct it as such, becoming stressed and agitated by a sound's violation of expected norms. Instead of trying to eliminate noise, we can focus on eliminating the need to control sound. Such reimaginings may challenge our very conceptions of property and space through which our norms and codes have formed.

In this space of active reconceptions, I will offer up a new metaphor for sound:

Sound is a bridge.

If seen as something that connects one person to another, sound can be accepted as the signal of human coexistence instead of the noise of an intruding stranger. Perhaps a culture that embraces this type of metaphor, and others yet to be conceived, could create an aural landscape that is not premised on territory and possession. The answer to Robert Baron's (1970) question 'when does sound become noise?' is simply this: it doesn't always have to.

17

Exploding the atmosphere:
realizing the revolutionary potential of 'the last street song'

Bruce Russell

What form do you suppose a life would take that was determined at a decisive moment precisely by the street song last on everyone's lips?

BENJAMIN, 1978, 182

Introduction

Walter Benjamin's apparently throw-away line, taken from his 1929 essay on the then-new French Surrealist movement, poses a challenge to sound culture which to date has not been seriously taken up. In considering today what influence auditory art forms may have upon life, even more than in the 1920s, the spotlight is immediately directed at the media through which we experience them. The key issue is the social utility of both the work and the media. One way to investigate what this use might be is to examine it from the most extreme position we can readily imagine. What if this 'last street song' was in fact the work of a noise artist?

In order to respond to Benjamin's challenge I will engage in my own reflections on the possible political significance of what I prefer to call 'improvised sound work' (ISW). While for clarity I will also use the term 'noise', this in my opinion is too freighted with a host of specific generic implications to be used without further gloss. Most current uses link it too closely to either geographical scenes ('Japanoise') or aesthetic choices not universally shared across the sector ('harsh noise'). 'ISW', in contrast, is nomenclature that is both descriptive and definitional.

It is my hope that in the early twenty-first century this kind of autonomous, as opposed to heteronomous (Bourdieu, 1993, 40), creative praxis will come to have a clear relation to forms of consciousness that are inherently counter-ideological and anti-capitalist. If this hope proves founded, then the form that such a life might take – if determined by it – could be presumed to be inherently antipathetic to the dominant ideology, which Mark Fisher has recently dubbed 'capitalist realism'. This he defined as: 'a pervasive atmosphere, conditioning not only the production of culture but also the regulation of work and education, and acting as a kind of invisible barrier constraining thought and action' (Fisher, 2009, 16). This is the ideology which at once supports and masks 'the order prevailing in the field of power' (Bourdieu, 1993, 44). Pierre Bourdieu memorably summarized this social phenomenon when he observed that while 'ordinary experience of the social world is a cognition, it is equally important to realize … that primary cognition is misrecognition' (Bourdieu, 1984, 172). His trenchant formulations relating to the 'theory of practice' will be heavily drawn upon in the analysis which follows.

My analysis adopts a framework of theory which incorporates Guy Debord's conception of the revolutionary role of 'minority tendencies' in culture. Specifically I am interested in the role of these tendencies in enabling the advance of revolutionary consciousness, in Lukács' famous formulation, 'beyond what was immediately given' (Lukács, 1977, 72). In other words, beyond the apparently limitless boundaries of what Debord dubbed the Spectacle, the social totality as a zone of ideological contestation. This development of consciousness may, I contend, be achieved by means of specific art practices analogous to those developed under the flag of Lettrism in the 1950s.

The key to any meaningful theory is grounded in practice – the actual life activity of historically specific individuals. So this analysis will be grounded in Walter Benjamin's insights into the revolutionary potential inherent in outmoded technologies. I will examine the way in which this impacts upon cultural practice embodied in media, using concepts developed by Rosalind Krauss. In my opinion the analysis of the structuring media is the key to understanding the continued vogue for analogue sound practice, and its potential social significance, viewed as one of the 'ways of using the products imposed by a dominant economic order' (De Certeau, 1984, xiii).

The authentic

In the penultimate chapter of *The Society of the Spectacle*, Debord made it plain that a 'unified critique of culture' necessarily implied a critique of the social totality. This was his practico-theoretical method throughout his career as a revolutionary: he saw no distinction between cultural work and political work (Kaufmann, 2006, 150). Indeed, the insights gained from the former were seen as essential to the establishment of success in the latter sphere, when 'this unified theoretical critique ... goes alone to its rendezvous with a *unified social practice*' (Debord, 1995, 147). He had already noted in 1963 that 'any fundamental cultural creation, as well as any qualitative transformation of society, is contingent on the continued development of this ... interrelated approach' (Debord in Knabb, 2006, 402).

Taking the ideal of a 'unified critique of culture' as my starting point, both as an artist and as a critic of social practice in what Fisher wittily terms 'Really Existing Capitalism' (Fisher, 2009, 45), makes the investigation of the significance of the 'last street song' both a challenge and an obligation. This is precisely the 'trick' by which Benjamin, in the sentence of his 'Surrealism' essay subsequent to the one quoted at the beginning of this chapter, says that 'this world of things is mastered' – in the replacement of the historical perspective with the political (Benjamin, 1978, 182). In this way, he goes on to say, 'art for art's sake' (autonomous cultural production) is to be simply seen as:'a flag under which sailed a cargo that could not be declared because it still lacked a name' (Benjamin, 1978, 183–4). The ideas both of a 'flag of convenience', and of the inadequacy of extant terminologies, are highly suggestive of our current state of understanding of the relationship of 'noise' to 'music', as well as many other fundamental ontological issues in the analysis of this developing field of cultural practice.

I have argued elsewhere that the Bourdieusian concept of the 'field' provides a workable tool for conceptualizing the cultural phenomena grouped under the broad heading 'sound culture' (Russell, 2011, 265). In Figure 17.1 the two axes are methodological continua stretching from 'composition' to 'improvisation' and from 'music' to 'noise'. In each case the first term

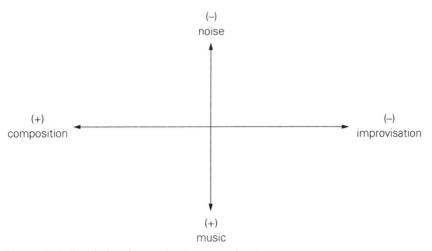

Figure 17.1 The field of sound culture production

is heteronomous and dominant (+) and the second is autonomous and dominated (−).

Benjamin had already, in a different context, provided a powerful argument in favour of seeking social meaning in marginal practices. In the Prologue to his *Habilitationsschrift*, he expounded in some detail on how the 'authentic' essence of a cultural product is most reliably identified in its most extreme, even aberrant forms:

> The authentic − the hallmark of origin in phenomena − is the object of discovery … and the act of discovery can reveal it in the most singular and eccentric of phenomena, in both the weakest and clumsiest experiments and in the overripe fruits of a period of decadence.
>
> (Benjamin, 1998, 46)

While my personal creative predilections are not without influence in my choice of subject area, I do feel strongly that Benjamin's argument may be applied to the analysis of avant-garde tendencies in audio culture under post-industrial capitalism, such as ISW. It is my belief that it is this 'authenticity' which explains the burgeoning growth in attention (both critical and creative) given to that part of sound culture coming under the general rubric of 'noise'.

It is precisely its location at the margins, in the 'most perfectly autonomous sector of the field of cultural production' (see the top right-hand corner of Figure 17.1), where the dominant economic model is 'loser wins' (Bourdieu, 1993, 39), which serves to give this ill-defined and theoretically contested practice its unique and double significance. On the one hand, its autonomy (distance from the popular market) guarantees that the sector's 'cargo' will be well ballasted with cultural capital, thus ensuring its potential interest to critics of the future, who will seek to define it as an example of a 'charismatic economy based on the social miracle of an act devoid of any determination other than the specifically aesthetic intention' (Bourdieu, 1993, 40). On the other hand, its 'singular and eccentric' status also makes ISW the ideal subject to serve as an exemplar for what Benjamin defined as 'the becoming of phenomena in their being' (Benjamin, 1998, 47). This understanding leads to the definition of the essence of a cultural form, which in Benjamin's terms is a 'monad', by which he means that 'every idea contains the image of the world' (Benjamin, 1998, 48). This is another way of defining art as 'neither a description nor an analysis ... rather an analogue of human reality – an attempt to map the process of integration of the subject and object in history' (Russell, 2010, 3).

The outmoded

Rosalind Krauss has furnished us with one of the most perceptive analyses of art in what she terms 'the post-medium age' (Krauss, 1997, 5). She has both formulated this problematic and identified one of the most potentially useful strategies adopted by visual artists seeking to escape from it. In this she draws liberally upon Benjamin's analysis of the history of photography and, in addition, upon his very fertile insights into the revolutionary role of the outmoded (Krauss, 1999). In the 'Surrealism' essay alluded to above, Benjamin famously (if gnomically) wrote of 'the immense forces of "atmosphere" concealed in these [outmoded] things' which artists may bring to 'the point of explosion' (Benjamin, 1978, 182). Krauss' development of these ideas over several journal articles at the close of the twentieth century provides many suggestive analogies to the praxis associated with ISW.

Krauss bases her analysis on the history of photography. She argues that after its initial flourishing as a fully developed artistic medium it entered a period of decline, eventually becoming what she calls a 'theoretical object' (Krauss, 1999, 290), and that this was due to a combination of economic and aesthetic desuetude. A theoretical object is not, she argues, either a historical or an aesthetic object, but an activity in which copies are made that have no originals – which she describes as one in a series of 'so many ontological cave-ins' (Krauss, 1999, 290). In thus becoming a theoretical object, she argues, a work of art 'loses its specificity as a medium' and becomes a purely subjective act of intention, a 'framing' of reality analogous to looking down a viewfinder whether or not a photograph is taken.

This is the art of the ready-made. In terms of classical composition this 'cave-in' occurred around 1960 to 1961 (Joseph, 2008, 91–101). Significantly, the way forward from this purely 'theoretical' impasse of avant-garde composition was described by Branden Joseph as 'the social turn', in which collective authorship and improvisation became important (Joseph, 2008, 101–8). In my opinion, these remain tell-tale indicators of significantly developed praxis in this field.

Within pop music, many critics are now arguing that a similar aesthetic impasse has been reached. A prominent example of this is Simon Reynolds' recent work (Reynolds, 2011), which is discussed below. Reynolds does not use Krauss' vocabulary, but he eloquently describes what is in effect a pop music tradition reduced to the status of a 'theoretical object'. In the same way in which film photography lost its original aesthetic specificity under the impact of digital convergence, so too has analogue sound recording technology. Only 20 years ago this was the last word in electronic sophistication, the site for the embodiment of breathtaking quantities of capital; now the multi-track tape-recorders and mixing consoles lie abandoned in the dust like the vast stone legs of Ozymandias.

Under the influence of the 'social turn' and in the hands of artists willing to employ old technologies to radically new ends, these outmoded 'objects that have begun to be extinct' (Benjamin, 1978, 181) have now taken on a new life. In the process the relation of the originator to cultural production has become, in the 'post-medium age', paradoxically more 'authentic' due to the very decay of the medium itself, which necessitates 'under precisely the guise of its own obsolescence … what has to be called an act of reinventing the medium' (Krauss, 1999, 296).

Krauss further quotes Benjamin as observing that the rejuvenation of photography in the inter-war period 'had an underground connection with the crisis of capitalist industry' (Benjamin, 2008, 274–5). She need hardly add that this analysis might apply even more forcefully in the era of the decay of industry itself, amidst today's comprehensive 'binary triumph' of the Spectacle. This reinvention is accomplished by, and further enables, the release of the concealed and pent-up Benjaminian forces of 'atmosphere'. While the rejuvenation of media described by Krauss is currently underway across the entire field of art, there is as yet little clarity on exactly what is unfolding.

My contention is that this process is most advanced within sound culture in the 'most autonomous' sector of the field, the so-called 'noise underground'. Here entire cadres of artists exploit terminally defunct modes of sound production, vintage equipment (yesterday's junk) is fetishized and 'inferior' modes of reproduction such as the cassette are ubiquitous. In line with this, a recent commentator has observed that 'in the mid-1980s, Noise music [*sic*] seemed to be everywhere', and, furthermore, that after two decades, growing social and economic dislocation has 'brought Noise back to the centre of attention' (Toth, 2008, 26). This attention is due in part, I contend, to the 'advanced' developments I am describing here.

One reality that everyone working with 'noise' or 'sound' has to address frequently is the firm assertion by individuals outside the field of production that what we do has no value because it's 'not music' (Russell, 2010, 85–8). Over time most of us have come to understand that this is in fact a positive or defining reality – which still leaves the question: 'so what is it?' For some time I have been working my way via practice towards an answer for which Krauss provides a full theoretical rationale: it is a distinct medium in its own right.

In her discussion of South African artist William Kentridge, Krauss defines a medium as 'not only a set of material conditions, but also a dense layering of economic and social history' (Krauss, 2000, 9–10). This she echoes elsewhere in saying that: 'a medium is a set of conventions derived from (but not identical with) the material conditions of a given technical support' (Krauss, 1999, 296). This identification of a medium, not only with a defined set of technologies but also with an overarching set of social relations, is brilliantly developed by Jonathan Sterne in his magisterial work on the original social meanings of sound reproduction.

Sterne defines a medium as 'a recurring set of contingent social relations and social practices', which therefore provides 'the social basis that allows a set of technologies to stand out as a unified thing with clearly defined functions'. He further observes that 'cultural context is essential to understanding the articulations of machines to forms of social organisation' (Sterne, 2003, 182, 192), and it is his account of the malleability which he attributes to sound technologies in their infancy that I find remarkably suggestive of the kind of media reinvention that Krauss ascribes to Coleman and Kentridge. While Krauss does not extend her argument about media reinvention to embrace a political perspective, I feel that this can legitimately be extrapolated by analogy with her own dependence on Benjaminian categories. Benjamin's own cultural criticism was unashamedly in the service of socially progressive tendencies, approaching 'a historical subject only where he encounter[ed] it as a monad ... a revolutionary chance in the fight for the oppressed' (Benjamin, 1968, 263).

It is thus the *fixing* of the malleable relationships between technologies and their surrounding 'cultural context' that creates a medium. Sterne explicitly and tellingly links this fixing to the thought of Georg Lukács, describing this as *reification* (Sterne, 2003, 182). While we may think that certain technologies are inextricably tied to specific social uses, this is in reality what Bourdieu called ideological 'misrecognition' (Bourdieu, 1984, 172). An example, as Sterne points out, is that in the past, point-to-point telephony (not broadcast radio) was used for broadcast programming; while today mobile 'telephones', which everyone understands and uses as point-to-point telephones, are actually (in terms of their technology) broadcast radio devices. So the role of technology in the creation of media, which is generally understood as an unproblematic form of technological determination, is in fact a more complex result of the interplay of technology within a 'structuring structure' of social relationships. So in fact the perceived model of technological determinism is an example of what Lukács termed 'phantom objectivity' (Lukács, 1977, 83), which serves to disguise the potential fluidity of social relations around the use of technologies to serve social ends.

The subjective effects of this have been well analysed elsewhere in relation to the role of the worker under capitalism, but it is worth remembering that 'the worker' finds the technological support 'already pre-existing and self-sufficient, it functions independently of him [*sic*] and he has to conform to its laws whether he likes it or not ... [and] his activity becomes less and less active and more and more *contemplative*' (Lukács, 1977, 89). Lukács goes on to note that this reified relationship of humanity to what in this context we call media is a 'perfectly closed system'. It is this 'contemplative' relation to technologies that hinders their use in socially critical or artistically original ways. *Retromania*, Simon Reynolds' widely reviewed recent survey of the state of popular music, identifies exactly this phenomenon, from the point of view of both consumption and production. He writes:

> Where retro truly reigns as the dominant sensibility and creative paradigm is in hipsterland, pop's equivalent to highbrow. The very people you would once have expected to produce (as artists) or champion (as consumers) the non-traditional and the ground-breaking ... [have] switched roles to become curators and archivists. The avant-garde is now an arrière-garde.
>
> (Reynolds, 2011, xix–xx)

His book details the many ways in which this atrophying of innovation is taking place. He discusses various possible causes but gravitates towards technological changes in production and consumption related to the adoption of digital tools, be they samplers or iPods, as well as the influence of universal availability of the totality of musical tradition via online archives such as YouTube (xiii). Obviously these phenomena are also linked to postmodernity's surface obsession with pastiche and ironic self-referentiality, cultural imperatives deriving from the 'Spectacular' shift in terms of economic logic, from industrial production to information management. As I suggested earlier, this cessation of invention is reminiscent of Krauss' 'theoretical object' – a copy with no original. Further investigation of this avenue of enquiry will no doubt prove at the least productive of much debate (Krauss, 1999, 290).

As Benjamin and Krauss have explained, media have what are in effect life cycles, and their 'malleability' comes into play both before and after their heyday in terms of their relevance to capital accumulation. When media are essential to the functioning of capital accumulation (when their technical supports are marketable commodities) then this reification is complete and the 'system' is closed, but as 'the vogue has begun to ebb from them' (Benjamin, 1978, 181), an opportunity appears to envisage an 'outside to the totality of technologized space' (Krauss, 2000, 34). In this space 'outside' the reified relations which surround technologies, the possible shapes of other media are at least potentially open to contestation. As we have seen earlier, Krauss argues that this redeployment of 'outmoded' technological supports within the subjectively established field of cultural production – in association with a new set of social relations – may constitute an entirely new medium. It is the invention of a new medium, with its correspondingly new social relations, that offers a chance for the Lukácsian 'advance beyond' in terms of previous forms of thought and human self-understanding.

Demonstrating this 'advance beyond' at a given stage of consciousness was the great practical contribution of Debord's early work with the 'lost children' of Lettrism (Kaufmann, 2006, 1). Kaufmann has even argued that the great strength of *The Society of the Spectacle* depends not on its status as a work of theory, but 'arises from the fact that it incorporates a way of life in a style' (2006, 74). By this he means that the Situationist understanding of life and the politics that provide its armature derive from a set of practices, principal among which are systematic idleness, the *dérive* and *détournement*. The virtue of these practices depends on the form of consciousness that they engender; the aim was to produce a new type of person to inhabit a new society. I believe that these same subjective effects may follow from the audio art practices of ISW, arising from the invention of a new medium. In particular these practices are anti-hierarchical, networked, improvised and limited to the field of restricted production, acting like Debord's anti-Spectacular cinema as an immanent critique of culture itself.

The *habitus* of technology

To step back for a moment to further our understanding of how media function, there is clearly a mechanism which must provide the glue for fixing social relations around technologies, which permits this invention and destruction of media. Neither Sterne nor Krauss attempt to analyse this in detail, and Benjamin characteristically only describes it elliptically and by implication. It is Bourdieu, in his analysis of what he calls elsewhere the 'logic of practice', who provides an intellectually brilliant and practically useful formulation which appears most compactly in the following equation:

'[(*habitus*) (capital)] + field = practice' (1984, 101).

If we understand the technological support as part of the 'capital' and the social relations as constituting the 'field', then the other factor which makes practice possible is the '*habitus*'.

Bourdieu defines *habitus* as:

> systems of durable, transposable dispositions, structured structures predisposed to function as structuring structures, that is, as principles which generate and organise practices and representations that can be objectively adapted to their outcomes without presupposing a conscious aiming at ends or an express mastery of the operations necessary in order to attain them.
> (Bourdieu, 1990, 53)

Bourdieu introduced this category in the context of his analysis of taste as a manifestation of class distinctions in French society (1984). He linked this explicitly to the perspective famously enunciated by Marx in the *Theses on Feuerbach* – stating that to apply this analysis 'one has to situate oneself *within* real activity as such' (Bourdieu, 1990, 52). Furthermore, he subsequently showed how the concept might be applied to the analysis of art practice, observing that 'collective invention' creates the position of the artist within a given field of practice and that this results from 'the objectification of past discoveries' in the field (Bourdieu, 1993, 63). The actual work undertaken by the artist relates to an act of 'position-taking' within the field, which is governed by 'the structure of the distribution of the capital of specific properties which govern success' (Bourdieu, 1993, 30).

It is my contention, in the light of the foregoing discussion regarding the invention of artistic media, that while Bourdieu does not explicitly discuss the relation between *habitus* and specific art practices, the adoption of this category as a 'structuring structure' or 'an acquired system of generative schemes' (1990, 55) with relation to the technological supports of specific art practices is wholly in accord with his aim to use this category to transcend 'the usual antinomies ... of determinism and freedom, conditioning and creativity' (ibid.). This view is strongly supported in the section of *Distinction* entitled 'The correspondence between goods production and taste production' in which Bourdieu writes that: 'It is always forgotten that the universe of products offered by each field of production tends in fact to limit the universe of the forms of experience ... that are objectively possible at any given moment' (1984, 230–1).

Thus if we speak of a *habitus* associated with a specific medium, this refers to the mode of use and social or aesthetic understanding associated with a given technology, as well as the characteristic structures of social relations which result from it and which in turn determine its further use. Bourdieu himself notes how artistic '"intention" is itself the product of the social norms and conventions which combine to define the always uncertain and historically changing frontier between simple technical objects and objets d'art' (Bourdieu, 1984, 29). This argument also applies not only to what is a 'work of art', but also to what constitutes an artistic practice. He observes that 'the *habitus* ... enables an intelligible and necessary relation to be established between practices and a situation, the meaning of which is produced by the *habitus* through categories of perception and appreciation' (Bourdieu, 1984, 101). This strikes me as a persuasive summary of how Krauss' 'redemptive reinvention' actually happens, and how one form of relation between people mediated by a reified technology can give way to another, once the economic and social underpinnings have become realigned in such a way as to permit what Lukács in the context of class struggle referred to as the 'advance beyond'.

Sterne's revealing discussion of the cultural context within which sound recording was invented (that is, the inventory of actual goals and intentions in play) supports Benjamin's contention that new technologies are always imbued with utopian promise. He argues that the repeated tropes of early sound recording experimentation – that the new technology might teach the deaf to speak or enable us to preserve the voices of the dead – were 'wishes that people grafted onto sound-reproduction technologies' (Sterne, 2003, 8) and furthermore that these 'wishes' reflect the intimate connection between technologies and social 'practices and institutions'(ibid.).

In the case of photography, Benjamin notes that 'the flowering of photography ... came in its first decade ... the decade which preceded its industrialization' (Benjamin, 2008, 274), and that the arc of time which follows during which photography succumbs to commercial exploitation builds the forces of 'atmosphere' inherent in the potentially correct alignment of technology and social relationships until the point at which the medium 'discharges its historical tension' (Benjamin, 2008, 295). He further explains that the genius of early photography lay in its social role as a portrait medium, at which period 'subject and technique were as exactly congruent as they became incongruent in the period of decline which immediately followed' (Benjamin, 2008, 283). This congruence is fundamentally a matter of the positioning of the technology and the artwork it supports within a field of social contestation, since, as Bourdieu points out, every artistic field is also a 'field of struggles' (Bourdieu, 1993, 30).

Contestation is, in my view, the prime evidence as to whether an art form is progressive or reactionary. Even the Jesuit De Certeau observed that 'the grid of "discipline" is everywhere becoming clearer and more extensive' (De Certeau, 1984, xiv) and that this 'centralised, clamorous, and spectacular production' (xii) in and of itself demands that we 'discover how an entire society resists being reduced to it' (xiv). The weapon we must take up against this *reduction* is the 'unified theoretical critique' that Debord called for: one that can only be termed creative if directed at the 'qualitative transformation of society' (Knabb, 2006, 402).

Reinventing the medium

I have argued thus far that the Bourdieusian *habitus,* in association with an understanding of media as reified technology, provides a highly developed and flexible theoretical apparatus for the analysis of actual cultural practice. I have also begun to show how this may be applied in the 'field of sound culture'. So what can this tell us about the possible social role of ISW? As I pointed out earlier, my perspective is that of Debord's search for a 'unified social practice'. Benjamin expressed this well in his discussion of film as a newly emerged medium when he said that: 'the most important social function of film is to establish equilibrium between human beings and the apparatus' (Benjamin, 2008, 37). Debord himself was quite clear that the 'unified critique of culture' was an 'immanent critique'. In the case of his own cinematographic work, this functioned as a critique of 'Spectacular' film. Moreover, he was not concerned that this work was confined to or directed at an advanced fraction of the non-dominant classes. In 1958 he characterized the Situationist International as 'an attempt at organizing professional revolutionaries in culture' (Knabb, 2006, 54) – the classic model of the 'vanguard party'. In the Situationist model of radical change, revolution starts from the development of a new consciousness, one that 'advances beyond', rather than follows behind, changes in objective social structures.

This raises the question of who may be regarded as the 'advanced social fraction' in terms of audio practice. My analysis seeks to suggest that it is those working in the 'most perfectly autonomous sector' of the field of music, the 'noise artists'. The current impasse of 'retromania' seems set to enmesh popular music in a perpetual past of nostalgia, pastiche and repetition; enmeshing both those artists who accept the potential blandishments of mass-market consecration, and those entering the cul-de-sac of retro-hipsterism. One way around this is to reject all the rules of music, forgo the market support potentially on offer in the field of general production, and decline the poisoned chalice of digital audio production. This offers the chance of side-stepping the mediatized *habitus* surrounding most popular and academic music.

As I have argued earlier, this 'noise side-step' (and ISW in particular) represents a classic instance of the Kraussian 'act of reinventing the medium' under the guise of the terminal obsolescence of a given technical support. It is also part of what Joseph has identified as the 'social turn' within sound culture, of which the *locus classicus* is Conrad's collective pragmatic activity of playing and listening (Joseph, 2008, 104–5). This represents the 'death of the composer' in the same way that 'noise' represents the 'death of harmony'.

Combining these two anti-hegemonic initiatives with the adoption of an outmoded technology from which the 'vogue', and hence the preordained reificatory *habitus* has leached, represents an opportunity for those artists at the 'most perfectly autonomous' pole of the sound culture field to generate a new practice. The possibility exists, I feel, that this could align with a new *habitus* not built on 'misrecognition', one furthermore that arises from a new relation between audience and artist. This latter development depends on the location of ISW within the 'field of restricted production, in which the producers produce for other producers' (Bourdieu, 1993, 39). This is where the Debordian 'cadre model' makes sense as a strategy for building an 'immanent social critique' which can be more broadly taken up as and when objective conditions favour it.

I am not arguing that the participants in the 'noise underground' are currently working from a perspective of fully developed revolutionary consciousness. However, it is certainly true that their autonomous position in the field of restricted production causes them to consciously question many of the ideological presuppositions of music as a cultural practice and also of capitalism as a structuring force in society as a whole. That this is taking place within a period of heightening social contradiction is undeniable. The oppositional social forces at play are undeveloped, but 'everyone agrees. It's about to explode' (The Invisible Committee, 2009, 9).

My position here is simply that engagement with non-commercial (that is, gratuitous) cultural practice in an invisible, non-hierarchically networked international community fosters precisely the perspective and the form of consciousness predisposing individuals to look outside 'the totality of technologized space' (Krauss, 2000, 34). This is the legacy of Debord waiting to be taken up. It was his constant assertion that the anti-artistic practices of

Lettrism were the foundation of his revolutionary practice: 'I think rather [than the events of May 1968] it is what I did in 1952 that has been disliked for so long' (Debord, 2004, 22–3). The question I am pointing towards here concerns what effect art practice has for the psychology and outlook of the practitioner. De Certeau's investigation of tactics looks to the same considerations: 'the intellectual synthesis of these given elements takes the form, however, not of a discourse, but of the decision itself, the act and manner in which the opportunity is "seized" ' (De Certeau, 1984, xix). The same point has been recently asserted from the point of view of revolutionary praxis: 'in truth, there is no gap between what we are, what we do, and what we are becoming' (The Invisible Committee, 2009, 15).

So in my view ISW is not simply the criticism of music by musical means; it may also be (albeit not necessarily intentionally) a cultivation of new forms of consciousness. In addition, from the point of view of practice it may also be an attempt at building a new medium with what Krauss (following Benjamin) describes as a 'redemptive role in relation to the very idea of the medium' (Krauss, 1999, 296). The creation of such a medium may support both new social structures within the practice community, as well as new ways of looking at the world that amount to a new *habitus*; a new *habitus* that offers, I believe, a possible exit from the cultural impasse of 'retromania' (Reynolds, 2011).

This impasse is closely analogous to the situation in art described by Debord in 1957 as 'total ideological decomposition' within 'modern culture', and which he identified as an opportunity for the 'experimental avant-garde' to engage in 'revolutionary action within culture' (Debord in Knabb, 2006, 32–6). Without wanting to engage in a prolonged discussion of the life and work of Guy Debord it may be timely to point out that the lessons which I am drawing derive from a 'consistent' reading of Debord's career. Some commentators assert a 'break' between the 'artistic' and the 'political' phases of the Situationist International and its principal theoretician (analogous to the fallacious opposition of the 'young' and 'old' Marx so prevalent in the 1960s and 1970s). I adhere to the position best represented by Kaufmann when he states that 'we thereby limit not only our ability to understand the continuity and specificity of the SI's activities ... but the overall consistency of Debord's life' (Kaufmann, 2006, 150). What I am interested in Debord for is both his 'sense of the poetic' (272) and his advocacy of a politics of 'immediate and authentic communication' (154). It is these consistent themes that underpin his practice of life, a practice which is a model of how one might train oneself for a total transformation of society from within. This is what Kaufmann designates a 'poetics of revolution' (2006, 165).

I see this ultimately as the answer to those who question the current proliferation of 'noise'. The value of this work, which seems entirely without aesthetic appeal, is equally devoid of economic benefits, and is largely unsupported by established institutions of artistic consecration, lies in the new forms of social relation that surround its technical supports – and in the new forms of consciousness that accompany its practice. These both structure the developing medium and are structured by it – and derive their charge from neither personal profit nor social advancement, but because they are 'structured around pragmatic activity, around direct gratification in the realization of the moment' (Tony Conrad quoted in Joseph, 2008, 104).

These new forms of cultural production are anti-hegemonic, collaborative and directed towards personal freedom because they are relatively independent from the almost seamless and irresistible 'totality of technologized space' which Krauss perceives as determining the individual's sphere of action in Spectacular society. It is only outside this, under the influence of the utopian charge inherent in outmoded technologies, that we can 'think our way back down the path of "progress" to ... earlier, stranger forms of expressiveness' (Krauss, 2000, 34).

Conclusion

It is in this way that we can begin to imagine what a life might be like that was determined by that 'last street song'. If my argument is not 'on everyone's lips' even within the field of noise practice, that is in itself no disqualification. Because Bourdieu makes plain that the operation of the *habitus* does not 'presuppos[e] a conscious aiming at ends', its operation is therefore not dependent upon individual consciousness. Instead it 'generates representations and practices which are always more adjusted than they seem to be to the objective conditions of which they are the product' – and this situation always precedes the 'raising of consciousness' (Bourdieu, 1983, 244).

Or, as Krauss puts it, the artist's specific choice of outmoded technology 'lodges itself in the domain of expression ... the traces of bodily production in the midst of the apparatus' (2000, 35). This is exactly equivalent to Lukács' observation, following Hegel, that history has its own 'cunning', and that 'the historically significant actions of the class as a whole are determined in the last resort by this [collective] consciousness and not by the thought of the individual' (Lukács, 1977, 51). And so the truth of my argument depends on the analysis of its suggestive power and its potential explanatory power in the light of future events, not on 'the naïve description of what men [*sic*] *in fact* thought, felt or wanted at any moment in history' (Lukács, 1977, 51).

It is precisely because this field of artistic praxis has, I believe, the potential to be thus directed towards radical human emancipation that the dreams once associated with the historical origins of its technological support – that is, sound recording and reproductive technologies – are able to approach expression (Sterne, 2003, 332). Benjamin argued that the fullest flowering of any art practice occurs when 'subject and technique' are 'exactly congruent' (2008, 283), as became the case with politically engaged photography in the anti-fascist period (Benjamin, 2008, 295). Simply because the coercive techniques of the dominant fraction are today more sophisticated than those of the Brownshirts is no reason to think that they should not be as firmly resisted, nor that the soundtrack to resistance might not be Kevin Drumm or Lasse Marhaug rather than the *Internationale* or *A las barricadas*.

Notes

Notes to Chapter 4

1 All translations from French my own.

2 'No doubt Plato was dissatisfied with his doctrine, since we see, thanks to the notes Aristotle left in the books M and N of his *Metaphysics* that towards the end of his life and in his initiatic teaching, Plato wanted to find a formulation able to explain becoming: instead of escaping this side of reality, he wanted to immortalize himself in the sensible' (Simondon, 2005, 536).

3 Atlan uses a probabilistic theory, based on Shannon's formalization of information theory, for a global understanding of processes of self-organization in complex systems, where detailed knowledge is lacking. Deterministic theories on the contrary use the concept of noise in the analysis of systems where the details of physico-chemical interactions are sufficiently well known. The deterministic approach is applied to systems of 'medium complexity' like that of cell-membranes that can be studied *in vitro* (without forgetting that they partake in far more complex, less determined network systems like that of the whole cell, whose metabolism remains subject to probabilistic theories). Quantitative network analysis is one such approach for the deterministic study of any kind of network system where elements, of any kind, are circulated and transformed. Another example of the deterministic approach are theories of 'order through fluctuations' by which unstable systems evolve towards states that are oscillating in time or space, or both – more familiar perhaps in the human sciences to readers of Isabelle Stengers, due to her collaboration with I. Prigogine (cf. Prigogine, 1976, 93–131; Glansdorff and Prigogine, 1976, 299–315, 1981; Prigogine and Stengers, 1992).

4 Contrary to the common emphasis on Bachelard's notion of the epistemological obstacle, Renault notes that Bachelard's notion of epistemological obstacle evolves throughout his work and that 'the dynamics of (an epistemological) rupture' will eventually 'no longer be those of a progressive reduction of epistemological obstacles' but that 'the discontinuity from the old to the new theory' will instead be projected 'in the form of tensions and contradictions'.

5 Atlan, 1979, 219 (see also Thoma, 1971, 109–20, 1975; Bell, 1952, 372).

6 Piaget, 1967, 1963.

7 Ashby, 1958, 1962.

8 Cowan, 1965a, 1965b.

Notes to Chapter 6

1 Schaeffer makes the distinction between the electronically 'pure' sounds (sine waves) and those sounds which have a recognizable instrumental timbre (Schaeffer, 1966, 450). Michel Chion, following Schaeffer, defines the mass criterion as a generalization of the notion of pitch, referring to the group of frequencies that constitute a sound. It includes those sounds where pitch is not precisely definable by the ear (Chion, 1983, 145). Complex sounds are those where the mass is fixed but not precise; in other words, sounds in which it is not possible to identify any fundamental frequency.

2 The morpho-typology proposed by Schaeffer tries to identify, classify and describe the sound objects from a perspective of reduced listening. Schaeffer, applying a sort of husserlian phenomenological reduction to the act of listening, is interested in the physical properties of sounds, ignoring any kind of causality or indexicality. When analyzing any sound object, we should privilege perception criteria.

3 When enumerating the differences between old and new media, Lev Manovich proposes some principles that should characterize the functioning of a new type of culture undergoing computerization. These principles include the automation of processes, the variability of forms in which new media objects are presented, and the possibility of transcoding certain formats into others, once they are all based on digital data. These would be dependent on two main principles that are the numerical representation of all media objects and their modularity, i.e. the construction of any type of media from discrete samples which can be combined almost indefinitely. Kittler's book *Gramophone, Film, Typewriter* is dedicated to analysing those communication technologies that exceeded a kind of symbolic mediation based on the alphabet and through the inscription of sound-waves or light on to a material surface, would present a certain *effect of the real*.

4 For detailed technical reference on digital, see Pohlmann's *Principles of Digital Audio*. (2005).

5 A French typographer who developed a mechanical process of registering vocal sounds as visual marks. In 1857, he presented his invention to the *Société d'Encouragement pour l'Industrie Nationale*. The *phonautographe* captured sounds through an acoustic shell, making a stylus attached to a diaphragm vibrate. It then created marks on a rotating cylinder of glass blackened by soot. In his communication, Léon Scott said:

> Gentlemen, I come to announce good news. Sound, like light, provides an enduring image from afar, the human voice is itself written (in the specific language of acoustics, of course) in a sensitive layer; after long efforts, I managed to collect the traces of almost all air movements

that make up the sound or the noise. Finally, by the same means, I may obtain, under certain conditions, an accurate representation of the fast movements, of the movements invaluable to our senses for their smallness, of the molecular movements. It is a case, as you can see in this new art, of forcing nature to constitute itself a general written language of all sounds.

(Scott de Martinville, cited in Pisano, 2004, 99–100)

Notes to Chapter 7

1 For more on the innovations in sound developed and utilized for *Star Wars* see Sergi (2004, 24–9, 51, 101–2).

2 Youngblood tentatively delineates and sketches out the various imminent spheres of image-making and image-exchange – shared images as an evolving and global forum for human communications, and a process which may be read therefore as forming or fomenting the next level of consciousness. Cinema is a near-obsolete stage in this transformation. When Youngblood conducted an interview with Lucas for the Los Angeles public television station KCET in 1971, their differences in conception of cinema were already apparent, with Youngblood talking of images and feelings and the desire to film dreams, and Lucas at times more concerned with 'what works' and dealing with 'studio executives'. The interview (*George Lucas: Maker of Films*, Jerry Hughes, 1971) is available at: http://www.slashfilm.com/votd-interview-with-27-year-old-george-lucas/.

3 On the matter of revolt in a *1984*-like future, Lucas' earlier films (*Electronic Labyrinth: THX-1138 4EB*, 1967, and *THX 1138*, 1971), which are the subject of his discussion with Youngblood, are key texts. On the shift from countercultural sci-fi to neoliberal sci-fi, see my discussion of the original and 'reboot' *Battlestar Galactica* series (Halligan, 2010).

4 Sergi's identification and formulation of a critical field for this endeavour ('Suggestions for Sound Analysis') is of limited use for this discussion of film sound. Chion (2009) also begins to assemble a glossary of terms and concepts. In this, and more generally, Chion's work is influenced by Pierre Schaeffer, whose writings on 'l'élément non visual au cinéma' (see Schaeffer, 1946, 45-8, 62-5, 51–4) and in 'Traité des objets musicaux' (1977), 'developed a universal classification of sounds that does not bother with distinctions between the sounds of noises, speech, or music' (Chion, 2009, 204).

5 Such a continuum allows Keane to talk of the 'unexpected pleasure to see the man who parted the Red Sea in *The Ten Commandments* [DeMille, 1956] get washed down the drain at the end of [*Earthquake*]' (Keane, 2001, 43–4).

6 Chion does not see this development so much as a belated equality between image and sound as the achievement of an aesthetic totality. For Chion, therefore, his first 'core idea' is that '*[t]here is no soundtrack*' (Chion, 2009, xi; emphasis in original): 'The inadequacy of the term *soundtrack* and of the kind of thinking it implies [...] leads to totally ignoring the sounds suggested by the image that we do not hear but that are as important as the ones we do hear' (Chion, 2009, 170; emphasis in original) – a reading then applied to *The Birds* (Alfred Hitchcock, 1963), a film in which, for Chion, the protagonists are at times attacked by sound alone (cf. Chion, 2009, 165–7).

7 In these respects other films from that period suggest themselves: the battles with the paranormal, the metaphysical and the limits of scientific possibility in *The Entity* (Sidney J. Furie, 1981), *Poltergeist* (Tobe Hooper, 1982), *The Exorcist II: The Heretic* (John Boorman, 1977), and *The Man Who Fell to Earth* (Nicholas Roeg, 1976) and *Brainstorm* (Douglas Trumbull, 1983), respectively.

8 At any rate, the answers provided by these two films represent a more proactive tangle of dissenting ideas than official stabs at clarifying mystifications: for Steven Spielberg's *Close Encounters of the Third Kind* (1977), the UFO encounter is presented in infantile, Disney-like terms. For Disney's own *The Black Hole* (Gary Nelson, 1979), a medieval vision of Hell is reintroduced as a possible endgame scenario – just as much for 'bad' computers and technology as for humans. Here experientialism gives rise to the immobilizing sense of wonderment. And a trip to Heaven for Warren Beatty, in *Heaven Can Wait* (Warren Beatty, Buck Henry, 1978), only lends him the enlightenment necessary to lecture businessmen on the economic advantages of responsible market capitalism back on earth.

9 Hence the impact of the Portsmouth Sinfonia's celebrated 'bad' rendition of the theme associated with *2001* – a performance art project associated with Brian Eno. At the crucial moment of the alignment of the planets, the appearance of the monolith and so forth, the uncouth noise of amateur and semi-amateur musicians trying to interpret their scores, all out of time, many out of tune, undermines the now grandiose associations of the music.

10 For Lacan, 'the real' resides, in psychoanalytical theory and practice, in or at the moment of trauma. To move beyond psychological strategies of displacement of guilt, for example, reveals or identifies such a structuring and difficult presence: 'the Real'. This may be a matter of flouting the authority of the big Other. For Žižek, 'the Real' becomes the 'irreducible kernel of *jouissance* that resists all symbolization' and so functions much as the notion of the aporia, in this discussion – repelling the looker, or asking for that look to be directed elsewhere; see Žižek (1999, 14).

11 The terms suggests a number of meanings in relation to the problematization of art and the figure of the artist-producer, typical of Gilbert and George's work in general, and retains the humour of Joyce's use of the self-aggrandizing description for his 1916 novel *A Portrait of the Artist as a Young Man*.

12 Hingley's translation adds a note of uncertainty not found in Frayn's of 1990: 'It seems to come from the sky' (Chekhov, 1989, 267). In Mamet's version the direction becomes: 'Suddenly a sound is heard as if from the sky, like the sound of a snapped string, dying away mournfully' (Chekhov, 1987, 49). All three translations reproduce Chekhov's original direction: the sound is not

necessarily located in the sky at its point of origin, but would merely seem to be.

13 'A little ere the mighty Julius fell,/The graves stood tenantless and the sheeted dead/Did squeak and gibber in the Roman streets –' (Act One, Scene One) (Shakespeare, 2005, 10).

14 One such piece of evidence is the Moscow Art Theatre's 1904 prompt book; even a cursory examination of letters between Chekhov and the producers illustrates Chekhov's profound disagreements with their interpretation (cf. Benedetti, 1995, 170–90). Rayfield cites instances of a similar sound in Chekhov's short stories, where clarity is given, as if the field of interpretation once established necessarily covers the entire oeuvre of an author.

Note to Chapter 8

1 The connection between *Irreversible* and Stanley Kubrick was kindly pointed out to me by Benjamin Halligan.

Notes to Chapter 9

1 For more on the sound of silent films, see Altman (2004).

2 For a fuller account of the effect of Dolby technology on film sound practice and aesthetics, see Sergi (2004).

3 The facts around the development of the Academy and X-Curves, and the statistical basis for the graphs, are covered in Allen (2006).

4 'Equalization' refers to any adjustment of the balance of frequencies within an electrical (or in this case audio) signal. Its most simplistic use is tone controls for boosting or lowering different parts of the frequency spectrum, i.e. bass and treble. In this case 'Academy Curve' and then subsequently 'X-Curve' were applied by default in cinemas to any film print being played with specified amounts of reduction in the relevant frequency ranges.

Notes to Chapter 11

1 'Head' refers to the physical start of a film.

2 The sublime: as developed from the eighteenth-century aesthetics of Kant and Burke where the sublime is associated with boundlessness and 'ideas' of danger as distinct from notions of beauty.

3 These include, among others, Chris Scarre (University of Durham), Iegor

Reznikoff (University of Paris X, Nanterre) and Michel Dauvois (Laboratoire d'Acoustique Musicale, Paris).

4 'Artwar' is also the title of a series of Jeff Keen Super 8 films and videos.

5 'Tail' refers to the physical end of a film.

6 'Autograph' is the title of Oxford's festival of sound art and contemporary music (Oxford Brookes University).

7 John Tilbury and Sebastian Lexer's performance of John Cage's *Electronic Music for Piano* (1964) was performed at *Café Oto*, London, on 22 January 2010.

Notes to Chapter 12

1 I use the terms 'process' and 'processual' in the sense that emerged from conceptual art practices of the twentieth century, where the activity or 'process' of *how* the work is made *is* the work (cf. Lippard, 1997; Stroud and Di Lallo, 2009, 122; Osborne, 2002; Williams, 2010).

2 *Amarillo Ramp* was commissioned by Stanley Marsh, who also commissioned *Cadillac Ranch* (1974) and several other sculptures on the land that his company The Marsh Enterprises owns, around Amarillo. Available at http://www.robertsmithson.com/earthworks/amarillo_300c.htm. Other Robert Smithson works referred to in this chapter may be viewed at http://www.robertsmithson.com/index_.htm.

3 For discussion of 'musique concrète' see Hegarty (2007, 32–3).

4 Sonic Youth was formed in New York City in 1981 with key musicians Thurston Moore, Kim Gordon, Lee Ranaldo, various drummers over the years, Richard Edson, Bob Bert, Jim Sclavunos, Steve Shelley, and further bass guitar with Mark Ibold.

5 For Ranaldo discussing his guitars, see http://www.youtube.com/watch?v=jPxgC35bTpQ&feature=related.

6 On the 'weather of music', see Herzogenrath (2009).

7 *Spiral Jetty* film clip. Available at http://www.youtube.com/watch?v=vCfm95GyZt4 and at http://www.robertsmithson.com/films/films.htm.

8 Gilles Deleuze discusses how individuation requires definition of a 'ground' (Deleuze, 1994, 152, 272), and this is what becomes defined as artistic territory as I have addressed elsewhere in relation to Smithson's earlier work in Rome (see Colman, 2007).

9 Following his code-breaking work for the British during the Second World War where he cracked the noise distortion of enemy communications, Alan Turing invented further coding ideas through experiments with the acoustic delays of 'sound pulses' (see Campbell-Kelly, 2005, 158).

10 Duration is a continuous whole that changes (see Deleuze, 1991, 37–49).

Autopoiesis refers to the auto-productive potential of living machines as open and thus processual forms (see Guattari, 1995; Stengers and Prigogine, 1984).

Notes to Chapter 13

1 Anti-copyright. Anyone can do whatever they want with the material contained in this chapter.
2 See http://www.youtube.com/watch?v=1jg_aDSGcMk.

Notes to Chapter 14

1 Massumi does state that affect is 'intensity that is qualifiable as an emotional state and a state that is static, temporal and narrative noise' (Massumi, 2002, 26). For Massumi's paradigm of affect, see Massumi, 2002.
2 For example, noise music is often described in relation to feelings of ecstasy, of being outside of oneself. For Merzbow, Japanese noise 'relishes the ecstasy of sound itself'(Akita, 2008, 60). For Michael Gira, the noise of Swans created 'an overwhelming sonic rush that could just erase your body' (Idov, 2005).
3 Paul Hegarty makes a similar point in relation to Japanese noise music. He states: 'If there is a noise body, it is between the participants, or how they relate; it is also the body in receipt of noise; also the subject struggling to be subject; but there is also ecstasy' (Hegarty, 2007, 147).
4 I borrow the notion of the ideology of immanence from my colleague Will Scrimshaw, who has sought to question the purported immediacy of hearing, which tends to inform dominant tenets in sound studies (see Scrimshaw, 2011).
5 Deleuze states: 'the face with its visual correlates relates to painting, the voice with its auditory correlates relates to music' (Bogue, 2003, 80). However, as Bogue warns, this opposition between face and voice is not as clear as it may initially seem, not least because the voice tends to belong to the mouth of the face. See Bogue, 2003, 80–1.
6 The track 'Vox' appears on Various Artists (2009) An Anthology of Noise and Electronic Music Vol.4 (CD) Sub Rosa (Ratkje, 2009).
7 Simon Reynolds is referring specifically to the use of noise in rock music. He states:

>the whole discourse of noise-as-threat is bankrupt, positively inimical to the remnants of power that still cling to noise. Forget subversion. The point is self-subversion, overthrowing the power structure in your own head. The enemy is the mind's tendency to systematize, sew up experience, place a distance between itself and immediacy.
>(Reynolds, 2004, 57)

Notes to Chapter 15

1 'Complaints about noise seem to be a part of all recorded history' (Bijsterveld, 2001, 45). For example, 'in 720 BC, the Greek colony Sybaris in Italy prohibited industrial noises in residential areas' (Bijsterveld, 2001, 64n).

2 dB(A) makes reference to the internationally accepted convention for measuring sound pressure levels. There is however some dispute as to whether this measurement scale is best suited for calibrating environmental noise.

3 'Typical neighbourhood noise comes from premises and installations related to the catering trade (restaurant, cafeterias, discotheques, etc.); or recorded music; from sporting events including motor sports; from playgrounds and car parks; and from domestic animals such as barking dogs' (WHO, 1999, v). Although reference is made to such things as discotheques, recorded music and motor sports, we can image analogous sounds that did not involve machine technology. For example, acoustic drums and other non-electronic musical instruments could equally be imagined as producing sounds that can be (could have been) interpreted as noise.

4 Serres provides us here with a conception of noise that exceeds a concern with just sounds. However, that this conception is meant to be applicable to sounds as well becomes especially evident in Serres (2008), particularly in Chapter 2.

5 It is also important to point out that the understanding of noise which we are developing exceeds the characterization of noise as simply unwanted or undesired sounds (Adams *et al.*, 2006; Bijsterveld, 2001, 42; Jones and Chapman, 1984, 3; Pelmear, 1985, 31; Riediker and Koren, 2004, 194; Rodda, 1967, 2; Stansfeld, 2006, 37). That characterization represents noise as a subjective matter, a matter of individual or collective preference: 'From the mid-thirties on … experts on psychoacoustics increasingly stressed that "reaction to noise is largely temperamental and varies greatly from person to person"; Everyday life had always shown that "some persons complain of noises which others find innocuous" ' (Bijsterveld, 2003, 182).

6 Another way to possibly understand noise is indirectly provided to us by Žižek (2008b) in his discussion of the figure of the tramp in Chaplin's *City Lights*:

> as Michel Chion pointed out in his brilliant interpretation of *City Lights*, the fundamental feature of the figure of the tramp is his *interposition*: he is always interposed between a gaze and its 'proper' object, fixating upon himself a gaze destined for another, ideal point or object – a stain which disturbs 'direct' communication between the gaze and its 'proper' object, leading the straight gaze astray.
>
> (Žižek, 2008b, 5)

Indeed, Serres (2008) also discusses noise as a kind of stain. Analogously, we might think of noise as that dissonance which interposes itself between engagement and its intended object.

7 It is claimed by science that sounds exceeding 120 dB(A) are harmful to human hearing.

8 That the city of Toronto's noise by-law, grounded in the understanding of noise as a metric, has been unable to resolve the conflict between The Docks and the residents of the Toronto Islands, seems to us, to confirm the inadequacy of a quantitative understanding of noise.

9 The transcription should have read 'decibels'.

10 The City of Toronto [Noise] By-law No. 111–2003 hints, in its appendix (52), at noise as exceeding quantification: 'In general, noises are annoying because they are heard over and above the level of the so-called "background" or surrounding environmental noise climate at a particular location.' Despite this articulation, the by-law itself formulates noise as if it is strictly a metric.

11 The transcription should have read 'Dr. Basrur'.

Notes to Chapter 16

1 This is a process that I am theorizing here through a close reading of relevant research. Each of these stages has either been implied or argued by the authors whose work I draw upon in this chapter, but have not been presented as a series of steps, as I do here.

2 Aside from deafness, some of the other physical ailments caused by sound are tied to the physical manifestations of anxiety surrounding unwanted sound. For instance, Kosko claims that noise causes stress sleep loss, and increased blood pressure (Kosko, 2006, xvi), yet sound at the same levels impacts upon people differently depending on a person's perceived control or familiarity with the sound. This type of evidence explains the causal ambiguity around noise/sound and its physical effects (Staples, 1996; Garcia, 2001).

3 It should be noted that Glass and Singer did find 'deleterious after-effects' of noise, even after adaptability. However, they posit that these effects could simply stem from the stress of adaptation to sound, rather than the noise itself (1972, 158–9).

Bibliography

Adams, M. *et al.* (2006). 'Sustainable Soundscapes: Noise Policy and the Urban Experience'. *Urban Studies*, 43 (13): 2385–98.

—(2007). 'The 24-hour City: Residents' Sensorial Experiences'. *Senses and Society*, 2 (2): 201–16.

Akita, M. (2008). 'The Beauty of Noise: An Interview with Masami Akita of Merzbow'. In *Audio Culture: Readings in Modern Music*, ed. C. Cox and D. Warner. London: Continuum, 59–61.

Alcohol and Gaming Commission of Ontario (2005). Transcripts of Hearing: The Docks by Cherry, Licence no. 804501. Toronto.

Allen, I. (2006). 'The X-Curve, its origins and history'. *SMPTE Motion Imaging Journal, July/August 2006* (accessed August 2011). Available at: http://www.dolby.com/uploadedFiles/zz-_Shared_Assets/English_PDFs/Professional/Dolby_The%20X-Curve__SMPTE%20Journal.pdf.

Althusser, L. (2002). *Lenin and Philosophy and Other Essays*, trans. B. Brewster. New York: Monthly Review Press.

Altman, R. (1992). *Sound Theory/Sound Practice*. London: Routledge.

—(2004). *Silent Film Sound*. Chichester: Columbia University Press.

Anon. (2011). 'One Pig' Album To Be Released On 10 October, *Matthew Herbert* (online). Available at: http://www.matthewherbert.com/news/2011/7/6/one-pig-album-to-be-released-on-october-10th.html. (Accessed 18 July 2011).

Ansen, D. (2003). 'How Far Is Too Far?', *Newsweek*. Accessed 28 February 2011. Archived at: http://www.newsweek.com/id/58610.

Arendt, H. (2000). 'The Two-In-One' (from *The Life of the Mind*, Vol. 1). In *The Portable Hannah Arendt*, New York: Penguin Books, pp. 408–16.

Arkette, S. (2004). 'Sounds like City'. In *Theory, Culture and Society*, 21 (1): 159–68.

Armstrong, E. and Rothfuss, J. (eds) (1993). *The Spirit of Fluxus*. Minneapolis: The Walker Art Center.

Artaud, A. (1958). *The Theater and its Double*, trans. M. C. Richards. New York: Grove Press.

Artaud, A. and O'Morgan, J. (1958). 'The Theatre and Cruelty'. *The Tulane Drama Review*, 2(3): 75–7.

Ashby, W. R. (1958). 'Requisite Variety and its Implications for the Control of Complex Systems'. *Cybernetica*, 1 (2): 83–99.

—(1962). 'Principles of the Self-organizing System'. In *Principles of Self Organization*, ed. Von Foerster et Zopf. Oxford: Pergamon Press, pp. 255–78.

Atlan, H. (1979). *Entre la fumée et le cristal*. Paris: Le Seuil.

Attali, J. (1985/2006). *Noise: The Political Economy of Music*, trans. B. Massumi. Minneapolis: University of Minnesota Press.

Badiou, A. (2003). *On Beckett*, ed. N. Power and A. Toscano. Manchester: Clinamen Press.

Bailey, P. (1996). 'Breaking the Sound Barrier: A Historian Listens to Noise'. *Body and Society*, 2(2): 49–66.

Balázs, B. ([1930] 2010). *Béla Balázs Early Film Theory: Visible Man and The Spirit of Film*, trans. R. Livingstone. Oxford: Berghahn Books.

Ballard, J. G. (1966). *The Crystal World*. London: Jonathan Cape.

—(2000). 'Robert Smithson as Cargo Cultist'. In *Robert Smithson: Dead Tree*, ed. B. Conley and J. Arnheim. Brooklyn: Pierogi, p. 31.

—(2009). *The Complete Stories of J. G. Ballard*. New York: Norton.

Baron, R. A. (1970). *The Tyranny of Noise*. New York: St Martin's Press.

Bataille, G. (1985). *Visions of Excess: Selected Writings, 1927–1939*, ed. A. Stoekl, trans. A. Stoekl, with C. R. Lovitt and D. M. Leslie, Jr. Minneapolis: University of Minnesota Press.

—(1986). *Erotism: Death and Sensuality*, Trans. M. Dalwood. San Francisco, CA: City Limits.

Baudrillard, J. (1983). *Simulations*, ed. P. Foss, P. Patton and P. Beitchman. New York: Semiotext(e).

Baxter, J. ed. (2008). *J. G. Ballard*. London: Continuum.

Beckett, S. (2006). *The Complete Dramatic Works*. London: Faber and Faber.

Begam, R. (1996). *Samuel Beckett and the End of Modernity*. Cambridge: Cambridge University Press.

Bell, D. A. (1952). 'Physical Entropy and Information'. *Journal of Applied Physics*, 23 (3): 372.

Benedetti, J. ed. (1995). *The Moscow Art Theatre Letters*. London, Auckland, Melbourne, Singapore, Toronto: Methuen Drama.

Benjamin, W. (1968). *Illuminations*, trans. H. Zohn. New York: Schocken.

—(1978). *Reflections*, trans. E. Jephcott. New York: Schocken.

—(1992). 'Theses on the Philosophy of History'. In *Illuminations*, 245–55 trans. H. Zohn. London: Fontana.

—(1998). *The Origin of Tragic German Drama*, trans. J. Osborne. London: Verso.

—(1999). *Illuminations*, trans. H. Zohn. London: Pimlico.

—(2008). *The Work of Art in the Age of its Technological Reproducibility and Other Writings on Media*, trans. E. Jephcott. Cambridge, MA: Belknap Press.

Berardi, F. [aka 'Bifo'] (2009). *Precarious Rhapsody: Semiocapitalism and the Pathologies of the Post-Alpha Generation*. London: Minor Compositions.

Bergson, H. ([1907] 1983). *Creative Evolution*, trans. A. Mitchell. Boston, MA: University Press of America.

—(1960/2001). *Time and Free Will: An Essay on the Immediate Data of Consciousness*, trans. F. L. Pogson. New York: Harper Torchbook.

Bijsterveld, K. (2001). 'The Diabolical Symphony of the Mechanical Age: Technology and Symbolism of Sound in European and North American Noise Abatement Campaigns, (1900–1940)'. *Social Studies of Science*, 31 (1): 37–70.

—(2003). '"The City of Din": Decibels, Noise, and Neighbours in the Netherlands, 1910–1980'. *OSIRIS*, 18: 173–93.

Biskind, P. (1999). *Easy Riders, Raging Bulls: How the Sex, Drugs and Rock 'n Roll Generation Saved Hollywood*. London: Simon & Schuster.

Blaker, H. and Giles, J. (eds) (2011). *BFI Performing Arts Catologue*. Available at http://www.bfi.org.uk/filmtvinfo/publications/performing-arts/BFI-Performing-Arts-Catalogue-2011.pdf.

Blanchot, M. (1989). *The Space of Literature*, trans. A. Smock. Lincoln: University of Nebraska Press.

—(1993). *The Infinite Conversation*, trans. S. Hanson. Minneapolis: University of Minnesota Press.

Blauert, J. (1997). *Spatial Hearing: The Psychophysics of Human Sound Localization*. Cambridge, MA: MIT Press.

Blechman, E. and Dannemiller, E. (1976). 'Effects on Performance of Perceived Control Over Noxious Noise'. *Journal of Consulting and Clinical Psychology*, 44 (4): 601–7.

Blum, A. (2003). *The Imaginative Structure of the City*. Montreal and Kingston: McGill-Queen's University Press.

—(2010). *The Grey Zone of Health and Illness*. Bristol, and Chicago, IL: Intellect Press.

Boettger, S. (2002). *Earthworks: Art and the Landscape of the Sixties*. Berkeley: University of California Press.

Bogue, R. (2003). *Deleuze on Music, Painting and the Arts*. New York and London: Routledge.

Bolter, J. D. and Grusin, R. (2000). *Remediation: Understanding New Media*. Cambridge, MA: MIT Press.

Bonefeld, W. and Psychopedis, K. (eds) (2005). *Human Dignity. Social Autonomy and the Critique of Capitalism*. Oxford: Hart Publishing.

Bourdieu, P. (1984). *Distinction: A Social Critique of the Judgement of Taste*, trans. R. Nice. Cambridge, MA: Harvard University Press.

—(1990). *The Logic of Practice*, trans. R. Nice. Stanford, CA: Stanford University Press.

—(1993). *The Field of Cultural Production: Essays on Art and Literature*, edited and introduced by R. Johnson, trans. R. Nice *et al*. New York: Columbia University Press.

Bragdon, C. R. (1979). *Noise Pollution: A Guide to Information Sources*. Detroit: Gale Research.

Brassier, R. (2007). *Nihil Unbound: Enlightenment and Extinction*. London: Palgrave Macmillan.

—(2007). 'Genre is Obsolete'. *Multitudes*, 28 (spring). Available at http://multitudes.samizdat.net/-Mineure-NOISE.

—(2009). 'Against an Aesthetics of Noise'. Available at *http://ny-web.be/transitzone/against-aesthetics-noise.html*.

—(2011). 'Concepts and Objects'. In *The Speculative Turn*, ed. L. Bryant, N. Srnicek and G. Harman. Melbourne: Re-press. Also available at http://www.re-press.org/bookfiles/OA_Version_Speculative_Turn_9780980668346.pdf.

Braun, E. (2000). *The Cherry Orchard*. In *The Cambridge Companion to Chekhov*, V. Gottlieb and P. Allain, ed. Cambridge, New York, Melbourne, Madrid: Cambridge University Press, 111–20.

Brock, D. (2004). *The Republican Noise Machine: Right-wing Media and how it Corrupts Democracy*. New York: Crown Publishers.

Brougher, K., Strick, J., Wiseman, A. and Zilczer, J. (2005). *Visual Music: Synaesthesia in Art and Music Since 1900*. London: Thames & Hudson.

Brown, S. D. (2002). 'Michel Serres: Science, Translation and the Logic of the Parasite'. *Theory, Culture and Society*, 19: 1–27.

Browne, D. (2009). *Goodbye 20th Century: Sonic Youth and the Rise of Alternative Nation*. London: Piatkus Books.

Bussy, P. (1993). *Kraftwerk: Man, Machine and Music*. London: SAF Publishing.

Cage, J. (1961). *Silence*. Middletown: Wesleyan University Press.

Campbell-Kelly, M. (2005). 'The ACE and the Shaping of British Computing'. In *Alan Turing's Automatic Computing Engine: The Master Codebreaker's Struggle*, ed. B. J. Copeland. Oxford: Oxford University Press: pp. 149–92.

Cascone, K. (2003). *Viral Space: The Cinema of Atmosphere*. Accessed 28 February 2011. Archived at: http://www.acs.ucalgary.ca/~tstronds/nostalghia.com/TheTopics/Tributes/another_kind_of_insert_2.jpg.

Casey, E. (2003). *Earth-Mapping: Contemporary Artists Who Map*. Minneapolis: University of Minnesota Press.

Catlin, F. (1986). 'Noise-induced Hearing Loss'. *The American Journal of Otology*, 7 (2): 141–9.

Chandler Jr, A. (1972). 'Anthracite Coal and the Beginnings of the Industrial Revolution in the United States'. *The Business History Review*: 141–81.

Chapuis, R. (2003). *100 Years of Telephone Switching*. Burke: IOS Press.

Chekhov, A. (1987). *The Cherry Orchard*, adapted by D. Mamet from a literal translation by D. Nelles. New York: Grove Press.

—(1989). *Anton Chekhov: Five Plays*, trans. R. Hingley. Oxford, New York: Oxford University Press.

—(1990). *The Cherry Orchard*, trans. M. Frayn. London, New Hamphire: Methuen Drama.

Chion, M. (1983). *Guide des objets sonores*. Bry-sur-Marne, Paris: Institut National de l'Audiovisuel; Buchet/Chastel.

—(1990/1994). *Audio-Vision: Sound on Screen*, trans. C. Gorbman. New York: Columbia University Press.

—(1999). *The Voice in Cinema*, trans. C. Gorbman. Chichester: Columbia University Press.

—(2007) 'The Silence of the Loudspeakers, or Why with Dolby Sound it is the Film that Listens to Us'. In *Soundscape: The School of Sound Lectures 1998–2001*, ed. L. Sider, D. Freeman and J. Sider. London: Wallflower Press, pp. 150–4.

—(2009). *Film, A Sound Art*, trans C. Gorbman. New York: Columbia University Press.

Classen, C. (1993). *Worlds of Sense: Exploring the Senses in History and Across Cultures*. London: Routledge.

—(1998). *The Color of Angels: Cosmology, Gender and the Aesthetic Imagination*. London: Routledge.

Coerver, C. ed. (2001). *Art in Technological Times*. San Francisco, CA: SFMoMA.

Cogan, B. (2006). *Encyclopedia of Punk Music and Culture.* Westport, CT: Greenwood Press.

Cohen, N. (1993). *Worksongs: A Demonstration Collection of Examples.* In *Songs About Work,* A. Green. Bloomington: Folklore Institute, Indiana University.

Colman, F. J. (2006). 'Affective Entropy: Art as Differential Form'. *Angelaki: Journal of the Theoretical Humanities,* 11 (1): 169–78.

—(2007). 'Affective Intensity: Art as Sensorial Form'. In *Sensorium: Aesthetics, Art, Life* ed. B. Bolt, F. J. Colman, G. Jones and A. Woodward. Newcastle, UK: Cambridge Scholars Press, pp. 64–83.

—(2009). 'Affective Sounds for Social Orders'. In *The Continuum Companion to Sound in Film and the Visual Media,* ed. G. Harper. London: Continuum, pp. 194–207.

Cook, P. ed. (1999). *Music, Cognition and Computerized Sound: An Introduction to Psychoacoustics.* Cambridge, MA: MIT Press.

Corbin, A. (1994). *Les Cloches de la terre: paysage sonore et culture sensible dans les campagnes au XIXe siècle.* Paris: Flammarion.

Corbould, C. (2007). 'Streets, Sounds, and Identity in Interwar Harlem'. *Journal of Social History,* 40 (4): 859–94.

Cornelius, A. (2008). *People Who Do Noise* (DVD). Cold Hands Video.

Court, P. (2007). *New York Noise: Art and Music from the New York Underground 1978–88.* London: Soul Jazz Records.

Cowan, J. D. (1965a). 'The Problem of Organismic Reliability'. *Progress in Brain Research,* 17: 9–63.

—(1965b). *Cybernetics and the Nervous System,* edited by Wiener et Schade. Amsterdam: Elsevier, pp. 9–63.

Cowie, E. (2003). 'The Lived Nightmare: Trauma, Anxiety and the Ethical Aesthetics of Horror'. In *Dark Thoughts: Philosophic Reflections on Cinematic Horror,* ed. S. J. Schneider and D. Shaw. Oxford: The Scarecrow Press, pp. 25–46.

Cox, C. and Warner, D. (eds) (2004). *Audio Culture: Readings in Modern Music.* London: Continuum.

Critchley, E. M. R. (1983). 'Auditory Experiences of Deaf Schizophrenics'. *Journal of the Royal Society of Medicine,* 76: 542–4.

Cross, A. G. (1969). 'The Breaking Strings of Chekhov and Turgenev'. *Slavonic and East European Review,* 47 (109): 510–13.

Cutler, C. ed. (2008). *Baku: Symphony of Sirens.* London: ReR Megacorp.

Debord, G. (1995). *The Society of the Spectacle,* trans. D. Nicholson-Smith. New York: Zone.

—(2004). *Panegyric, Vols 1 & 2,* trans. J. Brook. London: Verso.

De Certeau, M. (1984). *The Practice of Everyday Life,* trans. S. Rendall. Berkeley: University of California Press.

Deho, V. (2006). *Sound Zero: Art and Music from Pop to Street Art.* Bologna: Graphiche Damiani.

Deleuze, G. (1966). *Le Bergsonisme.* Paris: PUF.

—(1989). *Cinema 2: The Time-Image,* trans. H. Tomlinson and R. Galeta. Minnesota: Athlone Press, University of Minnesota Press.

—(1990). *The Logic of Sense,* trans. M. Lester and C. Stivale. London: Athlone Press.

—(1991). *Bergsonism*, trans. H. Tomlinson and B. Habberjam. New York: Zone.

—([1968] 1994). *Difference and Repetition*. Trans. P. Patton. London and New York: Continuum.

—(1997). *Difference and Repetition*, trans. P. Patton. London: Continuum.

—(2004). *Francis Bacon and the Logic of Sensation*, trans. D. W. Smith. New York and London: Continuum.

Deleuze, G. and Guattari, F. (1988/2010). *A Thousand Plateaus*, trans. B. Massumi. London: Athlone/Continuum.

—(1994). *What is Philosophy?*, trans. G. Burchell and H. Tomlinson. New York: Columbia University Press.

Derrida, J. (1993). *Aporias*, trans. T. Dutoit. Stanford, CA: Stanford University Press.

—(2003). 'And Say the Animal Responded?' In *Zoontologies* edited by Cary Wolfe. Minneapolis: University of Minnesota Press, pp. 121–46.

Derrida, J. and Attridge, D. (eds) (1992). *Acts of Literature*. London: Routledge.

Dia Art Foundation (2011). *Walter De Maria: The Lightning Field*. Available at http://www.diaart.org.

Dobnik, V. (2007) 'Drummers Clash with New Harlem Residents'. *USA Today,* 11 August. Available at http://www.usatoday.com/news/topstories/2007–08–11–345187240_x.htm (accessed 1 April 2008).

Dolar, M. (2006). *A Voice and Nothing More*. Cambridge, MA: MIT Press.

Dupont, F. (2007). *Species Being and Other Stories*. San Francisco, CA: Ardent Press.

Dyson, F. (2009). *Sounding New Media*. Berkeley: University of California Press.

Eco, U. (1986). *Travels in Hyperreality*, trans. W. Weaver. Florida: Harcourt, Brace & Co.

Eisenstein, S. M., Pudovkin, W. I. and Alexandrov, G. V. (1928). 'Statement on Sound'. In *S. M. Eisenstein: Selected Works, Volume I: Writings, 1922–34* (1988), ed. R. Taylor. London: British Film Institute, pp. 113–14.

Eno, B. and Kevin, K. (1995). 'Gossip is Philosophy': An Interview with Brian Eno, *Wired,* 3 May, pp. 1–14.

Evens, A. (2005). *Sound Ideas: Music, Machines, and Experience*. Minneapolis: University of Minnesota Press.

Feil, K. (2005). *Dying for a Laugh: Disaster Movies and the Camp Imagination*. Middleton, CT: Wesleyan University Press.

Firestone, S. ([1970] 1979). *The Dialectic of Sex: The Case for Feminist Revolution*. London: Jonathan Cape.

Fisher, M. (2001). 'Gothic Materialism'. In *Transmat: Resources in Transcendental Materialism*, available at http://www.cinestatic.com/trans-mat/Fisher/gothic.htm.

—(2009). *Capitalist Realism – Is There No Alternative?* Winchester: Zero Books.

—(2009). 'The Films of Jeff Keen'. *The Wire*, 302 (April): 22.

Flam, J. (1996). *Robert Smithson: The Collected Writings*. Berkeley: University of California Press.

Flusser, V. (2002). *Filosofia da caixa preta: ensaios para uma futura filosofia da fotografia*. Rio de Janeiro: Relume Dumará.

Focillon, H. ([1934] 1989). *The Life of Forms in Art*, trans. C. B. Hogan and G. Kubler. New York: Zone.

Frith, S. (1996). *Performing Rites: Evaluating Popular Music*. Oxford: Oxford University Press.

Frith, S. and Horne, H. (1987). *Art into Pop*. London: Routledge.

Fuller, M. and Goffey, A. (2009). 'Toward an Evil Media Studies'. In *The Spam Book: On Viruses, Porn, and Other Anomalies from the Dark Side of Digital Culture*, ed. J. Parikka and T. D. Sampson. Cresskill: Hampton Press, pp. 141–59.

García, A. (2001). *Environmental Urban Noise*. Boston, MA: WIT Press.

Garfinkel, H. (1967). *Studies in Ethnomethodology*. Englewood Cliffs, NJ: Prentice Hall.

Gaver, W. (1993). 'How Do We Hear in the World? Explorations in Ecological Acoustics'. *Ecological Psychology*, 5 (4): 285–313.

Gilbert, J. and Pearson, E. (1999). *Discographies: Dance Music, Culture and the Politics of Sound*. London: Routledge.

Gitelman, L. (1999). *Scripts, Grooves, and Writing Machines: Representing Technology in the Edison Era*. Stanford, CA: Stanford University Press.

Glansdorff, P. and Prigogine, I. (1976). 'Entropie, structure et dynamique'. In *Sadi Carnot et l'Essor de la thermodynamique*. Paris: Editions du CNRS.

—(1981). *Structure, Stability and Fluctuations*. Paris: Masson.

Glass, D. C. and Singer, J. E. (1972). *Urban Stress: Experiments on Noise and Social Stressors*. New York: Academic Press.

Goh, I. (2008). '"Strange Ecology" in Deleuze/Guattari's *A Thousand Plateaus*'. In B. Herzogenrath ed. *An (Un)Likely Alliance: Thinking Environment(s) with Deleuze/Guattari*, Newcastle Upon Tyne: Cambridge Scholars, pp. 195–215.

Goodman, S. (2010). *Sonic Warfare: Sound, Affect, and The Ecology of Fear*. Cambridge, MA: MIT Press.

Graziani, R. (2004). *Robert Smithson and the American Landscape*. Cambridge: Cambridge University Press.

Grosz, E. (2004). *The Nick of Time: Politics, Evolution and the Untimely*. Durham, NC, and London: Duke University Press.

—(2008). *Chaos, Territory, Art: Deleuze and the Framing of the Earth*. New York: Columbia University Press.

Guattari, F. ([1977 and 1980] 1984). *Molecular Revolution: Psychiatry and Politics*, trans. R. Sheed. New York: Penguin.

—([1992] 1995). *Chaosmosis*, trans. P. Bains and J. Pefanis. Bloomington: Indiana University Press.

Gumbrecht, H. U. (2004). *Production of Presence: What Meaning Cannot Convey*. Stanford, CA: Stanford University Press.

Hall, S., Critcher, C. *et al.* (1978). *Policing the Crisis: Mugging, the State, and Law and Order*. London: Macmillan.

Halligan, B. (2010). 'Disco Galactica: Futures Past and Present'. In *Battlestar Galactica: Investigating Flesh, Spirit and Steel*, ed. R. Kaveney and J. Stoy. London: I B Tauris, pp. 81–109.

Haraway, D. (1991). *Simians, Cyborgs and Women: The Reinvention of Nature*. New York: Routledge.

—(2004). *The Haraway Reader*. New York: Routledge.

Hardt, M. (2002). 'Exposure: Pasolini in the Flesh', in *A Shock to Thought: Expression After Deleuze and Guattari*, ed. B. Massumi. London: Routledge, pp. 77–84.

Hardy, T. (1877). *A Pair of Blue Eyes*. London: Henry S. King & Co.

Harkleroad, L. (2006). *The Math Behind the Music*. New York: Cambridge University Press.

Harman, G. (2008). 'On the Horror of Phenomenology: Lovecraft and Husserl'. *Collapse: Philosophical Research and Development*, 4: 332–64.

Hegarty, P. (2007). *Noise/Music: A History*. New York and London: Continuum.

Heinrich, M. *Critique of Political Economy: An Introduction to The Three Volumes of Marx's 'Capital'*, trans. A. Locasio (unpublished MS).

Herzogenrath, B. (2009). 'The "Weather of Music": Sounding Nature in the Twentieth and Twenty-First Centuries'. In *Deleuze, Guattari and Ecology*, ed. B. Herzogengrath. New York: Palgrave Macmillan, pp. 216–50.

Higbee, W. (2005). 'Towards a Multiplicity of Voices: French Cinema's Age of the Postmodern, Part II – 1992–2004'. In *French National Cinema*, ed. S. Hayward 2nd edn. London: Routledge, pp. 293–327.

Higgins, H. (2002). *Fluxus Experience*. Berkeley: University of California Press.

Hills, M. (2005). *The Pleasures of Horror*. London: Continuum.

Hobbs, R. (1981). *Robert Smithson: Sculpture*. London: Cornell University Press.

Hopkins, G. M. and Gardner, W. H. (1985). *Gerard Manley Hopkins: Poems and Prose*. London: Penguin Books.

Horeck, T. (2004). *Public Rape: Representing Violation in Fiction and Film*. London: Routledge.

Houellebecq, M. (2008). *H .P. Lovecraft: Against the World, Against Life*. London: Gollancz.

Huneman, P. and Kulich, E. (1997). *Introduction à la phénomènologie*. Paris: Armand Colin.

Hurley, K. (2004). *The Gothic Body: Sexuality, Materialism, and Degeneration at the Fin De Siècle*. Cambridge: Cambridge University Press.

Idov, M. (2005). 'Interviews: Michael Gira'. *Pitchfork*, 22 May 2005. Available at http://pitchfork.com/features/interviews/6048-michael-gira/ (accessed 16 July 2010).

Ihde, D. (2007). *Listening and Voice: Phenomenologies of Sound*. New York: SUNY Press.

Invisible Committee, The (2009). *The Coming Insurrection*. Los Angeles, CA: Semiotext(e).

Johnson, B. (2008). Early unpublished draft of '"Quick and Dirty": Sonic Mediations and Affect', the final draft of which is now available in *Sonic Mediations: Body, Sound, Technology*, ed. C. Birdsall and A. Enns. Cambridge: Cambridge University Press.

Jones, D. M. and Chapman, A. J. (1984). 'Audition and Man, Noise and Society'. In *Noise and Society*, ed. D. M. Jones and A. J. Chapman. New York: John Wiley & Sons, pp. 1–6.

Joseph, B. W. (2008). *Beyond the Dream Syndicate: Tony Conrad and the Arts after Cage*. New York: Zone.

Joshi, S. T. (1990). *The Weird Tale*. Holicong: Wildside Press.

—(2004). *The Evolution of the Weird Tale*. New York: Hippocampus Press.

Kahn, D. (1983). *The Latest: Fluxus and Music*. In *In The Spirit of Fluxus*, ed. E. Armstrong and J. Rothfuss. New York: Walker Art Center/D.A.P.

—(2001). *Noise Water Meat: A History of Sound in the Arts*. Cambridge, MA: MIT Press.

Kaufmann, V. (2006). *Guy Debord: Revolution in the Service of Poetry*. Minneapolis: University of Minnesota Press.

Kay, L. E. (1995). 'Who Wrote the Book of Life? Information and the Transformation of Biology'. *Science in Context*, 8:609–34.

Keane, S. (2001). *Disaster Movies: The Cinema of Catastrophe*. London and New York: Wallflower.

Kenny, T. (2000). *Sound For Picture*. Auburn Hills, MI: Mix Books.

Kilby, J. (2001). 'Carved in Skin: Bearing Witness to Self-harm'. In *Thinking Through the Skin*, ed. S. Ahmed and J. Stacey. London: Routledge, pp. 124–42.

Kim-Cohen, S. (2009). *In the Blink of an Ear*. London and New York: Continuum.

Kittler, F. A. (1999). *Gramophone, Film, Typewriter*. Stanford, CA: Stanford University Press.

Knabb, K. ed. (2006). *Situationist International Anthology* (revised edn). Berkeley, CA: Bureau of Public Secrets.

Kojève, A. (1969). *Introduction to a Reading of Hegel*, trans. E. De Vries. New York: Basic Books.

Kosko, B. (2006). *Noise*. New York: Viking.

Krauss, R. (1997). ' ":.. And then turn away?" An Essay on James Coleman'. *October*, 81: 5–33.

—(1999). 'Reinventing the Medium'. *Critical Inquiry*, 25 (2): 289–305.

—(2000), ' "The Rock": William Kentridge's Drawings for Projection'. *October*, 92: 3–35.

Krippendorff, K. (1991). 'The Power of Communication and the Communication of Power: Toward an Emancipatory Theory of Communication'. *Communication*, 12 (3): 175–96.

Kryter, K. D. (1970). *The Effects of Noise on Man*. New York: Academic Press.

LaBelle, B. (2006). *Background Noise: Perspectives of Sound Art*. London: Continuum.

Lacan, J. (1993). *The Psychoses: The Seminar of Jacques Lacan*, Book III (1955–56), ed. J. A. Miller, trans. R. Grigg. London: Routledge.

—(2005). *Le Sinthome*. Paris: Le Seuil.

—(2006). *Écrits*, trans. B. Fink. New York: Norton.

Lakoff, G. and Johnson, M. (2003). *Metaphors We Live By*. Chicago, IL: University of Chicago Press.

Langkær, B. (1997). 'Spatial Perception and Technologies of Cinema Sound'. *Convergence: The International Journal of Research into New Media Technologies*, 1997 (3): 92–107.

Lee, M. (2007). *Oceanic Ontology and Problematic Thought*. Brighton: Self-published.

LeGrice, M. (2001). *Experimental Cinema in the Digital Age*. London: BFI.

Levarie, S. (1977). 'Noise'. *Critical Inquiry*, 4 (1): 21–31.

Lévi-Strauss, C. (1966). *The Savage Mind*, trans. G. Weidenfeld. Chicago, IL: University of Chicago Press.

Lewin, M. (2005). *The Soviet Century*. London: Verso.

Lippard, L. ([1973] 1997). *Six Years: The Dematerialization of the Art Object from 1966 to 1972*. Berkeley: University of California Press.

Lloyd, W. H. (1934). 'Noise as Nuisance'. *University of Pennsylvania Law Review*, 82 (6): 567–82.

Lovecraft, H. P. (1963). *The Haunter of the Dark and Other Tales*. London: Panther.

—(1969a). *The Tomb and Other Tales*. London: Panther.

—(1969b). *Dagon and Other Macabre Tales*. London: Panther.

—(2002). *The Call of Cthulhu and Other Weird Stories*. London: Penguin Modern Classics.

—(2005). 'Supernatural Horror in Literature'. In *At The Mountains of Madness: The Definitive Edition*. New York: Modern Library, pp. 103–82.

—(2008). 'History of the Necronomicon (An Outline)'. In *The Case of Charles Dexter Ward*. London: Creation Oneiros, pp. 173–5.

Lozano-Hemmer, R. (2003). *Amodal Suspension. Relational Architecture No. 8*. Available at: http://www.amodal.net/index.html; http://www.lozano-hemmer.com/amodal_suspension.php.

Lukács, G. (1977). *History and Class-consciousness*. London: Merlin Press.

Manovich, L. (2001). *The Language of New Media*. Cambridge, MA: MIT Press.

Marinetti, F. (1992). 'Futurist Painting: Technical Manifesto'. In *Art in Theory*, ed. C. Harrison and P. J. Wood. Oxford, and Cambridge, MA: Blackwell.

Marks, L. U. (2000). *The Skin of the Film: Intercultural Cinema, Embodiment and the Senses*. London: Duke University Press.

Marquez, G. G. (1973). *One Hundred Years of Solitude*. London: Penguin.

Marx, K. (1990). *Capital, Vol. 1*. Trans. B. Fowkes. London: Penguin.

Massumi, B. (1993). 'Preface'. In *The Politics of Everyday Fear*, ed. B. Massumi. Minneapolis: University of Minnesota Press, pp. vii–x.

—(2002). *Parables for the Virtual: Movement, Affect, Sensation*. Durham, NC and London: Duke University Press.

Meillassoux, Q. (2009). *After Finitude*, trans. R. Brassier. London: Continuum.

Merriam-Webster's Collegiate Dictionary. Tenth Edition.

Metz, C. (2000). 'The Imaginary Signifier' In *The Film Studies Reader*, ed. J. Holloway, P. Hutchings and M. Jancovich. London: Arnold, pp. 213–18.

Metzger, G. (1965 [1959]). *Metzger at AA*. London: Destruction/Creation.

Metzinger, T. (2009). *The Ego Tunnel*. New York: Basic Books.

Miller, J-A.. (1988). 'Extimité'. *Prose Studies*, 11: 125–6.

Milner, G. (2010). *Perfecting Sound Forever: The Story of Recorded Music*. London: Granta.

Miéville, C. (2009). 'Weird Fiction'. In *The Routledge Companion to Science Fiction*, ed. M. Bould, A. M. Butler, A. Roberts and S. Vint. Oxford: Routledge, pp. 510–15.

Moore, T. and Coley, B. (2008). *No Wave: Post-Punk. Underground. New York 1976–1980*. New York: Abrams/HNA Books.

Morange, M. (2006). 'Information, biologie'. In *Dictionnaire d'histoire et philosophie des sciences*. Paris: PUF.

Morin, E. (1973). *The Lost Paradigm: Human Nature*. Paris: Le Seuil.

Motte-Haber, H. de la (2002). 'Soundsampling: An Aesthetic Challenge'. In *Music and Technology in the Twentieth Century*, ed. H-J. Braun. Baltimore, MD: Johns Hopkins University Press, pp. 199–206.

Mulvey, L., (2000) 'Visual Pleasure and Narrative Cinema'. In *The Film Studies Reader*, ed. J. Holloway, P. Hutchings and M. Jancovich. London: Arnold, pp. 238–48.

Nancy, J-L. (2007). *Listening*, trans. C. Mandell. New York: Fordham University Press.

Nietzsche, F. (1968). *The Will to Power*, trans. Walter Kaufmann. New York: Vintage Books.

—(1974). *The Gay Science*, trans. W. Kaufmann. New York and Toronto: Random House.

—(1998). *Twilight of the Idols*, trans. D. Large. Oxford and New York: Oxford University Press.

Noys, B. (2007). 'The Lovecraft Event'. Paper presented at the *Weird Realism: Lovecraft and Theory* Conference, Goldsmiths College, London, April. Version available at: http://leniency.blogspot.com/2008/06/lovecraft-part-2.html.

Oliveros, P. http://deeplistening.org/site/content/about (accessed 12 September 2011).

Osborne, P. (2002). *Conceptual Art (Themes and Movements)*. London: Phaidon.

O'Brien, F. (1974). *The Third Policeman*. London: Picador.

O'Rawe, D. (2006). 'The Great Secret: Silence, Cinema and Modernism'. *Screen*, 47 (4): 395–405.

O'Toole, M. (1995). *Tinnitus – Living with Noises in Your Head*. London: Souvenir Press.

Palmer, T. (2006). 'Style and Sensation in the Contemporary French Cinema of the Body'. *Journal of Film and Video*, 58 (3): 22–32.

Parikka, J. (2007). *Digital Contagions: A Media Archaeology of Computer Viruses*. New York: Peter Lang.

—(2008). 'Insect Technics: Intensities of Animal Bodies'. In *An (Un)Likely Alliance: Thinking Environment(s) with Deleuze/Guattari*, ed. B. Herzogenrath. Newcastle: Cambridge Scholars Publishing, pp. 339–62.

Passchier-Vermeer, W. and Passchier, W. (2000). 'Noise Exposure and Public Health'. *Environmental Health Perspectives*, 108 (suppl. 1): 123–31.

Patel, A. D. (2008). *Music, Language and the Brain*. Oxford: Oxford University Press.

Peirce, C. S. (1998). *The Essential Peirce: Selected Philosophical Writings*, Vol. 2, edited by the Peirce Edition Project. Bloomington: University of Indiana Press.

—(2008). *Semiótica*. São Paulo: Perspectiva.

Pelmear, P. L. (1985). 'Noise and Health'. In *The Noise Handbook*, ed. W. Tempest. London: Academic Press, pp. 31–46.

Phila.gov. (2008). Available at http://www.phila.gov/Health/units/noise.pdf (accessed 1 May 2009).

Phillips, C. (2007). *Gerard Manley Hopkins and the Victorian Visual World*. Oxford: Oxford University Press.

Phillips, N. and Hardy, C. (2002). *Discourse Analysis: Investigating Processes of Social Construction*. London: Sage.

Piaget, J. (1963). 'L'assimilation recognitive et le système des significations'.

In *La naissance de l'intelligence chez l'enfant*. Paris: Delachaux et Niestle, pp. 164–74.

—(1967). 'Les deux problèmes principaux de l'épistémologie biologique'. In *Logique et connaissance scientifique*, ed. J. Piaget, Paris: Gallimard, pp. 892–3.

Picker, J. M. (2000). 'The Soundproof Study: Victorian Professionals, Work Space, and Urban Noise'. *Victorian Studies*, 42 (3): 427–53.

Pisano, G. (2004). *Une archéologie du cinéma sonore*. Paris: CNRS Éditions.

Plantinga, C. (2009). *Moving Viewers: American Film and the Spectator's Experience*. London: University of California Press.

Poe, E. A. (1993). *Tales of Mystery and Imagination*. London: Everyman.

Pohlmann, K. C. (2005). *Principles of Digital Audio*. New York: McGraw-Hill.

Porteous, D. (1990). *Landscapes of the Mind: Worlds of Sense and Metaphor*. Toronto: University of Toronto Press.

Power, N. (2008). 'Woman Machines: the Future of Female Noise.' In *Noise and Capitalism*, ed. Mattin and A. Iles. San Sebastián: Gipuzkoako Foru Aldundia-Arteleku, pp. 96–103.

Prigogine, I. (1976). 'Order Through Fluctuations, Self-organization and Social Systems'. In *Evolution and Consciousness*, ed. E. Jantsch and C. H. Waddington. Reading, MA: Addison Wesley, pp. 93–168.

Prigogine, I. and Stengers, I. (1992). *Entre le temps et l'éternité*. Paris: Flammarion.

Projansky, S. (2001). *Watching Rape: Film and Television in Postfeminist Culture*. London: New York University Press.

Punter, D. (1996). *The Literature of Terror: A History of Gothic Fictions from 1765 to the Present Day (Volume 2: The Modern Gothic)*. Harlow: Pearson Education.

Ranaldo, L. (1985). 'Visiting Smithson Site '83–5' [tab] in *Stray Prose*. SONICYOUTH.com. Available at http://www.sonicyouth.com/dotsonics/lee/prose/index.html.

—(1991). Notebook. Available at http://www.youtube.com/watch?v=LqZn6DK VdaA.

—(1998). *Jrnls80s*. Berkeley, CA: Soft Skull Press.

Rancière, J. (2004). *The Politics of Aesthetics*, trans. G. Rockhill. London and New York: Continuum.

—(2009). *Aesthetics and its Discontents*, trans. S. Corcoran. Cambridge: Polity Press.

Rascal, D. and Van Helden, A. (2009). 'Bonkers' (audio recording on compact disc). London: Dirtee Stank.

Ratkje, M. (2009). 'Vox' on Various Artists. *An Anthology of Noise and Electronic Music Vol.4* (CD). Sub Rosa.

Rayfield, D. (1994). *The Cherry Orchard: Catastrophe and Comedy*. New York: Twayne Publishers.

Read, G. (1987). *Source Book of Proposed Music Notation Reforms*. Abingdon: Greenwood Press.

Reed, L. (2000) [1975]. *Metal Machine Music* (CD). Buddah Records.

Reich, S. (2004). *Music as a Gradual Process*. In *Audio Culture*, ed. C. Cox and D. Warner. New York and London: Continuum.

Renault, E. (2006). 'Rupture'. In *Dictionnaire d'histoire et philosophie des sciences*. Paris: PUF, pp. 982–3.

Reynolds, S. (1990). *Blissed Out: The Raptures of Rock*. London: Serpent's Tail.

—(2004). 'Noise'. In *Audio Culture: Readings in Modern Music*, ed. C. Cox and D. Warner, London: Continuum, pp. 55–8.

—(2006). *Rip it Up and Start Again: Postpunk 1978–1984*. London: Faber and Faber.

—(2011). *Retromania: Pop Culture's Addiction to its Own Past*. London and New York: Faber and Faber.

Reznikoff, I. (1995). 'On the Sound Dimension of Prehistoric Painted Caves and Rocks'. In *Musical Signification*, ed. E. Taratsi, Berlin and New York: Mouton de Gruyter.

Riediker, M. and Koren, H. (2004). 'The Importance of Environmental Exposures to Physical, Mental and Social Well-being'. *International Journal of Hygiene and Enviornmental Health*, 207: 193–201.

Rifkin, J. (2000). *The Age of Access: How the Shift from Ownership to Access is Transforming Capitalism*. London and New York: Penguin Books.

Rodda, M. (1967). *Noise and Society*. London: Oliver & Boyd.

Rodowick, D. N. (2007). *The Virtual Life of Film*. Massachusetts: Harvard University Press.

Rogers. S. (2010). *Neither Event nor Artifact*. Unpublished MA dissertation, Dartington College of Art (University College Falmouth).

Rubin, I. I. (2008) *Essays on Marx's Theory of Value*, trans. M. Samardžija and F. Perlman. Delhi: Aakar Press.

Rushton, R. (2002). 'Cinema's Double: Some Reflections on Metz'. *Screen*, 43 (2): 107–18.

Russell, B. (2010). *Left-handed Blows: Writing on Sound 1993–2009*. Auckland, NZ: Clouds.

—(2011). 'Lines of Flight: "The Most Perfectly Autonomous Sector of the Field of Cultural Production" '. In *'Sun, Land and Sea': Situating Music in Aotearoa New Zealand*, ed. T. Mitchell and G. Keam. Auckland, NZ: Pearson, pp. 265–79.

Russell, K. (1989). *A British Picture: An Autobiography*. London: Heinemann.

Russo, M. and D. Warner (2004). 'Rough Music, Futurism, and Postpunk Industrial Noise Bands'. In *Audio Culture: Readings in Modern Music*, ed. C. Cox and D. Warner. New York and London: Continuum, pp. 47–54.

Russolo, L. (2004). 'The Art of Noises: Futurist Manifesto'. In *Audio Culture: Readings in Modern Music*, ed. C. Cox and D. Warner. New York and London: Continuum, pp. 10–14.

Sacks, O. (2007). *Musicophilia: Tales of Music and the Brain*. London: Picador.

Sampson, T. D. (2009). 'How Networks Become Viral: Three Questions Cconcerning Universal Contagion'. In *The Spam Book: On Viruses, Porn, and Other Anomalies from the Dark Side of Digital Culture*, ed. J. Parikka and T. D. Sampson, Cresshill, NJ: Hampton Press, pp. 39–60.

—(2010). 'Viral Love'. Paper presented at the *Thinking Network Politics: Methods, Epistemology, Process* Conference, Anglia Ruskin University, Cambridge, March.

Sarig, R. (1998). *The Secret History of Rock: The Most Influential Bands You've Never Heard*. New York: Billboard Books.

Schaeffer, P. (1946). 'L'élément non visuel au cinéma'. *Revue du cinéma*, 1 (1–3): 45–8, 62–5, 51–4.
—(1977 [1966]). *Traité des objets musicaux: essai interdisciplines*. Paris: Le Seuil.
—(2004). 'Acousmatics'. In *Audio Culture: Readings in Modern Music*, ed. C. Cox and D. Warner. New York and London: Continuum, pp. 76–81.
Schafer, R. M. (1980). *The Tuning of the World*. Philadelphia: University of Pennsylvania Press.
Schulte-Fortkamp, B. and Nitsch, W. (1999). 'On Soundscapes and Their Meaning Regarding Noise Annoyance Measurements'. *Inter-noise 99*: 1387–92.
Sconce, J. (2000). *Haunted Media: Electronic Presence from Telegraphy to Television*. Durham, NC: Duke University Press.
Scrimshaw, W. (2011). 'Interiority, Immediacy and the Ideology of Immanence'. *Subtractions*. Available at http://willschrimshaw.net/subtractions/interiority-immediacy-and-the-ideology-of-immanence/ (accessed 9 March 2011).
Seifer, M. J. (1998). *Wizard: The Life and Times of Nikola Tesla, Biography of a Genius*. New York: Citadel Press.
Sergi, G. (2004). *The Dolby Era: Film Sound in Contemporary Hollywood*. Manchester, New York: Manchester University Press.
Serres, M. (1982). *HERMES: Literature, Science, and Philosophy*, ed. J. V. Harari and D. F. Bell. Baltimore, MD, and London: The Johns Hopkins University Press.
—(1995). *Genesis*, trans. G. James and J. Nielson. Ann Arbor: The University of Michigan Press.
—(2007). *The Parasite*, Trans. L. R. Schehr. Minneapolis and London: University of Minnesota Press.
—(2008). *The Five Senses: A Philosophy of Mingled Bodies*, trans. M. Sankey and P. Cowley. London and New York: Continuum.
Shakespeare, W. (2005 [c. 1599–1601]). *Hamlet*. London: Penguin Books.
Shannon, C. and Weaver, W. (1949) *A Mathematical Model of Communication*. Urbana, IL: University of Illinois Press.
Shapiro, G. (1997). *Earthwards: Robert Smithson and Art After Babel*.
Shaviro, S. (2010). 'Post-cinematic Affect: On Grace Jones, Boarding Gate and Southland Tales'. *Film-Philosophy*, 14 (1): 1–102.
Shiel, M. P. (2005). 'Vaila'. In *Late Victorian Gothic Tales*, ed. R. Luckhurst. Oxford: Oxford University Press, pp. 234–65.
Silverman, K. (1988). *The Acoustic Mirror: The Female Voice in Psychoanalysis and Cinema*. Indianapolis: Indiana University Press.
Sim, S. (2007). *Manifesto for Silence: Confronting the Politics and Culture of Noise*. Edinburgh: Edinburgh University Press.
Simondon, G. (2005). *L'individuation à la lumière des notions de forme et d'information*. Grenoble: Millon.
Singer, L. and Ranaldo, L. (2010). *Water Days*. Paris: Éditions Dis Voir.
Slater, R. and Terry, M. (1987). *Tinnitus: A Guide for Sufferers and Professionals*. Beckenham, Kent: Crook Helm.
Smith, N. (2005). 'The Splinter In Your Ear: Noise Music as the Semblance of Critique'. *Culture, Theory and Critique*, 46 (1): 43–59.

Smith, S. (1994). 'Soundscape'. *Area*, 26 (3): 232–40.

Sobchack, V. (2004). *Carnal Thoughts: Embodiment and Moving Image Culture*. London: University of California Press.

Stansfeld, S. (2006) 'Exploring the Link Between Environmental Noise and Psychiatric Disorder (Causes Of)'. *Psychiatric Times*, 23 (7): 37–41.

Staples, S. (1996). 'Human Response to Environmental Noise: Psychological Research and Public Policy'. *American Psychologist*, 51: 143–50.

Stengers, I. and Prigogine, I. (1984). *Order Out of Chaos: Man's New Dialogue with Nature*. New York: Bantam Books.

Sterne, J. (2003). *The Audible Past: Cultural Origins of Sound Reproduction*. Durham, NC: Duke University Press.

—(2006a). 'The death and life of digital audio'. *Interdisciplinary Science Reviews*, 31 (4): 338–48.

—(2006b). 'The mp3 as Cultural Artifact'. *New Media and Society*, 8 (5): 825–42.

Stewart, J. with A. Bronzaft, F. McManus, N. Rodgers and V. Weedon (2011). *Why Noise Matters: A Worldwide Perspective on the Problems, Policies and Solutions*. London: Routledge.

Stonehouse, R. and Stromberg, G. (2004). *The Architecture of the British Library at St. Pancras*. London: Spon Press.

Storr, A. (1992). *Music and the Mind*. London: HarperCollins.

Stroud, T. and Di Lallo, E. (2009). *Neo-Avant-Gardes, Postmodern and Global Art 1969–1999*. Milan: Skira.

Suter, A. and von Gierke, H. (1987). 'Noise and Public Policy'. In *Ear and Hearing*, 8 (4): 188–91.

Theorie Communiste, trans. Anon (2010). 'The Present Moment'. Available at *http://libcom.org/library/present-moment-theorie-communiste*.

Thoma, J. U. (1971). 'Bond Graphs for Thermal Energy Transport and Entropy Flow'. *Journal of the Franklin Institute*, 292: 109–20.

—(1975). *Introduction to Bond Graphs and Their Applications*. New York: Pergamon Press.

Thompson, E. (2002). *The Soundscape of Modernity*. Cambridge, MA: MIT Press.

Thrift, N. (2009). 'Pass It On: Towards a Political Economy of Propensity'. Paper presented at the *Social Science and Innovation* Conference, Royal Society of the Arts, London, February. Available at http://www.aimresearch.org/uploads/File/Presentations/2009/FEB/NIGEL%20THRIFT%20PAPER.pdf

Tiberghein, G. A. (1995). *Land Art*. New York: Princeton Architectural Press.

Toop, D. (1995/2001). *Ocean of Sound: Aether Talk, Ambient Sound and Imaginary Worlds*. London: Serpent's Tail.

—(2007). 'Paul Burwell 1949–2007'. *The Wire*, 277 (March): 10.

Toth, C. (2008). 'Noise Theory'. In *Noise and Capitalism*, ed. Mattin and A. Iles. San Sebastian: Arteleku, pp. 24–37.

Tulloch, J. (1980). *Chekhov: A Structuralist Study*. London: Macmillan.

Unknown, and Wolters, C. ed. (1978 [late C14]). *The Cloud of Unknowing*. London: Penguin Books.

Virilio, P. (1989). *War and Cinema: Logistics of Perception*, trans. P. Camiller. London: Verso.

—(2000). *Polar Inertia,* trans. P. Camiller. London: Sage.

Voegelin, S. (2010). *Listening to Noise and Silence: Towards a Philosophy of Sound Art*. New York and London: Continuum.

Vološinov, V. N. (1986). *Marxism and the Philosophy of Language*, trans. L. Matejka and I. R. Titunik. Cambridge, MA: Harvard University Press.

Von Neumann, J. (1956). 'Probabilistic Logics and the Synthesis of Reliable Organisms from Unreliable Components'. In *Automata Studies*, ed. C. E. Shannon and J. McCarthy. Princeton, NJ: Princeton University Press, 43–93.

Von Neumann, J. and Morgenstern, O. (1944). *Theory of Games and Economic Behaviour*. Princeton, NJ: Princeton University Press.

Vovolis, T. (2003). *The Voice and Mask in Ancient Greek Tragedy*. In *Soundscape: The School of Sound Lectures 1998–2001*, ed. L. Sider, D. Freeman and J. Sider. London and New York: Wallflower.

Walser, R. (1993). *Running with the Devil: Power, Gender and Madness in Heavy Metal Music*. Middletown, CT: Wesleyan University Press.

Westwood, S. and Williams, J. (1997). 'Imagining Cities'. In *Imagining Cities: Scripts, Signs and Memories*, ed. S. Westwood and J. Williams. London: Routledge, pp. 1–15.

White, N. (1992). *Hopkins: A Literary Biography*. Oxford: Oxford University Press.

WHO (1999). Guidelines for Community Noise. Available at http://www.tvsde.paho.org/bvsci/i/fulltext/noise/noise/pdf.

Williams, A. ed. (2010). *Nancy Holt: Sightlines*. Berkeley: University of California Press.

Wilson, S. (2011). 'Making Numbers Speak: JF Nash Jr and the Madness of Neoliberalism', *Culture/Clinic*, 1.2, in press.

Winograd, S. and Cowan, J. D. (1963). *Reliable Computation in the Presence of Noise*. Cambridge, MA: MIT Press.

Youngblood, G. (1970). *Expanded Cinema*. London: Studio Vista.

Zajonc, R. B. (2004). *The Selected Works of R. B. Zajonc*. New York: Wiley.

Žižek, S. (1999). 'The Undergrowth of Enjoyment: How Popular Culture can Serve as an Introduction to Lacan'. In *The Žižek Reader*, ed. E. Wright and E. Wright. Oxford: Blackwell, pp. 11–36.

—(2008a). *Interrogating the Real*, ed. R. Butler and S. Stephens. London and New York: Continuum.

—(2008b) [1998]. *The Plague of Fantasies*. London and New York: Verso.

Index

Made in the USA
Middletown, DE
10 August 2022

70986907R00169